Acknowledgments

I wish to acknowledge the support and encouragement I have received over the years from many friends. Their support and encouragement have helped me improve my Christian life in ways that would have not been possible without them. Much of what is presented in this book comes from hours of sharing and discussing our individual and joint spiritual journeys. For this, I will be eternally grateful.

I especially want to thank Ms. Winsome Jean of Winsome Expressions for her many suggestions and designs, which includes the cover of the book. Winsome's joyful and helpful spirit has been greatly appreciated.

My family has proven precious in this endeavor. My wife, Ruby Perry; my son, Reginald Perry Sr.; daughter, Rhonda Perry; and grandson, Reginald Perry Jr., all assisted me with information and advice that helped me complete the book.

Rubin Perry

Sun

Contents

Introduction..6
Beginning the Divine Journey to Peace..7
    God's Designer Role...8
    The Creation of Mankind..14
    Divine Preparation Processes..23
    Divine Processes and Mankind...31

Peace and the Divine Journey..49
    Mankind's Co-Creator Role..50
    Your Peace Journey...53
    Description of Meditation...64
    Meditation Exercises...81

Peace A Divine Substance..86
    Peace Definition..86
    Cause and Effect..95
    Divine Truth and Divine Righteousness An Overview.....................107
    The Search for Divine Truth...116
    Hunger and Thirst after Divine Righteousness................................132

Divine Peace Applied 139
    Customs, Changes, Conflict and Courage.......................................140
    War and Spiritual Influences..143
    Rhythm and Rest..152
    Peace and Healing...156

The Journey is Eternal...158

Sacred Heart of Jesus Christ

Fish

Earth

Bird

Milky Way Spiral

Full Moon

Introduction

Mankind is not some cosmological accident. A chance happening on a grand scale, no, mankind is an incomprehensible, creative delight of God with a destiny that far exceeds mankind's ability to understand. Glimpses of mankind's destiny are fleeting at best, but fragments are seen on occasion when spiritual eyes have been opened to the unlimited possibilities of an expanded God-inspired mind.

We must grow our mind to know God as He reveals Himself to us. This is vital. Education and knowledge are essential for life in the world. This book is about peace. Peace is obtained through knowledge and understanding of the divine nature of God and doing as He directs so that we become like Him.

Mankind has been created by God to assume responsibility for assisting God in the management of His creation. As the scripture states, mankind is to have *dominion over the fish of the sea, and over the fowl of the air, and over every living thing that moveth upon the earth"* **(Gen. 1:28).** We have a rightful place in God's world, a world designed with responsibilities yet with joyous, delightful, loving experiences for mankind. To be able to do this, we must obtain and use peace to develop divinelike abilities.

> **O LORD our Lord, how excellent *is* thy name in all the earth! who hast set thy glory above the heavens.**
> **²Out of the mouth of babes and sucklings hast thou ordained strength because of thine enemies, that thou mightest still the enemy and the avenger.**
> **³When I consider thy heavens, the work of thy fingers, the moon and the stars, which thou hast ordained;**
> **⁴What is man, that thou art mindful of him? and the son of man, that thou visitest him?**
> **⁵For thou hast made him a little lower than the angels, and hast crowned him with glory and honour.**
> **⁶Thou madest him to have dominion over the works of thy hands; thou hast put all *things* under his feet:**
> **⁷All sheep and oxen, yea, and the beasts of the field;**
> **⁸The fowl of the air, and the fish of the sea, *and whatsoever* passeth through the paths of the seas.**
> **⁹O LORD our Lord, how excellent *is* thy name in all the earth!**
>
> **Psalm 8:1–9**

Mankind is a creation of God, made to be a citizen of the universe and assigned to the earth for a reason, with responsibility for one another and all that is in it.

God, Jesus Christ, and the Holy Spirit are the personifications of the Divine Spirit in the life of mankind.

The implementation of the Divine Spirit in our being is the purpose of our life on earth.

Beginning the Divine Journey to Peace

Ancient of Days

God's Designer Role

This book is intended for all who desire peace. If you study the ideas and apply the principles outlined here, you will obtain peace. Many of you who desire peace are religious and are familiar with the use of the names or terms God, Jesus Christ, and the Holy Spirit as religious Christian names. Some of you who desire peace may not be religious or may not be Christian; and so the use of the terms God, Jesus Christ, and the Holy Spirit may be unfamiliar or contrary to your religious beliefs. For all of you, I want you to know that I do not wish to force anything upon you. It is just that through my understanding and use of these names and the beings they represent, a framework that enabled me to grow in peace was established. Peace is available to you if you consider what is presented here with an open mind.

I describe in this book my encounters with the spiritual world and God, through Jesus Christ and the Holy Spirit, and what I learned through them. Be assured that you too can obtain peace through them. I hope you become convinced, through trying the principles outlined in this book, that the names and roles of these high-level spiritual beings are indeed based on actual experiences and are effective in obtaining peace.

Attempts have been made by some to relegate these spiritual beings to particular religious denominations and creeds. I would ask you to expand your view if you think this and to accept the position that the nature of these spiritual beings surpasses our ability to relegate them to any particular religious denomination or creed. Their divine nature surpasses any religious denomination or creed. In fact, other religious names and terms may in fact describe the same spiritual beings.

I invite all to read this book with an attitude to prove for yourself whether what is presented here as truth is truth for you. For those of you who are not aware of these names or are doubtful about them, I only ask that you give what I describe a try. Prove for yourself the truth of what is described here.

The purpose of this book is to help you understand the source of peace. Many have thought that peace is an absence of conflict and strife in their personal life and in the world. This is only partially true. Peace is in reality a divine substance that must be acquired. Once you acquire peace, it then becomes active in your life. Peace is not the absence of anything, but a divine substance that is intended to reside within you to prevent and drive out conflict and strife.

It is a divine substance with quality and quantity that creates the same state of being that we normally think of as existing in heaven. It can be yours on earth. Its source is Jesus Christ. When you have obtained it, although you may be aware of potential dangers, you can rest in the knowledge and truth that Jesus Christ will not let it destroy your peace. You will know that all things will work for your good if you follow Him. Peace creates total assurance and well-being. It has the quality of assisting one to manage strife, unrest, and worry. In it is total trust in the protection of a divine being, Jesus Christ, who will shield you from danger. He is personally concerned about you and, if you follow Him, will not permit anyone or anything to harm you. This does not come easily and is hard work. It requires changes in your thinking, feeling, and willing. It is a total commitment to reinventing yourself. Not all desire to make these changes and as a result experience disappointments, grief, and disharmony in their life.

Throughout our discussion, we refer to God, Jesus Christ, and the Holy Spirit. They are described as the Holy Trinity and as three in one. They act as one. The divine attribute that best describes them is love. As we proceed with our discussion of peace, whenever they are mentioned, the divine quality love is implied. I say this because some might think that the love of God is being overlooked during our discussion. But that is not the case. We are specifically focusing on the unique role of peace in our discussion, but that is not to presume that the love of God is not fundamental to all we discuss.

I want to emphasize again that when the role of Jesus Christ is discussed, it is not intended to convey a narrow religious dogma, but I want you to consider that there exists a Spiritual Being whom Christians call Jesus Christ. He is the source of *all* life. He is more than a religious figure. He is a divine being who exceeds all physical and spiritual matters yet exists in them. Peace is among His many spiritual qualities. He has the ability to transfer peace from Himself to all who are willing to receive it. One of His primary purposes is to provide peace to those on earth. As you consider the thoughts and ideas discussed in this book, you will get to know Jesus Christ *personally*.

Jesus Christ also administers peace through another Spirit Being, the Holy Spirit, who will instruct you on how to obtain and use this peace. The Holy Spirit does this by teaching you how to awaken spiritual qualities that are asleep within you. This is necessary if you are to receive His peace. Under the personal administration of Jesus Christ and the transforming power transferred to you through the Holy Spirit, this peace, if you want it, will come to you and grow within you.

The Holy Spirit will first teach you how to obtain a clear understanding of the existence of this peace. He then will assist you with the reception of peace from Jesus Christ to you. Peace is first transferred into your spirit, then into your soul, and finally into your physical body. The role of the Holy Spirit in this transfer is to become your personal trainer and help you develop your spirit, soul, and body to receive the peace of Jesus Christ. The way it works is like this: Jesus Christ (often referred to as the Prince of Peace) is the sole ruler of peace and determines who gets peace. The Holy Spirit receives instructions from Jesus Christ to transfer peace. The Holy Spirit then assists with the transfer of peace to whom He is directed by Jesus Christ.

I ask you to view what you read here with an open mind and with an attitude of testing the ideas you read here for yourself. Spend time with the ideas and exercises presented in this book. They may not make sense at first, but test them for yourself. Stay with them. Spiritual Beings are there assisting you to obtain your peace. For many years, I have taught what you will be asked to do and can assure you that if you will be diligent in doing what is asked, you will experience the peace of Jesus Christ.

It is my intent with this book to provide you numerous opportunities to decide for yourself the truth or not of the existence of God, Jesus Christ, and the Holy Spirit and their role in your peace.

More about this will be presented later in this book, but as for now, I wish to give you a brief introduction. "Pinch yourself to see if you are awake." We often hear this in a playful setting spoken to get us to focus on the events or issues at hand or to get us to "wake up" and recognize the uniqueness of the situation at hand and our need to be involved with it.

Smart people have studied and debated about the history and purpose of man's existence for years. These debates are very complicated at times and hard to understand, but what one can understand is that one's own existence can be immediately demonstrated by "pinching oneself."

When we think about our own existence, it causes us to ultimately think about where we came from. We think about our parents, then their parents, then their parents, and so on. Eventually, we come to a realization that there has to have been an original parent. This parent, for the sake of our discussion at this time, is what I mean by God. God is divine as are Jesus Christ and the Holy Spirit. Their divine nature and state of being is higher than heaven and earth, yet their divine nature flows into both by sequence and order.

In the beginning, God created all that exists including mankind. This includes you, if you are reading this book. You are made of divine, precious, one-of-a-kind material. You are unique, with a special role in the perfecting of creation.

God, according to the Bible, declared all that He created as very good. Regardless of your current situation, God said that you, as a member of mankind, are very good. The Bible also indicates there was direct access between God and mankind. Not only was there direct communications between God and mankind, but God was also pleased with it. However, we also read in the Bible that because of disobedience on the part of the first human couple, Adam and Eve, the relationship between God and mankind changed; and they were driven out of the Garden of Eden.

Expulsion of Adam and Eve

Not only did the relationship between God and mankind change, but this very act of disobedience ultimately resulted in the changes in the nature of mankind and, ultimately, in his original form. Because of mankind's change of nature, it was determined by God that it would be best for mankind if the former relationship between them also change. One major result of this eventually was the shutting off of direct access to God. Mankind was unable to have the type of communion with God that existed in the beginning. This separation had the effect of being a type of perception by mankind as being "rejected" by God.

It has been suggested by some scholars that this perceived "rejection" by God has created a deep longing in mankind, a kind of divine depression and nostalgia that can only be cured by a return to the original communion of mankind with God. It appears God also has a sense of this longing because He has always provided a way and means for this relationship to be restored. One thing is for sure; and the purpose for this book is to highlight that not having direct access to God and God's peace has resulted in mankind being subject to conflict, wars, murder, trouble, strife, and the lack of peace. This separation from God has caused each of us to experience personal and environmental conditions lacking in peace.

Although mankind after this change in his nature and form did not enjoy the same type of communication and access to God as before, he still was able to call upon God through what is known as prayer, either directly or through others who had obtained a special nature that enabled them to communicate with God. These communications eventually took the form of rituals and practices that we have come to know as religious practices, doctrines, dogmas, and denominations—all intended to make possible mankind's continued communication with God.

God's overwhelming love for mankind also causes Him to devise new ways of communicating with Him.

One critical step He took to assist with restoring communication with mankind was to send Jesus Christ to earth. Jesus Christ is the Son of God, one with God who has all of the qualities of God—which includes love, peace, joy, faith, infinite power, eternal existence, just to name a few—and has come unto earth to reconcile mankind back to their rightful place with God.

One point that is of key importance to us in our discussion about peace that cannot be overemphasized is the role of Jesus Christ. He is called the Prince of Peace because He is in charge of how and in whom peace operates in the world. God has given Jesus Christ the responsibility to be the governor or ruler and source of peace. He is the first and final authority for peace in the earth.

The Holy Spirit, as well as other spiritual beings, assists Jesus Christ with this peace and its application. Jesus Christ, as a part of the process of administering peace, works directly with the Holy Spirit. The Holy Spirit distributes peace, as Jesus Christ authorizes.

Stars & Angels with infant entering the World

Let's take a moment to read passages of scripture from the Bible that describe the birth of Jesus into the earth.

The Birth of Jesus

> **And there were in the same country shepherds abiding in the field, keeping watch over their flock by night. And, lo, the angel of the Lord came upon them, and the glory of the Lord shone round about them: and they were sore afraid. And the angel said unto them, Fear not: for, behold, I bring you good tidings of great joy, which shall be to all people. For unto you is born this day in the city of David a Saviour, which is Christ the Lord. And this *shall be* a sign unto you; Ye shall find the babe wrapped in swaddling clothes, lying in a manger. And suddenly there was with the angel a multitude of the heavenly host praising God, and saying, Glory to God in the highest, and on earth peace, good will toward men.**
>
> **Luke 1:8–14**

The entrance of Jesus into the earth was a wondrous event involving divine beings and manifesting spectacular brilliance, announced by the praising of God for the fulfillment of a divine promise made in the early stages of mankind's placement on earth—a promise of the coming of a divine being that would restore mankind to his rightful place in the created universe.

We all have a common beginning. We all have a common destination. Regardless of nationality, we are all mankind and must come to a common knowledge of that fact, a knowledge that includes a search for and discovery of Jesus Christ and peace. The following words in the hymn "This Is My Song" capture the spirit that we have to recognize as mankind's common connection.

<u>This Is My Song</u>
This is my song, O God of all the nations,
A song of peace for lands afar and mine.
This is my home, the country where my heart is;
Here are my hopes, my dreams, my holy shrine;
But other hearts in other lands beating with hopes
and dreams as true as mine.

My country's skies are bluer than the ocean,
And sunlight beams on cloverleaf and pine.
But other lands have sunlight too and clover,
And skies are everywhere as blue as mine.
Oh, hear my song, thou God of all the nations,
A song of peace for their land and for mine.

This is my prayer, O Lord of all earth's kingdoms,
Thy kingdom come; on earth thy will be done.
Let Christ be lifted up till all men serve him,
And hearts united learn to live as one.
Oh, hear my prayer, thou God of all the nations,
Myself I give thee; let thy will be done[1].

---

1. Lloyd Stone wrote the first two stanzas in 1934, and Georgia Harkness added the last stanza in 1939. "This Is My Song" was copyrighted by the Lorenz Publishing Co. in 1964.

The Creation of Mankind

We mentioned the entrance of Jesus Christ unto earth, so it might now be helpful to discuss briefly the entrance of mankind on earth as described in Genesis 1:26, 27:

> **And God said, Let us make man in our image, after our likeness: and let them have dominion over the fish of the sea, and over the fowl of the air, and over the cattle, and over all the earth and over every creeping thing that creepeth upon the earth. So God created man in his own image, in the image of God created he him; male and female created he them.**

Mankind was created in the image and likeness of God. Although mankind was created in the image of God, he was not created as God. God is divine. He is eternal and not made of things that change or pass away. His nature is not the same as man. He is above man and made of substance that is superior to what exists in created forms. He manifests through these forms but is not them. He manifests in physical as well as in spiritual phenomena. He manifests as a Spirit. In John 4:24, Jesus stated:

> *God is a Spirit: and they that worship him must worship him in spirit and in truth.*

Since God manifests as a Spirit and man is made in God's image and likeness, then man, in addition to being physical, must be made in the image of God's spirit also. In our discussion throughout this book, think of man as having a ***human spirit***.

In Genesis 2:7, it stated:

> *And the Lord God formed man of the dust of the ground and breathed into his nostrils the breath of life and man became a living soul.*

This is a continuation of God's relationship with mankind. In this verse, we see God giving Man a soul form that is in addition to the spirit form Man received in 1:27. Therefore, also during our discussion, think of man as having a ***human soul*** and a ***human spirit***.

But Adam and Eve disobeyed God and as a result were put out of the Garden of Eden, for we read:

> **Therefore the LORD God sent him forth from the garden of Eden, to till the ground from whence he was taken. So he drove out the man; and he placed at the east of the garden of Eden cherubims, and a flaming sword which turned every way, to keep the way of the tree of life.**
> **Genesis 3:23–24**

After Adam and Eve's act of disobedience as described in Genesis 3, we read in verse 21 of that chapter that God does another creative act before putting them out. It stated in that verse:

> **Unto Adam also and to his wife did the Lord God make coats of skins and clothed them.**

The making of coats of skins and clothing them is another creative action God took in the construction of Man. So during our discussion, also think of man as having a ***human body***.

Some people I have taught have difficulty with these additions and the continual creative actions God takes on behalf of Man. God first created Man as a spirit, then formed in him a soul, and finally clothed him in coats of skins, a human body. The initial creation of mankind as described in Genesis 1:26, 27 was just the beginning. Eventually, Man took on a threefold nature. To help confirm this point, read what the apostle Paul wrote about the threefold nature of man when he writes in 1 Thessalonians 5:23 the following:

> **And the very God of peace sanctify you wholly; and I pray God your whole spirit and soul and body be preserved blameless unto the coming of our Lord Jesus Christ.**

Paul recognized the threefold nature of man in pointing out the need for our spirit and soul and body to be preserved. We all are composed of a **human spirit**, a **human soul**, and a **human body**. Each of these has been created as forms with defined bodies, systems, organs, and creative life processes.

Creative processes of life are specific for the **human spirit**, **human soul**, and **human body** and operate uniquely within each of them. These processes involve taking in external substances and extracting elements appropriate for each. The appropriate extracted elements are used to sustain life in each. Elements that are unused are eliminated as waste products.

Later, we will go a little deeper in our discussion of mankind's creation by God; but for now, I want you to think about the threefold nature and form of mankind. As we proceed with our discussion about peace, I will go deeper into the role peace plays in our human spirit, human soul, and human body. But first we will discuss peace and the human body, then the human soul, and finally the human spirit and the creative life processes in each that relate to peace.

Human Body

Your human body, the physical part of your threefold nature, is comprised of major physical body systems, organs, senses, and functions.

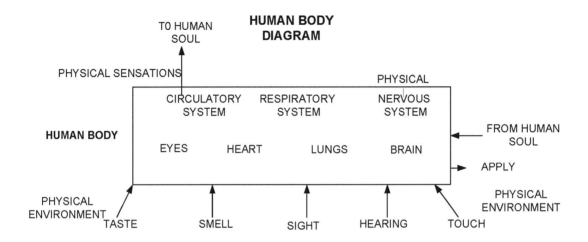

Diagram 1

The diagram shown above is a simple schematic diagram intended as an overview of the human body and its connections with the physical environment as well as with the human soul. Later, I will illustrate how all three—the human body, human soul, and human spirit—interact. The label "physical environment" to the right and left in the diagram indicates that our human body lives in an environment of physical objects. While the human body is self-contained, it is designed to interact with objects outside it and within it.

At the bottom of the diagram, the arrows depict the flow of sensations from the physical environment outside the human body to organs and systems within the human body. The arrows labeled "taste," "smell," "sight," "hearing," and "touch" signify the five major physical senses that receive sense information from different types of objects in the physical environment.

The arrow labeled "apply," to the right of the diagram, indicates that the human body is equipped with the ability to act upon objects in its physical environment.

There are thirteen (some sources list twelve) major systems in our human body. They include the circulatory, digestive, endocrine, integumentary, immune, lymphatic, musculoskeletal, muscular, nervous, reproductive, respiratory, skeletal, and urinary systems. For the sake of our illustration, I have only listed the circulatory, respiratory, and nervous systems.

The human body organs are many; but for the diagram, I have only included the eyes, brain, heart, and lungs. Major senses include seeing, hearing, tasting, touching, and smelling. These five major senses are considered to be the primary way man has contact with the physical world.

The arrow labeled "physical sensations" at the top of the diagram with an arrow "to human soul" is inside the human body and indicates that physical objects in the physical environment outside the human body once sensed can be converted internally to sensations that may then be conveyed to the human soul. These sensations, which result from physical objects interacting with our physical senses, are converted into internal sensations that are recognizable to the human soul. We will discuss more about this later.

The arrow labeled "from human soul" that soul sensations returning from the soul are conveyed to the human body and in due course are converted into physical sensations that affect the human body systems and organs. The arrow labeled "apply" indicates an act that typically results from converted soul sensations.

I think that a discussion of how the sense of sight works may generally serve to show further how this all works.

<u>Sight and the Eye</u>

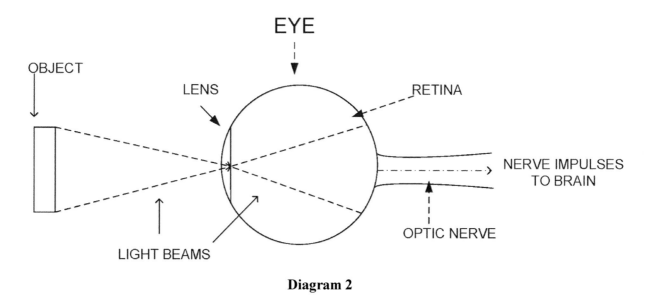

Diagram 2

The above schematic is intended to shows how the sense of sight operates within the eye. Light beams from an external object in our environment are reflected off the object and sensed by the eye. The lens of the eye focuses the light beams to the back of the eye onto an area called the retina, where the reflected light beams are converted into electrochemical nerve impulses and channeled to the optic nerve and then conveyed to the brain. The brain is not shown in the schematic, but the optic nerve is connected to the brain.

Once the nerve impulses reach the brain, another conversion occurs. In the brain, these nerve impulses are transformed to sensations that can be recognized by your soul. This transformation is possible because the brain is an organ with physical and spiritual capabilities. It not only processes physical sensations, but also has the capability to transform physical sensations into sensations recognizable to your soul and convert spiritual sensations from the soul that are recognizable to the human body. It may surprise some, but it is in your soul that you see, not in your brain. Physical brain sensations must be converted from physical sensations into spiritual sensations recognizable to your soul. I would ask you to think deeply about what has just been stated.

Objects in your physical environment are first recognized inside of you as sensations. The sense of sight conveys reflected light from objects outside of you into physical and soul sensations inside of you. The physical object of a car you see is outside of you, not inside of you. What is inside of you is the image of the car. The image of the car resides in your soul as a spiritual image, not the physical car.

Your soul is created to convert these physical-soul sensations into images. These images are then processed by your intellect and combined with other images to create ideas, concepts, and thoughts. These ideas, concepts, and thoughts are mixed with feelings and given names. These ideas, concepts, and thoughts, along with their names, are stored in us as memories. The combinations of these images, ideas, concepts, thoughts, and names are used to build our beliefs and truths about the world. When we choose to express these images, ideas, concepts, and thoughts, we give them names (sounds). These names are what we call words. Words are used to communicate what we have experienced and stored within us as images, ideas, concepts, thoughts, and names.

Words become containers for images, ideas, concepts, thoughts, names, memories, beliefs, and truths. These all vary in each individual because each of us vary in the operation of our physical and soul senses.

Hopefully, the following passage from Genesis 2:19 will give you further insight about this:

> **And out of the ground the LORD God formed every beast of the field, and every fowl of the air; and brought *them* unto Adam to see what he would *call* them: and whatsoever Adam called every living creature, that *was* the *name* thereof.**

In this passage, we are reminded again that the Lord God formed everything. Although the passage only mentions ***every beast of the field and every fowl of the air and intimates every living creature***, the Bible is very clear that all things were made by God. Mankind only reforms what God has originally made. In this passage, we see that Adam becomes a partner, a co-creator of sorts with God, because he is given the privilege of calling and naming what the Lord God formed. First, Adam must "see" what God has formed, and then and only then is he able to call what the Lord God has formed a name. The name Adam gave them was based on what he "saw."

Adam's words for the things formed by God contain the images, ideas, concepts, and thoughts that Adam "saw" they should have. In Adam's soul, the things took on the qualities and attributes that he imposes upon them. These qualities, attributes, and subsequent names were determined by Adam's sight and soul development. These things formed by the Lord God may or may not have the meaning to Adam and in Adam's soul that the Lord God intends them to have. It all depends on whether Adam's sense of sight and the state of his soul enable him to call these things formed by God the same name God intends for them.

I will point out that any defect or deformity in the physical and soul senses will affect the resulting accuracy and truth of the sensations. For example, color blindness will affect the ability of the eye to see certain colors. For one who is color-blind, their visual sensations will make it difficult to name the true color of the physical objects they observe. The resulting color images and names will not be the true colors of physical objects they see. The same limitations exist with hearing, tasting, and other physical senses.

Physical sensations must not be the sole means we use to determine the truth. We know the truth of a matter as the result of seeking what Jesus Christ would have us know about it. Peace is lacking in many of us because what we physically sense with our eyes may not be accurate and when viewed by our soul results in the forming of untruths. These inaccurate images, ideas, concepts, names, and resulting untruths cause unrest and are to be removed or transformed into real truths if we are to have peace. As we mature spiritually, we develop the ability to "see" spiritually. This ability enables us to see the reality or divine truth of what we experience.

Peace is built upon truth. Truth, although universal, grows as truth in you as an individual matter. What is seen as true by one may not appear as true for another. Therefore, if we are to have peace, we must be willing to seek and receive what God says about truth in what we experience in our world and be flexible in dealing with others because God may be showing them different things; and they may be unable to "see" and "name" as we because of individual differences.

Respiratory and Circulatory Systems

Let's spend a bit more time in our discussion of the human body by discussing the respiratory and circulatory systems and their interactions. A discussion of these two human body systems will prove helpful for us as we discuss how creative life processes in these human body systems and organs work; they will also show how there are similar creative life processes in the human soul and human spirit that relate to the acquiring of spiritual attributes like peace.

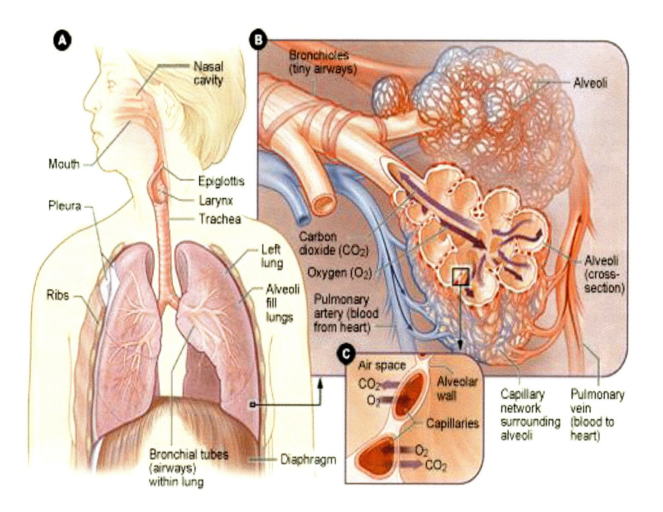

Diagram 3

Take a moment to look closely at diagram 3. It is from the U.S. government's National Institute of Health archives of images of the human lung. Image A in diagram 3 shows the major parts of the respiratory system of the human body. It shows the mouth and nasal cavity and the other body parts that channel air into our lungs. Air comes into our mouth and from the nasal cavity flows through several other body parts, including the trachea, then into the lungs, finally ending up in tiny air sacs in the lungs called alveoli. There are great numbers of these tiny alveoli in each lung. Image B shows what happens as air is channeled into the alveoli. Tiny airways called bronchioles serve as pathways for the air to finally reach the alveoli. Once the air reaches the alveoli, the oxygen in the air is exchanged with the carbon dioxide that is in the blood in the capillaries surrounding the alveoli. This blood has been pumped from the heart into the lungs. Image C shows how oxygen (O_2) in the air space inside the alveoli is exchanged with carbon dioxide (CO_2) from blood in the capillaries.

A major function of our respiratory system is to inhale oxygen (O_2) from the air outside our human body and to exhale carbon dioxide (CO_2), which is inside our human body. Without the constant replenishment of oxygen in our human body, we would die. Without the cleansing of the carbon dioxide (CO_2) from the blood within our human body, we would also die. The human body is constructed with this unique cycle. An element from outside of us that is necessary for our well-being is exchanged with an element inside of us, whose long-term effect inside of us could be harmful.

This process, as it relates to the respiratory system, is called breathing. Breathing takes in oxygen (O_2) from outside our human body into small saclike areas of our lungs called alveoli. These alveoli serve as switching stations where oxygen (O_2) is transferred from the alveoli to small blood vessels called capillaries and is exchanged for carbon dioxide in the capillaries.

Image C shows this transfer process, which is called diffusion. Diffusion occurs through a semipermeable membrane in the alveoli because of differences in partial pressure of the oxygen (O_2) on one side of the semipermeable membrane in the alveoli sac, causing the carbon dioxide (CO_2) on the opposite side to be diffused out. The result is that the composition of the blood is changed and sent back to the heart in a renewed form.

The effect is described as processing deoxygenated blood from the heart and replacing it with oxygenated blood from the lungs. Deoxygenated blood is blood that is lacking in the proper amount of oxygen (O_2) to sustain life or contains more carbon dioxide (CO_2) than it should.

What has just been described is a principle aspect of the creative life process as it applies to the blood system. In summary, oxygenated blood is pumped throughout the circulatory system to human body cells needing oxygen (O_2) and other nutrients necessary to sustain human cell life. Oxygen (O_2) is used by the human body cells to create energy, maintain health, and build new cells. One of the byproducts of this process is the creation of carbon dioxide (CO_2). The oxygen (O_2) content of the blood becomes less as a result. Now depleted, the deoxygenated blood must be renewed. The process of renewal occurs when the deoxygenated blood is returned to the heart and then pumped to the lungs, and eventually the alveoli areas, where the deoxygenated blood is renewed by the exchange of carbon dioxide (CO_2) for oxygen (O_2).

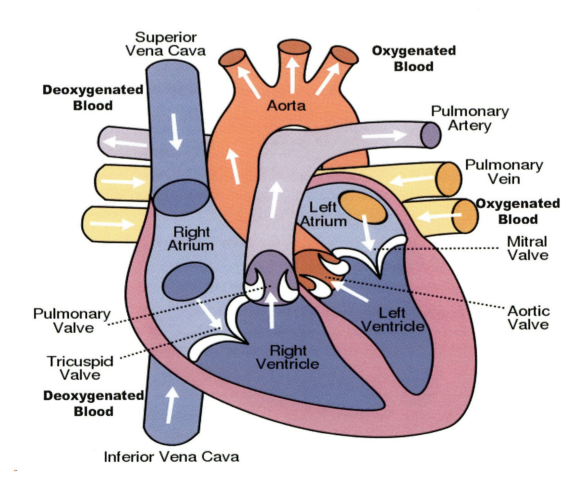

Diagram 4

Human Heart

Diagram 4 is of the human heart, which shows the superior vena cava in the upper left area of the diagram and the inferior vena cava in the lower left area of the diagram. They convey deoxygenated blood, which has too much carbon dioxide (CO_2) from the human body, and that blood is channeled through the right atrium and subsequently the right ventricle and out the pulmonary artery to the lungs. As stated above, it is in the lungs where carbon dioxide (CO_2) in deoxygenated blood is exchanged for oxygen (O_2). The pulmonary vein transport the oxygenated blood back from the lungs, channels it through the left atrium and subsequently the left ventricle, to be pumped by the heart through the aorta and out to the human body.

<u>Now I would like you to consider that one fundamental principle in our life is the process of renewal through exchange. We are constantly confronted with the need to renew ourselves through the removal of old toxic things and the acceptance and use of new life-giving things. New-life-filled air must replace old-life-depleted air, new ideas of truths and actions must replace old ones that no longer apply, and new knowledge must replace old knowledge if we are to live and grow</u>.

Even many things that have served us well in the past must be renewed or exchange if we are to become transformed. These include physical as well as spiritual things. This is the process of life. Otherwise, we cease to live.

From James 1:17–21, we read:

> **Every good gift and every perfect gift is from above, and cometh down from the Father of lights, with whom is no variableness, neither shadow of turning. Of his own will begat he us with the word of truth, that we should be a kind of firstfruits of his creatures. Wherefore, my beloved brethren, let every man be swift to hear, slow to speak, slow to wrath: For the wrath of man worketh not the righteousness of God. Wherefore lay apart all filthiness and superfluity of naughtiness, and receive with meekness the engrafted word, which is able to save your souls.**

God is the source for the word of truth. We must be patient in expressing our thoughts, especially if they are thoughts spoken in angry. The correct approach is to humbly seek to hear from God, through Jesus Christ and the Holy Spirit, what God would have us hear and do what He would have us do. Know that old ideas and thoughts must constantly be reviewed and renewed as appropriately with new ones.

God is a Spirit. Let us pause at this time and be reminded that man has a human body, a human soul, and a human spirit—all created by God and all interrelated. Although man's human soul and human spirit are made of spiritual substances, these substances also functions in ways that are similar to those of the human physical body.

I bring this to your attention for in my discussion with many people I find that this simple concept of man having a spiritual nature like God and later a physical body is difficult for some to grasp. Think along with me about this. When the Bible states that man was made in the image and likeness of God in Genesis 1:26, it literally means that man was made as spirit. This reference is made to man as a spirit being. Mankind is made in the image of God primarily as a spiritual being.

Mankind was later given coats of skins; see Genesis 3:21. This too was an act of God's love and no after thought but was given purposely to accommodate mankind's spiritual nature, which had changed as a result of disobedience.

Our physical body is constructed to house our changed spiritual image and likeness of God but is not the original spiritual image or likeness of God created in the beginning of our creation. The physical body houses man's spiritual image and has a representation in some way to the image of God. Your physical body houses physical forms with systems, organs, and creative life processes that are physical representations of godly spiritual systems, organs, and creative life processes.

If you read and think about what is stated in 1:26 and 27 of the book of Genesis, you will see that it states:

> **And God said, Let us make man in our image, after our likeness: and let them have dominion over the fish of the sea, and over the fowl of the air, and over the cattle, and over all the earth, and over every creeping thing that creepeth upon the earth.**
> **So God created man in his own image in the image of God created he him; male and female created he them.**

This shows that man is made in the image and likeness of God. So a study of what is meant by image and likeness will reveal, when related to God, how the composition of our human body though physical also contain spiritual components that are representative in nature to God.

For a simple illustration, think about this: in Genesis 6:6, it is stated that "The LORD was grieved that he had made man on the earth, and His **heart** was filled with pain,"

And

In Genesis 6:8: **"But Noah found favor in the eyes of the LORD."**

Statements about the "heart of God," the "eyes of the Lord," and many more references are made to show representations of physical attributes to spiritual attributes. Mankind is intended to be a living manifestation of godly attributes. We are challenged to study and understand the relationship and representation of spiritual attributes to physical attributes we possess in our physical body.

<u>Here is another fundamental principle I would ask you to consider. Just as there is the need to exchange physical oxygen from outside our human body for carbon dioxide inside our human body as representative of healthy human life, there is also the need to exchange spiritual truths from outside our human soul and human spirit for physical and spiritual untruths and partial untruths inside our human soul and human spirit that are harmful. Just as breathing is a necessary function of physical life that enables our spiritual life, so is divine spiritual inspiration necessary for our physical and spiritual life. This inspiration comes from God through Jesus Christ and the Holy Spirit.</u>

Allow me the opportunity to take our discussion in a slightly different path and discuss a revelation I have received (it may be apparent to some of you), but it was certainly new to me. The revelation is that in God's creative design, there are processes I define as **life force, function, feature**, and **form**.

Bear with me as I attempt to describe what I mean. This will involve a side journey for a while from our discussion of the human body, human soul, and human spirit. This side journey will involve a discussion of **life force, function, feature**, and **forms**, as well as **divine design and creation** in general and **divine peace** in particular. We also will touch on God's **divine design and creation of the world** as written in the first chapter of Genesis of the Bible and end with a brief statement about **divine law and order.** So let's begin.

Divine Preparation Processes

Life Force, Function, Feature, and Form

Life Force

Life force consists of the divine spiritual life and energy that animate all of God's creation, both physical and spiritual. God's creation is often divided into mineral, plant, animal, human, and divine kingdoms, which exist in the world's physical and spiritual environments. Spiritual life and energy operate uniquely in each kingdom, physical and spiritual. For instance, plant, animal, human, and divine kingdoms reproduce themselves in all variety by means of the life force acting upon the specific seeds that God implants within them. God places in each specific seed His creative design, growth processes, and power to enable the seed to reach the potential that is enclosed within it. Each seed produces fruit uniquely after its kind as a result of the life force working within it.

We each are the fruit that came from the life force operating in the human seed within us and in our parents. We all are born with life force operating within us, and although each new born infant contains some life force, other life forces external to the new born infant must be provided to enable the infant to become what God intends. Good food from minerals, plants, and animals and care from our parents or caregivers are required for survival and proper growth of our human life.

The cycles of growth of our human life require our dependence upon other elements outside of ourselves for us to survive. However, as we grow older, we are expected to make our own survival choices as they relate to our environment and depend less on the choices of others.

But there is more to us than our human life. Within our human seed is the potential of becoming divine. Part of our human seed waits to be born as a divine being acceptable to God the Father. For this to occur, the human seed within us must receive life force from the divine kingdom. Divine life force is born within us when our human life force is combined with the divine life force, which only comes from Jesus Christ. As Jesus Christ said:

> **Verily, verily, I say unto thee, Except a man be born again, he cannot see the kingdom of God. Nicodemus saith unto him, how can a man be born when he is old? can he enter the second time into his mother's womb, and be born? Jesus answered, Verily, verily, I say unto thee, Except a man be born of water and of the Spirit, he cannot enter into the kingdom of God. That which is born of the flesh is flesh; and that which is born of the Spirit is spirit. Marvel not that I said unto thee, Ye must be born again.**
>
> *John 3:3–7*

And

> **Jesus saith unto him, I am the way, the truth, and the life no man cometh unto the Father, but by me.**
>
> *John 14:6*

Divine spiritual life force from Jesus Christ creates a new birth in our spirit. This new birth in our spirit occurs when our human spirit join with the divine spirit of Jesus Christ. Divine life force from Jesus Christ is external to our human life force and is designed by God to combine with the human life force within us to produce divine spiritual fruits.

Divine spiritual fruit comes from the combination of our human spirit with God's divine spirit. A list of divine spiritual fruit is described in Galatians 5:22-23 and Ephesians 5:9:

> **But the fruit of the Spirit is love, joy, peace, longsuffering, gentleness, goodness, faith, meekness, temperance, righteousness and truth.**

This fruit will not be present in us without the involvement of Jesus Christ, and just as there comes a time in our human life cycle when we must take responsibility to ensure the survival of our human life, there comes a time when we must take responsibility for the survival of our divine spiritual life. It is essential that we receive the proper divine spiritual food and care if life force is to properly operate in our spirit.

As you can see by the above passage, peace is only one of the varieties of spiritual fruit that springs forth when the Spirit of Jesus Christ combines with our human spirit. Although there are eleven varieties of spiritual fruit, the purpose of this book is to focus only on peace. This is not to imply that the others are less important because they are all interrelated. You cannot have one without the other. Peace is presented to you because it plays such a vital role in the recognition and growth of the others. Jesus Christ emphasized to His followers during His last days to them that peace was going to be given to them to sustain them and keep their heart from being troubled.

> **Peace I leave with you, my peace I give unto you: not as the world giveth, give I unto you. Let not your heart be troubled, neither let it be afraid.**
> *John 14:27*

Divine spiritual fruit like peace are not initially sensed by physical sense organs and systems. This is because there are boundaries between man's spiritual and physical perceptions. These boundaries are crossed only by those whose spiritual and physical systems have been developed to enable them to do so. Just as the transfer of oxygenated blood from the lungs to the heart and thence throughout the physical body requires the cooperation of different physical system, so on a higher level, the cooperation of spiritual and physical systems is necessary for the reception of divine spiritual fruit.

The development of our spiritual and physical systems to perceive the divine life force of God is a part of God's design for each of us. The human part is within us waiting for the entrance of the divine part. The divine part comes from Jesus Christ when we believe in Him and receive the inspiration sent by Him through the Holy Spirit. The Holy Spirit comes to our spirit and begins a work in us that causes a transformation in our spirit, soul, and body, if we are willing, so that we might perceive and partake of divine spiritual fruit.

As stated earlier, this divine life force can be likened to the creative life force in a seed. It carries all the qualities and possibilities that God intends. In a larger sense, this divine life force has specific functions, features, and forms to accomplish the multitude of purposes God has for His creations. We are discussing only peace, but all of God's spiritual and natural creations come from divine seeds.

Physical seeds carry the potential of physical life, but they must be combined with the proper physical soil, physical water, and physical sunlight to grow. Embedded in the seed is what later comes forth as the fruit. The same is true of spiritual seed. Spiritual seed carries the potential for spiritual life. It also must be combined with the proper spiritual soil, spiritual water, and spiritual sunlight in us to grow. Embedded in the spiritual seed is what later comes forth as spiritual fruit. The spiritual seed of peace must be planted in us for us to grow the fruit of peace. The spiritual peace seed comes from Jesus Christ. It has to be properly received by us as a seed for the fruit of peace to grow in us.

With physical seeds, the soil of the earth furnishes conditions for growth, but without the rain and sunlight, there would be no fruit. The soil is earthy and in the earth, but the rain water and sunlight come from outside the earth and are "heavenly." So is it with spiritual growth.

Our spirit and soul furnished the soil for conditions of growth, while Jesus Christ who operates from outside us before coming inside of us (if permitted) furnishes the seed referred to in the Bible as the "Word." The rain water and the sunlight are referred to in the Bible as the former and latter; rain and the light are spiritual forces that act like water and sunlight upon our spiritual seeds.

A more detailed look at the functions of water and sunlight might serve to explain this further. Sunlight displays its transforming nature when its effects upon things are studied. In plant life, sunlight is important in the process of photosynthesis, whereby the energy in sunlight along with minerals from the earth and air is used by plant life to grow and produce fruit as well as convert carbon dioxide into oxygen, which is essential for human life.

Sunlight has qualities that range within and beyond the range of our physical senses. It is not visible to the naked eye and is mostly recognized by its effects and reflections. Sunlight is composed of particles that affect us. For example, sunlight assists the physical body in producing vitamin D, which is necessary for a healthy life, but we are not aware of this process and only experience the result. It has been proven that a lack of sunlight or the substance it provides can result in physical and emotional disorders.

Sunlight is composed of light particles that are both visible and invisible. Its effects vary according to the nature of the object upon which it shines. Similarly, the effect of the force of life that comes from Jesus Christ varies when acting upon our human spirit, our human soul, and our human body based upon our nature or, as explained in the Bible, upon our willingness to receive Him.

Spiritual substances from Jesus Christ when correctly combined with life forces within our human spirit, human soul, and human body causes spiritual, emotional, and physical changes that lead to peace.

God intends for you to choose life. He states:

> **I call heaven and earth to record this day against you, that I have set before you life and death, blessing and cursing: therefore choose life, that both thou and thy seed may live: That thou mayest love the Lord thy God, and that thou mayest obey his voice, and that thou mayest cleave unto him: for he is thy life, and the length of thy days:**
> **Deuteronomy 30:19–20**

You have been given the free will to choose life—that is, to choose Jesus Christ. He is the source of your life, and any other choice results in spiritual death. In the course of your life, you experience the opportunity to make a variety of choices. The choices you make may be as God intends or not. You will ultimately sense the effects of your choices in your human spirit, in your human soul, and in your human body. Ideally, you are to develop the ability to make godly choices in the use of your life force by becoming obedience to the written and living Word of God.

Peace is an attribute that results from obedience to the written and living Word of God. As you believe in Jesus Christ, receive Him, and are obedient to His commandments and the guidance of the Holy Spirit, you will receive guidance, truth, and peace. Jesus Christ said in John 14:6 the following:

> **Jesus saith unto him, I am the way the truth, and the life no man cometh unto the Father, but by me.**

And in John 14:27:

> **Peace I leave with you, my peace I give unto you: not as the world giveth, give I unto you. Let not your heart be troubled, neither let it be afraid.**

Peace is in the life force that Jesus Christ gives to you. The lack of peace in your physical body and especially in your heart can be caused by your refusal to accept the peace that Jesus Christ offers. Peace works from the human spirit and human soul to your human body. Peace in your human spirit, human soul, and human body is greatly dependent upon the choices you make in the use of the life force in you when you were born and your acceptance of the divine life force given to you by Jesus Christ through the Holy Spirit.

Peace is not from the world, but from Jesus Christ. It is important to realize that you can never acquire peace from the world. It is a divine quality and is not available from physical things. It comes from the divine life force and is formed in us when this divine life force is used as Jesus Christ wills. This book is prepared to show you what you can do to learn how to perceive and receive the peace of Jesus Christ.

Function

The life force performs functions. These functions I will describe include organs and processes in our spiritual and physical bodies that direct the operation of life forces within them. These functions are also called systems. In the physical body, the major functions or systems include the respiratory, circulatory, nervous, digestive systems, and others for a total of twelve major functions or systems. These functions or systems are necessary in order for our physical body to function properly and to enable us to complete the purposes for which we were created.

The respiratory system is necessary for the replenishment of oxygen in the body and the removal of carbon dioxide. The circulatory system is necessary for the transport of oxygen-enriched blood and other nutrients to cells in the body to sustain their life and so on. The life force uses each function or system to enable you to exist as God intends.

Just as there are specific physical functions in our human body so are there spiritual functions in our physical functions as well. These spiritual functions are also active within our human soul and human spirit.

Peace is one such function. It is not my intent to describe the life force processes in all the various spiritual functions of the human spirit, human soul, and human body, but to ask you to consider that just as the life force affects physical functions or systems to enable them to exist as God intends, life force also affects spiritual functions or systems within our human spirit, human soul, and human body to enable them to exist spiritually as God intends. However, it might be helpful at this time to address the *what* question as it relates to the function of peace.

Just *what* is the function of peace in our human spirit, human soul, and human body?

Peace functions to assist us to connect with Jesus Christ and receive from Him additional divine qualities that in divine order follow grace and peace. As it is written in 2 Peter 1:2–4:

> **Grace and peace** (notice peace is mentioned along with grace as needing to be multiplied or increased to partake of the divine nature) **be multiplied unto you through the knowledge of God, and of Jesus our Lord, According as his divine power hath given unto us all things that pertain unto life and godliness, through the knowledge of him that hath called us to glory and virtue: Whereby are given unto us exceeding great and precious promises: that by these ye might be partakers of the divine nature, having escaped the corruption that is in the world through lust.**

The divine nature that peace prepares us to partake of includes faith, virtue, knowledge, temperance, patience godliness, brotherly kindness, charity, and other divine qualities described in 2 Peter 1:5–8 and other scriptures in the Bible.

Peace opens a pathway within our human spirit through which the entire divine nature of God comes into us. As this occurs, the human spirit becomes transformed and is then enabled to assist in providing leadership to the human soul and lead the human soul to its own renewal.

As a result of the leadership of the human spirit, the human soul becomes renewed and subsequently able to perform its major function, which is to provide spiritual guidance to the human body.

Ultimately, the human body becomes obedient to the leadership of the human soul so that it does the will of the Father on earth.

Peace functions in the human spirit, human soul, and human body so that they all work as one harmonious unit. Peace is a divine attribute that functions at all three levels to remove unrest and anxieties. Peace creates harmony in our human spirit, human soul, and human body and prepares us to be able to receive the inflow of the forces of truth, righteousness, wisdom, and love from Jesus Christ without interference.

Feature

Just as you have functions throughout your human spirit, human soul, and human body, these also are created with minor parts called features. If we look at the human body for an example, we find that the human body consists of various external and internal organs, processes, etc., which are parts of the functions. For example, the human body's respiratory function or system consists of the trachea, lungs, alveoli, etc., and the circulatory function or system consists of the heart, blood, arteries, veins, etc., and so it is with all the human body functions that there are features for all of them. These features play a role in accomplishing the tasks of the functions.

Features are operational parts of functions created to enable functions to be accomplished. Features, since they are a part of functions, also use the force of life from Jesus Christ. Features are subparts of functions. They perform various aspects of the function. In our discussion of the sense of sight, some of the features for the function of sight include the lens of the eyes for the reception and focus of light beams, the retina for the conversion of light beams into nervous signals, the optic nerves for the transport of nervous signals to the brain, etc. These features are all the elements that make up the function of sight. Features are used by functions to accomplish their purpose, but to do this, they must take on a form.

Peace consists of many features, but I will just touch upon a few. One of the features of peace is the spiritual power to guard your spirit and soul against those things that would cause you to worry or have a troubled heart and mind. Notice what is described in Philippians 4:7:

> **And the peace of God, which passeth all understanding, shall *keep* your hearts and minds through Christ Jesus.**

The word *"keep"* in the passage above is sometimes used to describe a military term that means to guard or protect. So peace consists of a spiritual feature that guards our hearts and minds. This feature acts in ways that we cannot logically understand.

Another feature of peace is power. When we have developed our spiritual and human nature to an advance degree, we will be empowered by Jesus Christ to use the word *"peace"* to stop forces that seek to frighten us. We see this as demonstrated by Jesus Christ on the Sea of Galilee when a storm arose that frighten the disciples but not Jesus Christ. Jesus spoke to the storm, and the storm ceased:

> **And there arose a great storm of wind, and the waves beat into the ship, so that it was now full. And he was in the hinder part of the ship, asleep on a pillow: and they awake him, and say unto him, Master, carest thou not that we perish? And he arose, and rebuked the wind, and said unto the sea, *Peace be still*, And the wind ceased, and there was a great calm. And he said unto them, Why are ye so fearful? how is it that ye have no faith? And they feared exceedingly, and said one to another, What manner of man is this, that even the wind and the sea obey him?**
> **Mark 4:37–41**

Another feature of peace is that it can exist in a specified place. We get a glimpse of this as described in Leviticus:

> **And I will give peace in the land, and ye shall lie down, and none shall make *you* afraid: and I will rid evil beasts out of the land, neither shall the sword go through your land.**
> **Leviticus 26:6**

A place can have peace within it, while another place does not. One who is sensitive to the spirit can sense this when they travel. Some places are more peaceful than others. In some cases, there is even a sweet fragrance that signals the presence of peace in that place.

Peace has a transferable nature. In John 14:27, Jesus said: **"Peace I leave with you, my Peace I give unto you: not as the world giveth, give I unto you. Let not your heart be troubled, neither let it be afraid."**

Peace can be transferred from one to another. The peace we have within us or that another has within them can be transferred to another who is open to perceive and receive it.

Form

Form is the shape that all created objects and beings become. Within human beings, forms develop as a result of the coming together of divine substance with human spiritual, soul, and physical substance. At the spirit stage, the form is made of spiritual substance; at the soul stage, the form is made of soul substance; and at the physical stage, the form is made of physical substance. There is an interaction of all three of the resulting substances, which affects their individual form with the intent that each becomes as God intends. When this occurs, there is peace at each stage, showing forth that God's design has been perfected. Therefore, peace may be perfected at the spiritual stage and yet not manifested in perfected form at the other levels until later. Ultimately, the peace that dwells within the spirit and soul of an individual is intended to also affect his physical being, environment, and world.

Form develops in order and in an arrangement based upon God's prior design. Form takes up space. Some forms move from space to space. Form contains life force, function, and feature. Every manifestation of life force, function, or feature has a unique form. When perfected, the form has within it all the Creator intends. In order for us to become aware of the various manifestations of life forces, functions, and features, their forms must be known or sensed. We are born into the world with this need to know these things, and we grow individually in knowledge through our recognition of forms.

New born babies eagerly look at, touch, feel, taste, and smell objects and beings in their environment in their desire to know. They primarily recognize these things through their use of their physical senses. We recognize objects and beings primarily through the use of physical senses. What we recognize is the physical forms that the life forces, functions, and features have shaped. It is only later that we come to know the features, functions, and life forces within these forms.

We recognize physical forms with our physical sense organs. Likewise, we recognize spiritual forms with our spiritual sense organs. The use of meditation, prayer, Bible study, and application of the teachings of Jesus Christ through the guidance of the Holy Spirit will equip you to correctly recognize all of these.

The spiritual forms of peace are best described by their effect upon our human spirit, human soul, and human body. Our total being is affected by the spirit of peace that first starts in the human spirit. Peace affects our human spirit to enable it to become sensitive to the divine spirit of God. Our human spirit is changed so that we replace our judgment of objects and beings in our world with God's judgment of objects and beings. Our prior and new judgments are now shaped by the peace of God. This occurs in that part of our human spirit known as our mind. These new judgments change the forms that exist in our human soul. Our intellect, feeling, and will are all affected by this change in our mind.

Spiritual forms (together with their enclosed life force, function, and features) affect physical objects and beings. Spiritual forms often become assimilated into the physical objects they affect. Because of this, the distinctness of spiritual form is not readily perceived and is only recognized when spiritual senses are developed, which can perceive their presence. For those whose spiritual senses are not developed, the effects of spiritual forms are only recognized by changes in the nature of the physical objects or beings that have been affected. The distinctness of spiritual forms after their encounter with physical forms is most often known only by their effects.

One example of this in nature is the pleasant fragrance of a flower. The pleasant fragrance of the flower acts upon the air around it to change the nature of the air. Its very encounter with the air causes the air to change. The air continues to exhibit the characteristics of a gas except that now the fragrance from the flower has changed its aroma. The combination of fragrance and air will diffuse through the space as one, even though the air now contains the fragrance from the flower. The fragrance takes on the form of the air now carried by it. The fragrance within the air changes the effects of the air on those who smell it, which then causes changes to occur in them.

This would occur if the fragrance had also been absorbed by clothing. However, this would not be the case with all things. Some things would not be affected by the fragrance and so would not be changed. It would only affect those substances that were prepared to accept it.

The same is true for the peace form. It affects only those things, places, and beings that are prepared to accept it. The life force, function, features, and form of peace will be exhibited wherever peace is permitted to dwell. One only has to believe in Jesus Christ and seek His peace to receive it. It will combine with you and change your spirit, soul, and physical nature to the degree you are prepared to accept and use it. What you do with the form of peace will change your state of being. Its form in you will change the effect you have on your environment and others.

> **Be ye therefore perfect, even as your Father which is in heaven is perfect.**
> **Matthew 5:48**

Life force, functions, and features create in us a final form that is perfected when we become completely what God intended us to be from the beginning of His creation. We are to become divine. We are a part of God's divine plan. The final form we take is the result of God's spirit interacting with the life force He gave us at our birth. Our final form is to consist of the divine forms of our spirit, soul, and body that all are to be perfected according to God's original plan for each of us. God's divine plan is for us to have divine recognizable spirit, soul, and body forms that the life force creates as it perfects our spirit, soul, and body.

Our spirit, soul, and body forms are constantly changing. They are perfected when they have become completely what God intended them to be when He designed us. Your final form is purposed to be the completed (perfected) reality of the divine design for you.

Let's take a further look at the **Divine Design and Creation**.

Divine Design and Creation

Divine designs, creative plans and processes produce life forces, functions, features, and forms. Divine designs, creative plans, and processes are first prepared by the Creator then used to create life forces, functions, features, and forms.

Life forces are active in functions, and life forces and functions are active in features, and life forces, functions, and features are all active in forms. These do not come into existence at once but appear within each other in order, in sequence. I show this in the following illustration. The red circle (life forces) is contained within the green circle (functions), which is contained within the blue circle (features). Finally, all of them are contained within the yellow circle (forms). They are designed to come into being in a predesigned order, not all at once, yet eventually to become combined in all creation, including us, and to work within each other as a unified whole.

Although the illustration shows the life forces, functions, features, and forms as separate discrete circles, think of them as integrated. Also, think of them as growing from the center outwardly. The life forces are the cause of the creations of all the others. The life forces cause the functions to come into being. The life forces create the features to enable the functions to operate correctly. Eventually, the life forces create the forms to enable the functions and features to perform as God intends.

After the form is created, additional divine substance as content is infused into the form. This divine substance comes from God through Jesus Christ and the Holy Spirit. Organs are subsequently formed within the form. More divine substance is inserted into the organs. Processes unique to the specific organs act upon the substance within them, further changing the substance and eventually distributing it to the total being for use.

For example, on the physical level, the human heart is formed to receive blood and oxygen from other parts of the body and the lungs, which receive oxygen from external air. Both the blood and oxygen become contents in the heart. Our heart carries out functions, contains features, has a form, and performs processes that act upon the blood and oxygen, preparing them to be pumped out of it to the rest of our body organs and systems for their use and existence.

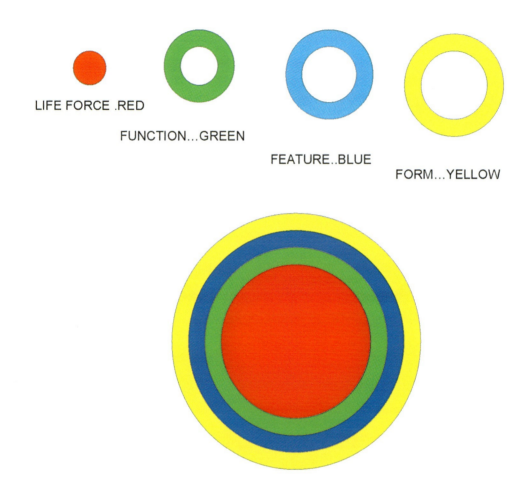

Within all creation is the divine design. God first designs within Himself the object, thing, or life form He later creates. The designs and the order of His creation are spiritual at the beginning that later become physical. Physical creation comes after spiritual creation, not the other way around. The design and order of God's spiritual and physical creation are predetermined before the process of creation begins. Imagine this with me.

Think of this as the thinking process you go through when planning an automobile trip. Typically, you determine many of the details of the trip before you start the journey—where you are going, what routes you will take, what you will carry on your trip, how much will it costs, and so forth. So it is that the life forces, functions, features, and forms of our spiritual and physical world, including the life forces, functions, features, and forms in you, existed spiritually in God's before He created them and you. The design process involves designing the appropriate life forces, functions, features, and forms initially so that when they are spiritually and physically created the intended object, thing, or life form might reach its intended purpose.

Divine Processes and Mankind

Divine Design and Divine Peace

Life Force of Divine Peace

Divine peace is included in God's divine life force. It affects both spiritual and physical substances. It has particular functions in you as well as specific features and forms. Think of it as a sunbeam. God's divine life force acts like the sun. Divine peace is like one of its sunbeams. Divine peace is one of the attributes of God that shines on all things and object. For mankind, who has the freedom to receive or reject God, it shines on them but only becomes a part of those who believe and receive Jesus Christ, the Holy Spirit, and Him.

Functions of Divine Peace

The major function of divine peace is to prepare your spirit, soul, and body to receive the truth and righteousness that later is to be transferred to you from Jesus Christ and the Holy Spirit. Divine peace functions as a necessary preconditioning of our spirit, soul, and body to enable us to identify what is true and right from what is false and wrong.

Therefore, it is necessary that our spirit, soul, and body become peaceful if we are to unmistakably understand and respond correctly to the truth and righteousness that comes from Jesus Christ and the Holy Spirit.

This growth involves cleansing and purifying of our thinking, feeling, and willing processes. Cleansing and purifying of our spirit, soul, and body is not without tests and storms in our life. But with the peace of Jesus Christ, the tests will be passed, and the storms of life with be quieted. However, I must add that in no way will divine peace be obtained without going through these tests and storms. But be of good cheer with Jesus Christ and you will overcome them!

Features of Divine Peace

Peace consists of features that include joy, patience, calmness, stability, thoughtful responses, and reactions, just to name a few, all which are intended for distribution throughout your entire being. Joy is a major outcome of divine peace. Along with joy, you will also come to possess a quiet strength that will give you extraordinary endurance of seemingly overwhelming injustices.

Form of Divine Peace

The spiritual organ **Conscience** is the form created in mankind by God to contain peace. The conscience is formed by the Spirit of God to house divine peace. Although divine peace is a spiritual substance that affects all components of our spirit, soul, and body, the organ that has the capacity to house it is the conscience. From the conscience goes forth a spirit of peace that affects the understanding (truth) and will (righteousness) and from there our total being.

Divine peace flowing from our conscience enables us to transform our thinking, feeling, and willing. We gain the ability to follow the directions of Paul when he urges us (Phil. 4:8):

> **Finally, brethren, whatsoever things are true, whatsoever things are honest, whatsoever things are just, whatsoever things are pure, whatsoever things are lovely, whatsoever things are of good report; if there be any virtue, and if there be any praise, think on these things.**

Our feelings are transformed in us so that we possess feelings of gladness of heart in pleasing God.

Thou hast put more than in the time *that* their corn and their wine increased. I will both lay me down in peace, and sleep: for thou, LORD, only makest me dwell in safety.

Psalm 4:6–7

Our will becomes formed to be more in line with the will of God. As expressed in the *Lord's Prayer* in Mathew 6:10:

Thy kingdom come. Thy will be done in earth, as it is in heaven.

Divine Design of the World

Having laid a foundation of the divine formative powers of God as demonstrated in life forces, features, functions, and forms in general and divine peace in particular, let's end this side journey by a discussion on how God applied them in His creation of the world.

Let us begin with the Bible—Genesis 1:1–2:

> ¹**In the beginning God created the heaven and the earth.**
> ²**And the earth was without form, and void; and darkness was upon the face of the deep. And the Spirit of God moved upon the face of the waters**

God existed before the first verse. He was prior to the beginning. He existed prior to the creation of heaven and earth. In Genesis 1:1, where it states "in the beginning God created the heaven and the earth," I would have you consider that God existed before the scene described in this verse. This verse describes God developing the designs, creative plans, and processes for the life forces, functions, features, and forms of everything that later comprised heaven and earth. This occurred before they were brought into existence. All of these were within God as divine designs and plans before they were actually made into spiritual and physical matters.

These existed in God prior to their coming forth into existence within the spiritual world and the physical world as we know them. God designed all He intended for heaven and earth within Himself first before they appeared. I hope this is not too difficult to imagine. The point I want you to grasp is that not only had God existed before heaven and earth, but that God created the designs and creative plans and processes for all objects and things that would exist in heaven and earth, and that they all were within Himself before they were made. This includes you!

Genesis 1:2 continues to describe conditions within God. The earth *was*, but was without form and was void or empty of the creative plans and processes God intended for it. Although the condition of the earth is stated as void, it does not mean that it was "nothing" for it does consist of "darkness" and "water." This "darkness" is not nothingness, but the potential substance that would be used by divine forces, functions, features, and forms for earth that would later be created.

We do see that this earth contained "water." This water is not as we know water today, but water of a different type. I ask you to think of it as water of an undefined spiritual nature that is made up of spiritual substance that God uses to make His designs a reality, a reality that can be revealed to others. For we see that the Spirit of God moves upon it, which suggests it has substantiality. This all occurs within God Himself. If you read further on, you will see in 2:5 that this could not have been water as we currently think of it because God had not yet caused it to rain.

For the LORD God had not caused it to rain upon the earth.

Genesis 2:5

In Genesis 1:3, we begin to get insight into the way God makes the divine designs that are within Himself real within the spiritual world first and later within the physical world. Consider this explanation. First, He **says something** about the thing, object, or entity, then He **does something** to create or affect the thing o existence.

What He says *states the design* for the thing, object, or entity. What He does *makes or affects the design for the* thing, object, or entity. The design precedes the creative plan and process. This seems wise. First, you design, then you create. Look at the following verses:

> ³And God said, Let there be light: and there was light.
> ⁴And God saw the light, that it was good:
> and God divided the light from the darkness.
> ⁵And God called the light Day, and the darkness he called Night.
> And the evening and the morning were the first day.
>
> *Genesis 1:3–5*

Let us take a look at this further. God *said*. What He said was what He had earlier designed within Himself. Then after He *said*, He activated the creative plans and processes, which also were already within Him. The activation of these plans and processes made what He said a reality. The light appears. Bear in mind that this is not the physical light of the sun, moon, or stars, for they don't appear until later in the creation process. This is a spiritual light that consists of supernatural spiritual substance of warmth, illumination, and infinite variety from which all known creation is made. Included in it are the spiritual life forces, functions, features, and forms that will later come forth in the created spiritual and physical worlds. This spiritual light is not knowable through our five senses but is known through spiritual senses.

Then He inspects, *saw*, the light that was created. He determines whether it conforms to His design and creative plan and process. It does, and He judges it as *good*. This light has the quality of God within it and is capable of being revealed so that God senses it outside Himself. As we develop our spiritual senses, we too will be able to have this light within us. This is so because Jesus said when He was on earth.

> Ye are the light of the world. A city that is set on an hill cannot be hid.
> Neither do men light a candle, and put it under a bushel, but on a candlestick; and it giveth light unto all that are in the house.
> Let your light so shine before men, that they may see your good works, and glorify your Father which is in heaven.
>
> **Matthew 5:14–15**

In Genesis 1:4, God continues His creative plan and process in regard to the light. He distinguishes between the created *light,* which is revealed as a spiritual substance that has become what God intends, and *darkness*, which is a spiritual substance that is yet to be revealed and become what God intends it to be. This does not mean the substance represented by *darkness* does not exist; it just means that it has not yet been revealed as God intends. *Darkness* is often experienced as what some call chaos. *Darkness*, or chaos, is what we define as a state of being currently unknown or unacceptable to us.

> ⁵And God called the light Day, and the darkness he called Night.
> And the evening and the morning were the first day.

He *divided* the *light* from the *darkness*. Keep in mind that all this is coming forth from the original design of the heaven and earth that existed within God in the beginning. In verse 5, He further clarifies the distinction He has just made between light and darkness. He *called* the light *Day*, and the darkness He *called Night*. For God to call an object or thing is to give it qualities, characteristics, and boundaries. To *call* light *Day* is to state its qualities, characteristics, and boundaries. To *call* darkness *Night* is also to state its qualities, characteristics, and boundaries. *Light* is the created and known; *darkness* is what is unknown to us, thus uncreated. Although darkness represents the uncreated and unknown, it is not uncreated and unknown to God as is evident by the fact that He "called" it and gave it its qualities, characteristics, and boundaries.

We also can begin to see the power of God's spoken word. He says something, it happens. When He gives an object, thing, or entity a name, it takes on the qualities of the given name. From what we have been discussing, it can be said that light has now been revealed as different from darkness and is given a quality called *Day*. Light, as we described earlier, can be seen and is a revealer. So *Day* represents life force, function, feature, and form revealed. ***Night***, or ***Darkness***, as we described earlier, represents potentiality of life force, function, feature, and form that are not seen and are objects and things not yet revealed. At the end of verse 5, we read ***And the evening and the morning were the first day.*** This describes that the ***Day*** contains a condition consisting of fading light (evening), where objects, things, or entities are not clearly revealed, and increasing light (morning), where objects, things, or entities become more clearly revealed.

As we discuss divine peace, this process, when applied to the creation of divine peace in us, has meaning for us. We must first grow in the understanding of what divine peace is and then grow in using God's ordained processes to obtain it. Our understanding will not be clear at first but will become clearer as we receive and use divine peace. Another aspect is that the forming of divine peace in our human spirit, soul, and body starts gradually. We hardly notice its growth in us at first. However, slowly, we become more aware of it as it increases and becomes more pronounced in us.

Verse 5 describes the end of the first period of God's creative process.

> ⁶And God said, Let there be a firmament in the midst of the waters, and let it divide the waters from the waters.
> ⁷And God made the firmament, and divided the waters which were under the firmament from the waters which were above the firmament: and it was so.
> ⁸And God called the firmament Heaven. And the evening and the morning were the second day.

In verse 6, God ***said***, and again what He said was what He had earlier designed within Himself. Then after He ***said***, He activated (***made***) the creative plans and processes that also were already within Him. The activation of these plans and processes made what He said a reality. This time, a ***firmament*** is created, and the ***firmament*** divides the ***waters*** from the ***waters***. The ***firmament*** is ***called heaven***, which gives the ***firmament*** its qualities, characteristics, and boundaries. ***Heaven*** is described in the Holy Scriptures as a place where spiritual beings dwell. All this occurs in the spiritual realm. Please keep this in mind. These actions are not yet occurring in the physical world as we understand the physical world.

This ***firmament***, or ***heaven***, is the spiritual home of angels, other created beings, and, ultimately, mankind. In verse 6, God ***divided*** and placed a boundary between these ***waters***. These ***waters***, as we stated earlier, is this preexisting spiritual substance that existed within God that He uses to construct His creation. God creates a boundary by dividing the ***water*** into two portions. One portion is above the ***firmament***, or ***heaven***, and the other portion is below ***heaven***. As we noted earlier, ***heaven*** is a dwelling place for angels and other created beings, including mankind. Some of these angelic beings later assist with the creation and maintenance of both the heavens and the earth. That there is ***water*** above the ***heavens*** tells us, if we are willing to accept it, that there exists spiritual substance and beings that are even more exalted than the ***heaven*** we typically imagine.

Verse 8 also states ***And the evening and the morning were the second day***. Again, this describes that the ***Day*** contains a condition consisting of fading light (evening) where objects and things are not clearly revealed and increasing light (morning) where objects and things become more clearly revealed. In this case, the slow but sure separation and revelation of spiritual substances out of it own midst to form a spiritual place called heaven. Let me suggest to you at this point that while heaven is a place, it is also a state of being. It has characteristics that create a divine state in those who dwell within it. Heaven also serves as a boundary between the "waters" or spiritual substance above it and the spiritual substance below it.

Verse 8 states the end of the second period of God's creative process. Please note this.

> ⁹And God said, Let the waters under the heaven be gathered together unto one place, and let the dry land appear: and it was so.
> ¹⁰And God called the dry land Earth; and the gathering together of the waters called the Seas: and God saw that it was good.

In verse 9, again, God ***said***; and again what He said was what He had earlier designed within Himself. Then after He ***said***, He activated the creative plans and processes that also were already within Him. The activation of these plans and processes made what He said a reality. In this case, the *waters* that was below heaven are gathered together, and *dry land* appears. This indicates that within the *waters* under the heavens existed a spiritual substance called *dry land*. This *dry land* is called *Earth*. Again, I remind you that this is not the earth as we know it. Please don't become confused. God is still creating this out of this mysterious spiritual "water" substance we read about in verse 1.

God gives qualities, characteristics, and boundaries to this *dry land*. He *called* it *Earth*, and the gathering together of the *waters* He called *Seas*. Both the *Earth* and the *Seas* are made from this mysterious spiritual "water" substance, and all are different from what we now know as water, earth, and seas. Please keep this in mind.

> **¹¹And God said, Let the earth bring forth grass, the herb yielding seed, and the fruit tree yielding fruit after his kind, whose seed is in itself, upon the earth: and it was so.**
> **¹²And the earth brought forth grass, and herb yielding seed after his kind, and the tree yielding fruit, whose seed was in itself, after his kind: and God saw that it was good**
> **¹³And the evening and the morning were the third day.**

In verses 11–12, again, God *said*, and again what He said was what He had earlier designed within Himself. Then after He *said*, He activated the creative plans and processes that also were already within Him. The activation of these plans and processes made what He said a reality.

This time, He continues to state His design for the earth and create what He had designed for it. This earth is this spiritual "water" substance that God creates to bring forth growing things out of itself from seeds that is within it. You will note that the growth was specific and **after its kind.** A boundary limits the growth. The product that comes forth is totally dependent upon the seed that is within it. Seed produces grass, herb, or fruit, which produces seed, which later produces grass, herb, or fruit and so on.

Verse 13 states **And the evening and the morning were the third day**. Again, this describes that the *Day* contains a condition consisting of fading light (evening) where objects and things are not clearly revealed and increasing light (morning) where objects and things become more clearly revealed. In this case, the revelation of how the designs that exist in God will come forth from the earth.

Not only growing operations where living things grow from seed after its kind but also that the composition of grass, herb, or fruit is determined by the composition of the seed. I want to keep reminding you that the earth as described here was produced from **water**. This is the spiritual substance we described above. The earth, which was derived from this **water,** was created by God to reproduce substances out it from seeds placed in it.

Things are produced in this **water-earth** substance as the result of the seed. And so it is the seed that is placed in this **water-earth** substance that produces the resulting grass, herb, or fruit. Peace is described as a fruit of the spirit in Galatians 5:22. Peace can only come to you from the seed of peace that is placed within you. If there is to be peace in you, it can only come and grow as a result of Jesus Christ placing it in you. Jesus Christ is the Prince of Peace. We can only obtain peace from Him.

I have provided comments on the first three days of the Genesis creation story to stimulate your thinking about the ways of God's designs and creative processes. I suggest you might read on through chapters 1, 2, and 3 of Genesis to gather more insight into the world as created by God. My purpose in describing these first thirteen verses is hopefully to give you a sense of the rhythms and phases of God's creative designs and processes and perhaps some insight into God's design and creative processes that do not happen all at once.

Later, in Genesis 1:26–27, you will note where God makes man in His image and likeness. And in Genesis 2:7, you will note where the Lord God formed man of the dust of the ground and breathed into his nostrils the breath of life and man became a living soul. God continues His creative work on man by giving him a soul, which is created from this same **water-earth** substance we described above. Man now consists of both a spirit and soul.

It very important for us to recognize that since man now has a soul created from this ***water-earth*** substance, he now has been given plantlike qualities and like plants has the potential to produce spirit and soul fruit from seed. Peace is one of the fruits that is produced in man. The seed of peace comes from Jesus Christ. Keep this in mind as we continue with our discussion of how peace is formed in you.

Also you should note that God is and has always been active in the affairs of the world. He has not stopped His activities in the affairs of Man. Some would have you believe that God does not actively care about His creation. This is not true. He has always cared about what happens in the world and what happens to you.

One of His major interventions was the sending of His Son, Jesus Christ, into the world to restore it to Him. Jesus Christ continues to labor in world processes and in us if we are receptive of Him. This process in us involves showing us how to grow peace in us. We can only grow peace and thereby become restored to God by letting the peace of Jesus Christ be planted and grown in us.

Divine Law and Order

I must end this side journey with this. Divine designs and creative plans and process are often referred to in the Bible as laws, precepts, statutes, and commandments. They are God-given designs, creative processes, and ways that He uses to achieve His divine purposes. They are not afterthoughts.

What we call "the laws of nature," when properly understood, are divine designs and creative processes in action. Not a creation of the scientist or the philosopher who "discovered" them. All creation is governed by divine orders or commands. Divine orders and commands are invisible yet real powers organized as frameworks of creation. These divine frameworks determine boundaries within which created forces, functions, features, and forms must operate. They are ordained by God.

The Lord describes divine orders and processes in many scriptures in the Bible but none any more profound than in Job 38–40, which I encourage you to read. Especially in Job 38:1–11, we see this when He questions Job on his knowledge of divine orders and processes as they relate to the things God creates and the framework or foundations and boundaries He sets:

> **Then the Lord answered Job out the whirlwind and said,**
> **Who is this that darkeneth counsel by words without knowledge?**
> **Gird up now thy loins like a man; for I will demand of thee, and answer thou me.**
> **Where wast thou when I laid the foundations of the earth? Declare, if thou hast understanding.**
> **Who hath laid the measures thereof, if thou knowest? Or who hath stretched the line upon it?**
> **Whereupon are the foundations thereof fastened? Or who laid the corner stone thereof; when the morning stars sang together, and all the sons of God shouted for joy? Or who shut up the seas with doors, when it brake forth as if it had issued out of the womb? When I made the cloud the garment thereof, and thick darkness a swaddling band for it, and brake up for it my decreed place, and set bars and doors, and said, Hitherto shalt thou come but no further: and here shall thy proud waves be stayed?**

Divine designs and creative plans and processes affect all created things, including our human spirit, soul, and body. Divine designs and creative plans and processes affect the reception of peace by you. Divine peace as imparted by Jesus Christ through the Holy Spirit to you must conform to divine designs and creative plans and processes if you are to receive it. One of the purposes of this book is to assist you with understanding enough about how God, through Jesus Christ and the Holy Spirit, designs and implements creative plans and processes so that you willingly receive the peace Jesus Christ intends you have when He said:

> **Peace I leave with you, my peace I give unto you: not as the world giveth, give I unto you. Let not your heart be troubled, neither let it be afraid.**
> **John 14:27**

I hope you come to recognize that in all of God's creations, He works by divine designs, creative plans, and processes with life force, features, functions, and forms. One of His major creations is divine peace.

Now let us return to the main discussion of our threefold makeup consisting of the human body, human soul, and human spirit. We will pickup with a discussion of the human soul.

Human Soul

Thank you for going along with me on our excursion into a discussion of deeper aspects of the divine creative processes. I believe this will serve us well later in our journey to peace to know that divine creative processes are active in our human body, in our human soul, as well as well as in our human spirit. So let us pick up where we left off with the human body by a discussion of the human soul.

The human soul is where you think, feel, will, and store your memories, beliefs, and "truths." Our soul is not physical. It is spiritual and serves as an intermediary for the life force of Jesus Christ, which gives life to your human soul as well as your human body and human spirit. One function of your human soul is to serve as an intermediary between your human spirit, which we will discuss in a few moments, and your human body, which we mentioned above. It is because of your human soul that you are able to think, have emotions, and make choices that not only affect your human soul but your human body as well. The human soul houses that part of your makeup that receives physical and spiritual sensations and attempts to make "sense" of them.

It is where you attempt to fit together your experiences into a logical, meaningful pattern, where you attempt to build a view of the world and how you fit in it. The human soul also stores your memories, beliefs, and "truths." "Truths" are shown with quotation marks because although truths are eternal, your knowledge of truth may be partial and not the divine truth of Jesus Christ. Because we are all different, we see things differently, and our truth is subjective and relative. As you grow in spiritual knowledge, your grasp of the eternal truth changes. This does not mean that truth changes, but your understanding of truth changes.

Memories, beliefs, and truth all help you think, feel, and choose what actions you should take when confronted by life experiences.

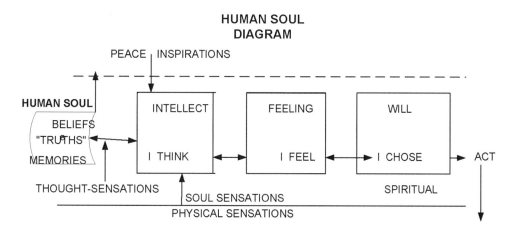

Diagram #5

Diagram 5

The diagram shown above is a simple schematic diagram intended to explain how the human soul interacts within the human body and human spirit as well as internally within itself.

Starting from the bottom of the diagram, **soul sensations**, with its arrow, represent **physical sensations** that originated in the human body that have been converted in the brain to be recognized by the soul. This was mentioned earlier when we discussed the human body. The **thought sensations** indicated on the left are thoughts that are created by our thinking about the **soul sensations** we receive. These **thought sensations** are what we use to develop our **beliefs**, *truths*, and **memories**. The **peace inspiration** label and arrow at the top of the diagram are shown to illustrate that peace is an inspiration (revelation, perception) from the human spirit (not shown but will be discussed a little later), which affects the soul organs. Peace is of a godly nature and has a different nature than the soul, although they both are spiritual. Peace is not recognized by the soul, unless the soul senses and organs have been developed to recognize peace.

In the diagram, you see that the **Human Soul** has distinct parts that I want you to think of as soul organs where I Think, Feel, and Choose. There also are soul organs that house our beliefs, "truths," and memories. These beliefs, "truths," and memories are stored in our soul (we become conscious of them through our brain) and are transmitted to our human spirit, where they become a part of it. All these organs are affected by each other. The arrows are intended to show that there is a constant interchange of beliefs, "truths," and memories among our intellect, our feeling, and our will. These do not work in isolation but interact with each other. The *Act*, with its arrow, indicates that once we chose to do something, soul sensations are converted into sensations that are recognizable to the human body and sent from the human soul to the human body for action. These soul sensations, which originate in the soul, intended for the human body also affects the human soul and human spirit because of the interrelationship of the three.

The human soul is the foundational center of activity of the intellect, feelings, and will. In your intellect, you construct thoughts; in your feeling, your emotions are active; and in your will, you process the results of your thinking and feeling and activate your choices. The results of these activities are sent forth to the human body and human spirit where the effects are felt as life-sustaining or as death. The soul is very vital to our obtaining peace.

Just as the human heart serves as a transfer center of oxygenated blood and as a distribution center for dispatching life force to the entire body, so does the human soul act as a transferring center for the distribution of thinking, feeling, and willing from the human spirit and human soul to the human body.

I want to emphasize that thinking in particular is an aspect of the soul that is of prime importance. Thinking separates mankind from the lower animal. It is a key part of the soul that enables us to reach our divine destiny. The correctness of your thinking determines who you are and who you become. The process of growth in peace starts with sound thinking.

It is with your thinking that you attempt to make "sense" of the world. Those objects, people, and experiences that are encounter in the world become input into your thinking, which assist you in constructing your individualized view of the world. It is within this individualized view of the world that you try to discover how and where you fit. These discoveries will be a continuous undertaking for those who search for truth for themselves, but for those who cease searching for their own individual truth, the result is they will fail to reach God's desired end for them. To reach God's desired end requires a systematic search that starts with thinking and ends with freely believing in Jesus Christ and understanding and doing what He requires of us.

Believing is a process of persuading oneself of something based upon thinking about it. When we are persuaded of something, we have thought about it, analyzed, and compared it with something else to come to a conclusion about what it means and how it fits in with our previous world beliefs. So often Jesus Christ would ask His disciples, "Do you believe?" This challenged them to think and to decide on a reason or reasons that would or had persuaded them to accept the matter that was being considered.

Primary in this believing is the challenge to believe in the divinity of Jesus Christ. There are numerous situations in the life of Jesus Christ where we read where He challenges those around Him on this. In the Gospel of John, Jesus challenges Phillip, one of the twelve disciples:

> **Jesus saith unto him, Have I been so long time with you, and yet hast thou not known me, Philip? he that hath seen me hath seen the Father; and how sayest thou then, Shew us the Father? Believest thou not that I am in the Father, and the Father in me? the words that I speak unto you I speak not of myself: but the Father that dwelleth in me, he doeth the works. Believe me that I am in the Father, and the Father in me: or else believe me for the very works' sake. Verily, verily, I say unto you, He that believeth on me, the works that I do shall he do also; and greater works than these shall he do; because I go unto my Father. And whatsoever ye shall ask in my name, that will I do, that the Father may be glorified in the Son.**
>
> *John 14:9-13*

Believing comes from our thinking, which takes place in our intellect.

The human soul uses its thinking, feeling, and willing capabilities to produce reasons for doing things that stimulate feelings and thereby produces emotions that stimulate a willingness to act. When we reason, we affect our emotions and our choices. If our reasoning is sound, we affect our feelings properly, which produces truthful emotions, and we make good choices. When our reasoning is unsound, just the opposite occurs, and we sin.

> **Come now, and let us reason together, saith the LORD: though your sins be as scarlet, they shall be as white as snow; though they be red like crimson, they shall be as wool.**
>
> *Isaiah 1:18*

And

> **And the scribes and the Pharisees began to reason saying, Who is this which speaketh blasphemies? Who can forgive sins, but God alone? But when Jesus perceived their thoughts, he answering said unto them, What reason ye in your hearts? Whether is easier, to say, Thy sins be forgiven thee; or to say, Rise up and walk? But that ye may know that the Son of man hath power upon earth to forgive sins, (he said unto the sick of the palsy,) I say unto thee, Arise, and take up thy couch, and go into thine house. And immediately he rose up before them, and took up that whereon he lay, and departed to his own house, glorifying God.**
>
> *Luke 5:21–25*

One noteworthy benefit to reasoning is that sound reasoning based upon faith in Jesus Christ opens one up to receive divine life force from Jesus Christ. This results in one developing the ability to permit divine healing and cures in our physical body.

The human soul is an intermediary between the human body and human spirit and has communication with both. As a result, it has capabilities to share life force and godly attributes to integrate the two together. This causes continual interaction of the forces of both.

A major principle in obtaining your individual peace is the godly alignment of the Human Soul with your Human Spirit and then to align the Human Body with it. This alignment will be the result of you receiving and following the guidance of the Lord Jesus Christ through the Holy Spirit.

Jesus said that the Holy Spirit of God will receive from Him and show to His disciples what He desires His disciples to have:

> **Howbeit when he, the Spirit of truth, is come, he will guide you into all truth: for he shall not speak of himself; but whatsoever he shall hear, that shall he speak: and he will shew you things to come. He shall glorify me: for he shall receive of mine, and shall shew it unto you. All things that the Father hath are mine: therefore said I, that he shall take of mine, and shall shew it unto you.**
>
> *John 16:13–15*

And again in Romans:

For as many as are led by the Spirit of God, they are the sons of God. For ye have not received the spirit of bondage again to fear; but ye have received the Spirit of adoption, whereby we cry, Abba, Father. The Spirit itself beareth witness with our spirit, that we are the children of God.
Romans 8:14–16

Divine influence works like this. Divine influences flow from the highest to the lowest through intermediaries or intermediary stages. God's purpose for our lives flows from God the Father, through Jesus Christ the Son who is the administrator of divine life forces in the world. Jesus Christ petitions the Father on our behalf. The Father then sends the Holy Spirit at the request of Jesus Christ to our human spirit; then our human soul, which serves as the intermediary between our human spirit and human body, dispatches the life force finally to our human body. The Bible, in speaking of this in regard to mankind, defines the states as the human spirit being ***born again***, the human soul being ***saved***, and the human body being ***redeemed***.

The human soul is where our belief system is developed. Because it is an intermediary between our human spirit and human body, it plays a major role in the regeneration of both. It plays a pivotal role in the regeneration of our human spirit and our human body in developing in them the divine qualities God intends. We have to reexamine and eventually discard many things we have previously believed that appear to be godly but are not. This means we must change some of our previously held beliefs. This is a continuous process as we grow in spiritual maturity. One of the major changes that will be required is what we believe about our own makeup and nature and the nature of Jesus Christ.

We struggle with who we are and how we relate to this world. We wonder about our very existence, who are we, why are we here, what are we to do, unaware that there already exists a specific divine design order established by God through Jesus Christ into which we are to fit.

Reconnecting with God

After much study and experience, I ask you to consider that there exists in all of us a deep spiritual loneliness that can only be satisfied by communion with God. The first stage of reestablishing this communications is to find out how to reconnect with God. To do this, we must replace former untrue beliefs with new true beliefs about who we are, why we are here, and what we are to do.

This process is referred to in the Bible as cleansing or purifying. In other words, we "clean out" or replace former untrue beliefs with new true beliefs. We become free of those beliefs and impediments in our makeup that block our awareness of our true nature and where we fit in God's divine order. The Holy Spirit, under the Leadership of the Lord Jesus Christ, guides us in developing true beliefs and hence cleansing our self.

Beliefs are developed from our thinking. Our normal thinking consists of thinking about sensory experiences we receive from external objects, people, and things. We develop ideas and concepts about these experiences and keep them in our mind as memories. These memories become the basis of our belief systems. However, this is a belief system based only on five-sense knowledge. This knowledge is limited. The five senses are themselves limited as anyone who has experience failing eyesight and hearing loss will acknowledge. So a belief system based solely on five-sense knowledge will be imperfect. Our belief system must incorporate spiritual knowledge if our beliefs are to become true.

Truth come from Jesus Christ and is spiritual. Our truth becomes divine when it is purified by the divine truth of Jesus Christ. We make divine truth alive in us when we incorporate it in what we believe, think, feel, and do in our human soul and human body.

That brings us to the last subject in this section, the Human Spirit.

Human Spirit

One question that seems to plague mankind is who am I? Great thinkers have pondered this question. Many seeking an answer often turn to the writings of philosophers and theologians for answers. Although there are often conflicting views, the prevalent opinion and the one that is fundamental to our discussion about peace is that we are created beings made in the image of God. That our Creator is God, a supernatural being whose nature is superior to Man and yet made Man in His image and likeness. I would say made Man as a reflection of Himself.

SPIRIT DIAGRAM

REALM OF HOLY TRINITY AND DIVINE SPIRITS

HUMAN SPIRIT

- I AM BORN AGAIN
- GOD
- JESUS
- CONSCIENCE
- HOLY SPIRIT
- PEACE | INSPIRATIONS
- SPIRITUAL SENSATIONS

In Genesis, it is written:

> **And God said, let us make man in our image, after our likeness: and let them have dominion over the fish of the sea, and over the fowl of the air, and over the cattle, and over all the earth, and over every creeping thing that creepeth upon the earth.**
> **So God created man in his *own* image, in the image of God created he him; male and female created he them.**
>
> **Genesis 1:26–27**

In Psalms, it is recorded:

> **I have said, Ye are gods; and all of you are children of the most High.**
>
> **Psalm 82:6**

As we indicated earlier, and this may be difficult for some to accept, if mankind is made in the image and likeness of God and like God has godly qualities, why does he still have so much trouble? Many scholars that accept the existence of God believe that Mankind is designed with the potential to have divine godlike qualities like peace but as a result of events in mankind's past has strayed from his original connection with God and must now somehow remedy what has been lost.

Our Human Spirit exists in us in a seed-type form with the potential to assist us to become what God intended in His original creation. This process is not a simple one. Man has to properly participate in preparing his human spirit to become what it should be. This is hard. As we stated earlier, mankind lost his original status with God because of disobedience.

The mistake caused by this disobedience must be corrected. Mankind's original godlike nature was changed because of this disobedience. As a result, the peace of God, which is the subject of this book, should be present in us but is not. So to accomplish His original plan, God instituted a plan that included Jesus Christ. This plan involved God sending Jesus Christ unto earth to help us.

Our role, if we want divine peace, is to believe in Jesus Christ and follow His instructions on how to receive divine peace into our human spirit. We first must decide we want divine peace. We then must believe that Jesus Christ can provide the divine peace we seek. We lastly must believe that we have in us the capacity to be peaceful and that this capacity is a part of our human spirit.

When we believe Jesus Christ is who He says He is, He begins to act on our behalf by asking God the Father to send the Holy Spirit to dwell in us; thus, the Holy Spirit enters our human spirit and activates the divine seed that is already in us and the process of making alive our human spirit began. This process enables our human spirit to receive the divine peace that comes from Jesus Christ.

The Holy Spirit, under the direction of Jesus Christ, comes into us and guides us to work together with Him to prepare our human spirit to receive the spirit of peace from Jesus Christ. A divine principle is revealed here. In God's divine order, preparation first occurs; then spiritual power is transferred. Without preparing the way, there can be no access to God's presence. So it is with peace. You must first be made ready by the work of the Holy Spirit before the Spirit of Peace is given to you by Jesus Christ.

When the process begins, the Holy Spirit working with us begins to transform our human spirit. For some, the perception of this process is immediate; for others, it becomes perceptible over time. The process is expressed in simple terms in Christianity as being "born again."

Please note the "born again" process first starts in our human soul with belief in Jesus Christ. But there is an introductory phase where God provides to all creation a spiritual formative power called grace. Grace is a formative spiritual power that is freely given to all to start the process that opens up our human spirit and soul to receive faith. Faith is what enables us to believe in Jesus Christ.

When we believe in Jesus Christ, He sends the Holy Spirit to begin a work in our human spirit. The effect of the Holy Spirit working in our human spirit first causes a sense of joy that comes from the entrance of divine peace into our mind. We wonder where this new joyful feeling is coming from; and after attempts to sustain it, for it subsequently begins to fade away, we realize it is not caused by something we can do, but comes from God. Later, we began to doubt our ability to sustain it. This doubt is indeed well-founded, for this peace and joy that come from the presence of the Holy Spirit fade after a short time but begin to return as we grow spiritually. This experience is described in the Bible as *the earnest of the Spirit*:

> **Who hath also sealed us, and given *the earnest of the Spirit* in our hearts.**
> **Moreover I call God for a record upon my soul, that to spare you I came not as yet unto Corinth.**
> **Not for that we have dominion over your faith, but are helpers of your joy: for by faith ye stand.**
> **2 Corinthians 1:22–24**

This initial joy is just a foretaste of what is to come if you permit the Holy Spirit to have His proper role in your life. You must actively participate in growing your faith in Jesus Christ. One of the major truths we must grow to understand is that we must have total faith in God, Jesus Christ, and the Holy Spirit.

We learn about our physical body by experiences our physical body has with other beings and things that affect it. The same is true of our human spirit. We learn about our human spirit as a result of the experiences that affect it, such as encounters with God, Jesus Christ, and the Holy Spirit and other spirit beings and forces.

The Holy Spirit is initially active with our human spirit to teach us under the administration of Jesus Christ about these things. The more we learn about spiritual beings and things, the wiser we become.

As we surrender ourselves to the Holy Spirit, marvelous supernatural things begin to happen to us. Our sensitivity to others increases, and our insight into our need to assist others increases. In many persons, their dream life become more vivid, and they remember more of what they experience in dreams. In some, they have the experience described in the Bible as the "baptism of the Holy Spirit." This causes them to speak in a different language than their native language and exhibit supernatural abilities called "gifts of the spirit." These are all signs of their permitting the Holy Spirit to work in and with them.

One of the major outcomes of these experiences is the development of a true sense of self, of who you really are. Through these encounters with the Holy Spirit, you grow to realize that your real nature is divine and spiritual, and that you have within you the capability under the guidance and power of the Holy Spirit to become a guardian of your own spirit, soul, and body. You come to realize that the "I" you talk about when you refer to yourself is in your divine spirit, not your physical body or your soul, but your divine spirit.

The "I" used to define you is in your human spirit. You are a divine being made in the image and likeness of God. Your "I" is that part of you given responsibility to lead your human spirit to become what God intended it to be from the beginning of your creation by Him.

The "I" in you is placed in you to enable you to guide your human spirit as well as your human soul and your human body. The Human Spirit through your "I" makes use of your spiritual and physical functions. For example, when I think, it is the "I" of the human spirit that is using my intellect to think. Remember that the intellect is a function of the soul. So the "I" uses the human spirit to manage the intellect that is in the human soul. When "I" eat, it is the "I" in my human spirit that is using the physical organs of my human body to eat.

This knowledge of who I really am is major. Just as my physical body grows from childhood to maturity, so must my human spirit grow from childhood to maturity. I become mature spiritually when my "I" take responsibility for the leadership of my human spirit. I take that responsibility when I humble myself and recognize that the Holy Spirit is to guide my "I" to that maturity. and my role is to willingly follow His leadership.

The first place the Holy Spirit begins to work on in our human spirit is our conscience. The Holy Spirit transfers the divine power of divine peace to our conscience to wake it up. The conscience is a major organ of our human spirit, but in most of us, it is barely active. One of the earliest signs of being "born again" is an alive and active conscience.

Our conscience is that part of our human spirit that informs our "I" of what is good, true, and righteous in the mind of God. When the Holy Spirit stimulates our conscience to become active, we know that a spiritual change is occurring in us.

As our "I" follows our conscience, which has received guidance from the Holy Spirit, it becomes perfected. As our conscience becomes perfected, we become more Christlike. On the other hand, our conscience withers when we act contrary to the revealed truth and will of God. As it withers, we move closer to physical and spiritual death. This is first manifested in our physical body as diseases of the heart.

Our conscience affects our heart. The action of the conscience is felt in the heart as agitation. This is often referred to as a troubled heart. All of us are subject to this. The troubling of one's heart is the physical result of our spiritual conscience.

The Bible states that the conscience is a judge. The conscience is a witness. The conscience can be defiled. The conscience may be good or evil. The act of one person can affect the conscience of another for good or evil. The conscience grows to contain the mystery (hidden truth) of faith. The conscience may be pure. The conscience can become as "seared" as with a hot iron or scarred and insensitive through speaking in hypocrisy. This manifests as a lack of conscience and is seen in human acts that are called "beastly." The conscience may become corrupted when one is mentally dishonest and unbelieving. Life force from Jesus Christ flows in and purges the conscience of those who believe in Him and follow His commandments.

The reality or truths of physical matters or actions are not to be confused with the reality of spiritual matter or actions. They are not the same. Although physical reality does shows forth as an image of spiritual reality, this physical image is the outer covering of a hidden spiritual truth or mystery that can be known only though the use of spiritual senses. Our conscience is one such spiritual sense. Using our conscience, that has been transformed by Christ, helps us to act in the physical world in ways that Christ desires and hence enable us to become more peaceful.

There is a condition of conscience that occurs after the purging by Jesus Christ and the Holy Spirit, where the conscience becomes so pure that it no longer is affected by sin. This happens when the person totally surrender to the will of God.

The prayer of the righteous affects the conscience for good, not only by prayer for one's own conscience but also by prayer for that of another. Our conscience guides us in doing God's will even when we are enduring grief and suffering. There is a working out of our own salvation through the following of our conscience in faith in Jesus Christ even when we appear in the physical sense to suffer wrongly. As the measure of God's Spirit increases in us, so does our awareness of the activity of our conscience increase.

The Spirit of God is given to each individual in proportion to what is needed for them to grow in love and wisdom at that specific moment. These are given in accordance with their ability to receive it. The Holy Spirit knows just what and how much of the divine nature to impart to us at any given moment.

Peace is just one of the divine qualities that is imparted to our nature by God, Jesus Christ, and the Holy Spirit if we are willing and prepared to receive it. We will say more later about the role peace plays in the development of conscience in the section where we discuss the definitions of peace.

Putting It All Together

Putting It All Together

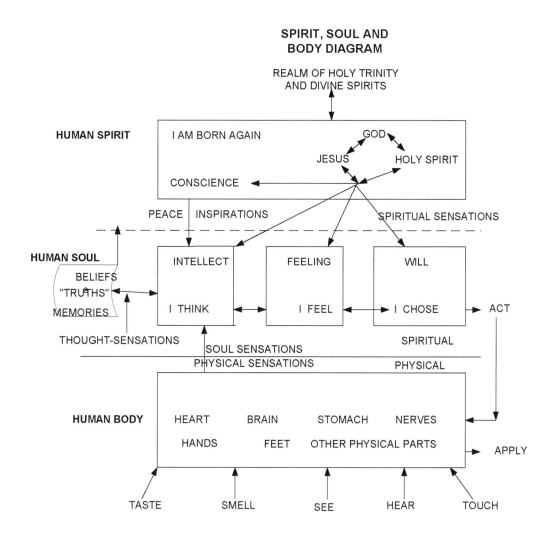

The **Putting It All Together** illustration shown above is an attempt at showing how our spirit, soul, and body all interact with each other. As described earlier, physical sensations from the world around us are conveyed from our human physical body to our human soul where they are processed and become thoughts, memories, "truths," and beliefs. These are transmitted to our human spirit and used by our human spirit to become what we understand to be truth and right. These truths and rights are then used to form what we decide to do and are sent to our human soul and human body as impulses to be acted upon.

This is the composition of our being before we decide to let Jesus Christ and the Holy Spirit work in our life. However, when we decide to accept Jesus Christ and let Him guide us through the Holy Spirit, we discover that His first words to us are we *must be born again*. Jesus Christ came to tell us that what we are as spirit, soul, and body is just the beginning, and we must be "born again." We must be changed.

We come to understand that our current human construction of spirit, soul, and body is just the first stage in a growth to perfection. We are to become divine. This human body, soul, and spirit all eventually will be reborn into a being that will become eternal. Paul mentions this in 1 Corinthian 15 where he states that *flesh and blood cannot inherit the Kingdom of God.* He states in the same chapter that our corruptible body, that is our perishing body, must become immortal, that is everlasting. Our current being must be changed by us working with the Spirit of God so that we become a new composition that like the being of Christ is incorruptible. *We become a new creation that will assist God in worlds yet to be revealed.*

Our current composition is a mixture of good and evil influences that are active in our thinking, feeling, willing, memories, "truths," and beliefs. These influences are to become all good, which require work on our part as we obey the guidance of the Holy Spirit.

In a later section titled **Divine Truth, Divine Peace, and Divine Righteousness**, we illustrated a more advance model of this diagram. In it, we show in more detail how our spirit, soul, and body interact with our thinking, feeling, willing, memories, "truths," and beliefs to enable us to reach immortality. Our spirit, soul, and body are dynamically transformed as we receive and obey the inspirations of divine truth, divine peace, and divine righteousness from Jesus Christ and the Holy Spirit. Divine peace plays a major role in this development. Divine peace, working through our conscience to our understanding (truth) and will (righteousness), assists in the production of spiritual fruit.

The summary of it in this discussion is that we are to become like Jesus Christ. The intricate, awesome being that we are, although simply illustrated in our diagrams, is to become even more wonderful. From our birth, we are created to become an eternal spiritual being. We are not born into this world just to live under natural laws only but to become recipients of more heavenly characteristics. We are to become filled with divine attributes. We are to grow to exhibit the spiritual fruit describes in the scriptures. We are to be the fruit of the earth mentioned in James 5:7:

> **Be patient therefore, brethren, unto the coming of the Lord. Behold, the husbandman waiteth for the precious fruit of the earth, and hath long patience for it, until he receive the early and latter rain.**

We are to grow to become divine spiritual fruit. The intended purpose of our mission on earth is to willingly work with Jesus Christ and the Holy Spirit to produce from within our spirit, soul, and body these divine attributes. These fruit are:

> **But the fruit of the Spirit is love, joy, peace, longsuffering, gentleness, goodness, faith, Meekness, temperance.**
> *Galatians 5:22,23*

And

> **For the fruit of the Spirit is in all goodness and righteousness and truth.**
> *Ephesians 5:9*

FRUIT OF THE SPIRIT

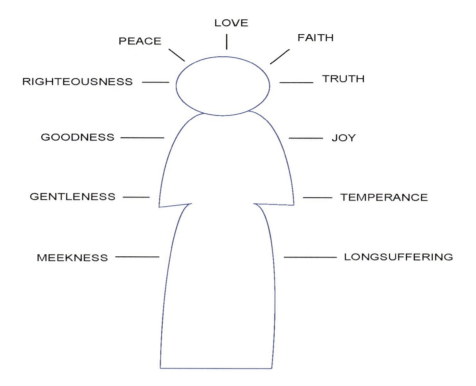

The following are brief statements about the spiritual attributes shown above that will give us a sense of their role in our lives:

Love

Love is the divine attribute of God from which all the others come. It is the creative life force of God. It creates benefits for all creation. It manifests in each of us as willing obedience to God's commandments.

Joy

Joy is the divine attribute that confirms that peace and the other fruit of the spirit are active in you. It results from being pleasing to God.

Peace

Peace is the divine attribute that enables us to maintain harmony in the midst of disharmony. It creates steadfastness and stability and opens one to the other divine attributes. It begins its work in our mind, in the spiritual organ, the conscience, and proceeds to work throughout our total being in due course.

Long-suffering

Long-suffering is the divine attribute that enables one to operate in accordance with the times and seasons of God.

Gentleness

Gentleness is the divine attribute that prevents us from causing harm to any and is exhibited physically by kindness to all.

Goodness

Goodness is the divine attribute that is the outcome of all that God does and wills for us to do.

Faith

Faith is the divine attribute that causes things to be created first in the spiritual world and manifest later in the physical world in accordance with God's will.

Meekness

Meekness is the divine attribute of humility and openness to the influx of the spirit of God.

Temperance

Temperance is the divine attribute that assists in controlling the activities of our spirit, soul, and body as God wills.

Righteousness

Righteousness is the divine attribute that judges an action or behavior as being in accordance with God's will.

Truth

Truth is the divine attribute that enables one to understand the reality of what is experienced. It is what God says a thing is.

We ultimately are to shine forth with a glorious spiritual light created by the spiritual fruit of love, joy, peace, long-suffering, gentleness, goodness, faith, meekness, temperance, righteousness, and truth.

The destiny we seek is a divine one where the qualities of divinity as listed above become our innate character. Until this occurs, we labor in the progress of becoming divine.

Peace and the Divine Journey

Peace Dove

The Trinity

Mankind's Co-Creator Role

Blessed are the peacemakers for they shall be called the children of God. So goes the saying of Jesus Christ in the Bible. Peace and peacemakers are essential to the world today. It seems that the world is becoming more disquieted through the rapid changes occurring in it. We are in an age of tremendous changes. Many of these changes appear to be beneficial to mankind, while others challenge the very foundation upon which our lives are built and appear to be harmful. The result is often confusion and turmoil for many.

It has become clear that changes in our life and on earth are unavoidable, and for peace to occur on earth, these changes must be understood and managed. This involves, at times, doing away with former things and adopting newer ones. Failure to meet the challenges of these changes causes unrest in many.

Many who share the desire for peace on earth come to recognize that these changes are replacing familiar and cherished things. But they should not be discouraged and misread these changes. They are the signs that former things are being done away with in order that we may grow to an understanding of what is needed if we are to live in peace. We must not become dismayed nor discourage by these signs. Jesus Christ came into the world to help us grow in peace. We do that as we grow in understanding as how to manage the various changes we experience in the earth.

Our human spirit, human soul, and human body—like the earth—are intended by God to become places of peace and harmony. However, the early phases of the establishment of peace in us are a breaking up of our old thinking processes, beliefs, and habits. Many of us desire such a peace immediately, but as you will discover as you read and study the material in this book, to experience peace in your life is a process. To become a peacemaker in the world is an even more lengthy process, one we are all asked to undertake.

This book combines the description of various aspects of peace for your reflection and a process of interaction between you, Jesus Christ, and the Holy Spirit that will help you obtain peace. The approach you will take will require your daily active participation. The rewards are eternal.

You will be asked to regularly exercise your spiritual nature and strengthen your ability to guide your human spirit, human soul, and human body in line with the increased knowledge and wisdom you are gaining. You need to obtain a *notebook or diary* where you will record what you receive from the Spirit of God and learn from your experiences. This notebook or diary we will call your *Peace Journal*.

This discussion about peace is intended to help you with your search for peace. A peaceable nature is a recognizable sign in someone who has sought after peace and has become transformed by it. If you seek peace in your life, it must start with you. For some, this statement may seem foolish. We believe our lack of peace is because of others. Often our attention is drawn to other people and aspects of events that cause disturbances in our lives, and we decide that these things are the cause of the disturbances in us. Although it may appear true on the physical level that these disturbances are caused by others, it is not spiritually true. The disturbances in ourselves are disturbances that we have permitted. There may be physical sensations, but the physical and spiritual results are what we have permitted to occur in our spirit.

External conditions of chaos and confusion will occur in our lives. However, our reactions to these conditions can be such that through it all, we maintain a state of peace in our human spirit, human soul, and human body.

If you wish to become a seeker after peace, then eventually, your search will lead to the spiritual nature of things and to Jesus Christ. To obtain true peace, not the false peace of the world, you will eventually come to realize that Jesus Christ is the source of that peace.

Jesus Christ, who is described in the Bible as the Prince of Peace, directs the Spirit of peace to those who believe in Him and earnestly seek Him. The approach we have taken in this book is to leave open to the reader the option of proving that a belief in Jesus Christ will or will not lead to peace in their lives. This proving will require time and physical and spiritual effort on the part of the reader. As you proceed in a sincere effort with this book, you will be led step-by-step on a journey that is intended to grow peace in you. The question you need to answer is, Are you willing to put in the sincere effort to receive the peace that is already promised to you by Jesus Christ?

A major benefit of this search for peace will be your personal recognition of your life's purpose. I like to think of it as coming to where you "fit" in the circumstances of your physical and spiritual environment. Whether it's with loved ones, coworkers, the community, the larger world, and with God. This starts with trust in God. When I think about our need to trust God, I am reminded of a saying I read in ***Sabbath Shiurim***, a book by Rabbi M. Miller on the Torah. In it, he quotes words from a prayer that goes something like this: "May you be seated in the place to which you belong." Trust in God, and He will lead you to the place prepared by Him for you.

Peace includes knowing where you belong! You have a purpose that requires daily actions. Your purpose is achieved one day at a time. Know that those around you ***today*** are a part of your purpose. Family, friends, foes, and others who are encountered during your daily activities are necessary parts of your purpose. There is no need to set yourself apart from your daily life in order to find peace. In fact, the experiences of daily living are essential to the development of your peace,

The peace development exercises portion of the book is to help you develop the discipline to know what God has for you ***today***. When you discipline yourself to daily peace exercises, you increase your knowledge of peace. Through the use of your peace development exercises, you, under the guidance of the Lord Jesus Christ and the Holy Spirit, will participate in physical and spiritual exercises. The Holy Spirit will lead you in completing these exercises and in exploring other questions and areas that He knows are needful for you.

Jesus Christ victory over the grave

Gandhi Smiling

Praying Hands

Angels The Awakening

Peace Dove

White Heaven Beach Water

The Quiet Hour

Bible

Your Peace Journey

Your peace development will be a lifelong journey where you will discover peace. It will take you on a path that leads to transformation for you and reconciliation with God. Along the journey, you will encounter exciting new life-changing experiences. It is important that you record these. So I am asking you to keep a ***peace journal***. Purchase a notebook and make it your ***peace journal***. In it, you should record what you experience during meditation. You also should record in it the experiences that result from you applying in your daily life the principles set forth in the Bible and those that occur when you follow the guidance of Jesus Christ and the Holy Spirit.

The Holy Spirit will guide you, as directed by Jesus Christ, by words, spiritual revelations, thoughts, spiritual, and physical experiences. The Holy Spirit's role is to help you complete your peace journal. You will recall that we stated earlier that you are a spirit made in God's own image, with a soul all residing inside a physical body. You are precious and wonderfully made. The Holy Spirit will guide and help you become a more magnificent divine being.

Be diligent in recording your experiences in your peace journal. It will be an invaluable chronicle of your journey toward peace. I hope you enjoy the trip.

During your journey, you will encounter:

Divine Beings:

1. God
2. Jesus Christ
3. Holy Spirit
4. Angels

Your Self:

1. Your Human Spirit
2. Your Human Soul
3. Your Human Body
4. Your Human Mind
5. Your "I AM"—Ego

The diagram that follows is an insightful symbol that illustrates the relationship between God, Jesus Christ, the Holy Spirit, and mankind. As you look at the diagram, it shows two triangles. But the diagram is intended to show the top one as representing the real triangle and the bottom triangle as a reflection of the top one. Light reflecting off the top triangle creates the bottom triangle, which is its image. The triangle on the bottom is a reflection or image of the one on the top.

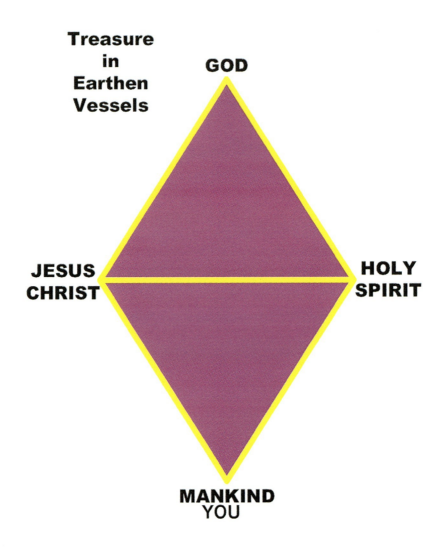

This may be made clearer by another illustration. If you have ever been beside a clear pool of water or a lake when the waves are still, you can see the surrounding trees or structures reflected off the surface of the water.

Reflection on Lake

So it is with mankind. We are created to be a reflection of God. Matter is a type of spiritual water and is intended to assist with God manifesting in mankind. Man is to be a reflection of God in the world. The psalmist declares, **"he leadeth me beside the still waters. He restoreth my soul"**. The psalmist tells us that the Lord leads him to places where we experiences divine peace, places where his soul returns to the godly life form intended for it.

The Bible further states *we have this treasure in earthen vessels.* **Meditating of this symbol has proven to be beneficial to many in their efforts to develop an understanding of mankind's relationship to God, Jesus Christ. and the Holy Spirit.**

Sin causes turbulence in us and distorts God's image; consequently, mankind's knowledge of its divine nature has become distorted and blurred. Jesus Christ and the Holy Spirit have been sent to mankind to assist with the restoration and reconciliation of mankind back to God by regenerating the original God image and nature in mankind. Jesus Christ has ordained His peace as a life force in this mission of restoration and reconciliation. If we are to be peacemakers, we must initially have a clear, undistorted view of Jesus Christ, the Holy Spirit, and their role with us in regard to peace.

Jesus Christ as the Son of Man (God in Man) demonstrated mankind's true capabilities while He was on earth. He challenges us to awaken, to become restored to our true nature, and to become all we were intended to become. He has asked God our Father to send the Holy Spirit to help us and guide us in becoming regenerated and restored to our rightful place in God.

The diagram shows that we have direct contact with Jesus Christ and the Holy Spirit and contact with God through them. As you continue with your personal discoveries of peace, it is vital that you must become a disciple of Jesus Christ through the leading of the Holy Spirit.

You are indeed a treasure in an earthen vessel. Your spirit and soul are housed in a physical (earthen) body. As you commune with Jesus Christ, recognize that your spiritual development and growth in the spirit of peace will greatly depend upon your obedience to Him and through the work of the Holy Spirit who will come and abide within you. Jesus Christ when describing the role of the Holy Spirit says:

> **Howbeit when he, the Spirit of truth, is come, he will guide you into all truth: for he shall not speak of himself; but whatsoever he shall hear, that shall he speak: and he will shew you things to come. He shall glorify me: for he shall receive of mine, and shall shew it unto you. All things that the Father hath are mine: therefore said I, that he shall take of mine, and shall shew it unto you.**
> **John 16:13–15**

Divine peace is one of the things you will receive. God, through Jesus Christ and the Holy Spirit, will work with you to show you what you need to do to achieve your rightful place in Him.

Meditation, prayer along with the right applications of God's written and communicated word, will be vital to you as you develop your peace. As you are persistent, you will become co-creator with Jesus Christ in the growth of peace in you. Meditation and prayer are vital parts of your daily exercises as you commune more with Him and grow peace in your spirit. The meditation exercises will strengthen you as you perform them and the acts of faith that result from them. A major reward for you will be the discovery of your life purpose. At the same time, you will receive and be asked to record on daily basis very valuable personal up-to-date information about your efforts in pursuit of your life's purpose. You also will obtain an understanding of the role peace plays in you fulfilling your life's purpose.

The information in this book is constructed to assist the person who has made a decision to seek the peace of Jesus Christ. They may be tired of not knowing what to do and now want to get answers about their life. They may sense that there is more to living than they are experiencing. This seeking is itself a spiritual signal that Jesus Christ is reaching out to them.

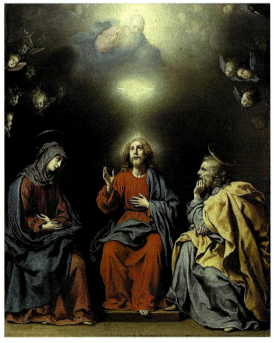

The Trinity

Divine Beings

God the Father

Our earth is changing. It is moving into a phase where peace is essential. If we are to accomplish God's purpose on this earth, we must know the will of God for peace. God has entrusted the stewardship of His earth into our hands. Mankind was given responsibility to assist Him in the management of all aspects of the earth. And despite what some might believe, that responsibility has not been changed. Mankind still has responsibility for the earth.

> **And God said, Let us make man in our image, after our likeness: and let them have dominion over the fish of the sea, and over the fowl of the air, and over the cattle, and over all the earth, and over every creeping thing that creepeth upon the earth.**
> **So God created man in his own image, in the image of God created he him; male and female created he them. And God blessed them, and God said unto them, Be fruitful, and multiply, and replenish the earth, and subdue it: and have dominion over the fish of the sea, and over the fowl of the air, and over every living thing that moveth upon the earth.**
> **Genesis 1:26–28**

Keep in mind we are all on a mission of discovery and accomplishment. We are helpers sent to fulfill a plan designed and developed in heaven. The mission is a noble one that manifest in earthy or physical things, but at its core is spiritual. Many persons see this. Others who are spiritually blind do not see the spiritual nature of their mission. It is therefore difficult to perform the mission if one cannot see it. When we acquire peace, we calm down our mind so that we can spiritually recognize our life mission and purpose.

Time on earth is essential. Our time should be spent wisely. God's perfect will for us is revealed in time. These revelations come in God's time. God's timing is often referred to in the Bible as the "fullness of time." To receive God's revelations, we must be in a state of peace. As the earth enters in to this new place in God's time, it becomes subject to greater confusion and chaos. When these changes occur, peacemakers are surely needed.

In the book of Genesis, in the Bible, the Spirit of God moved upon the waters of the creation to bring about order. This need to bring manifested order is a godly principle that the astute disciple "see." This need for manifested order grew even more evident with the introduction of mankind into the Garden of Eden. God placed Adam in the Garden of Eden to "dress" it and "keep" it. This signifies that work, order, and supervision are necessary. As the story of Adam and Eve further reveals, Adam and Eve, in their attempt to accelerate God's process, took matters into their own hands and disobeyed God's orders. This brought about separation from God, death, and disruption of God's creative process for mankind. But God continue to seek ways to reconcile mankind back to Him and to reach mankind's divine destiny.

Sacred Heart of Jesus Christ

God the Son—Jesus Christ

Jesus Christ, the Prince of Peace, came into the world to restore mankind back to God. He had participated in the creation of man and now He participates in man's restoration. His plan includes transmitting the divine attribute of peace to mankind to rebuild harmony and restore the earth to a peaceful state.

Jesus Christ's Prayer of Peace
(received during meditation)

Our Father which art in heaven and the earth, Holy is thy name.
Come unto me all who labor and are heavy-laden and I will give you peace.
My peace is not like the world's peace.
My peace surpasseth all understanding. Be not afraid

Peace, my peace comes to those of you who diligently seek me.
You must seek if you are to receive.
I don't want to hurt or harm, or interfere with your will.
So you must seek peace if you are to receive peace.
Therefore, come those who seek to know me, and I will show my peace unto you.
Come you who are weak and heavy-laden and I will give you rest.
Come you down trodden and despondent and learn of me and I will give you my kingdom privileges.
Don't be deterred by the things of this world for they will soon fade.
I, the God of your fathers and mothers have spoken it.
I laid down my life that you would have eternal life.
Let it not be in vain.

Peace in the heart. What joy there is, in peace in the heart.
Love of the heart. What peace there is in love of the heart.
I love you, I love you, I love you, I love you, I love you.

As we speak of peace, we must mention love. Love is the cornerstone of peace. Without love, there is no peace. God is love and sends His love through Jesus Christ to perfect His love in us. As we move about our lives, we must become aware of the work of the Spirit of Love in us. Without this awareness, our lives become void, and emptiness overtakes us. With love in our lives, we care. It is in this caring that peace has an opportunity to blossom and grow. The seed of peace once implanted in us will flourish and grow when love is supplied to it. Love nurtures in our spirit and in our soul the seed of peace. Love will furnish the nutrients that assist the growth of peace. As peace grows and spreads to all parts of us, we began to become more and more aware of the sweetness of the spirit of peace.

The journey to peace is not an end in itself, but its purpose is to learn to love God and love our neighbor as we love ourselves. We learn to do this. It is not innate.

The Lord Jesus Christ comes to prepare mankind to know this love and by doing so to reconcile mankind back to their rightful relationship with God the Father. This was paramount. He did not fail. The pattern for the rescue has been completed. His plan involves you and me. Our role must now be fulfilled. Jesus Christ still labors hard to obtain our participation and reestablish this reconciliation.

Peace has been defined by world standards as:

1. Freedom from disagreement or quarrels.
2. A condition of harmony, accord, and concord.
3. An undisturbed state of mind; absence of mental conflict filled with serenity, calmness, quietness, and tranquility.
4. Freedom from war or civil strife. An agreement to end hostilities.
5. Freedom from public disturbance or disorder. A condition of public security where law and order prevails.

What the above definitions ignore is that Jesus Christ must be in midst for these conditions to exist. Mankind has struggled for ages to find peace. We have looked for ways to live together in peace, but with little success. We have searched endlessly for peace in our lives, while all the time peace was as close as a heartbeat. God's gift of peace is available to all for the asking. Since the beginning of time, His peace has flowed unto earth. Mankind, because of self-will and disobedience, has lost the ability to recognize and to share peace.

> **And the peace of God which passeth all understanding, shall keep your hearts and minds through Christ Jesus.**
>
> **Philippians 4:7**

How wonderful is the peace of God. Peace has within it the joy of life. This joy helps us endure the fiery darts of the wicked until our faith is in place. Search your heart for those thoughts that hinder the peace of God. Seek to know the truth of yourself. Study the thoughts of your mind and judge them by the scales of Christ's justice. Search your affections. Determine if God's divine spark of love or the fires of infernal deceit from the devil, others, or yourself ignite the emotional fires within you. Know that the influences and personalities we follow become our masters.

Remember we are created to be joint heirs with Christ. Look to Christ for the real understanding. Know that the peace of God is bestowed upon us. Peace is placed in us. There is a fitted place, a part of us reserved to house God's peace. God knows where it is. We sense it at times, but we must learn to be still to permit peace to dwell and work in us. Peace desires to abide. God who is rich in blessing and full of mercy, grace, and love longs to fill us with His peace.

Peace Dove

<u>God the Holy Spirit</u>

The Holy Spirit is often referred to in the Bible as the Spirit of God, as well as other titles such as Comforter and Spirit of Truth. Jesus Christ said in John 15:26:

> **But when the Comforter is come, whom I will send unto you from the Father, *even* the Spirit of truth, which proceedeth from the Father, he shall testify of me:**

Jesus Christ said He would ask the Father to send the Holy Spirit to guide us in our search for truth, which is a search to know Jesus Christ, who is the Truth. Jesus Christ says to one of His disciples, Phillip, in John 14:6, that He is the Truth:

> **Jesus saith unto him, I am the way, the truth, and the life: no man cometh unto the Father, but by me**.

He also said He gives peace (John 14:27):

> **Peace I leave with you, my peace I give unto you: not as the world giveth, give I unto you. Let not your heart be troubled, neither let it be afraid.**

So the Holy Spirit has the responsibility to guide those who are willing to Jesus Christ and peace.

God the Father, Jesus Christ, and the Holy Spirit are all involved in your successful travel on your peace journey. The Holy Spirit comes to assist you from the moment you make up your mind to take the route described in this book. For many, the role of the Holy Spirit remains a mystery. This will no longer be the case if you are diligent in your meditation and prayer. The Bible is very clear about the functions of the Holy Spirit in the life of those who choose to follow Jesus Christ. The Holy Spirit will affect their spirit, soul, and body.

The Holy Spirit will come to you if you are open to receive Him. He will talk to you, teach you, encourage you, assist in your healing, inform you, strengthen you, and guide you. His role is to prepare you to receive the divine nature of Jesus Christ and God the Father. One of the ways this is done is by cleansing and purifying you of those false beliefs that close the door of your mind and prevent you from receiving the Truth of Jesus Christ.

The effects of the Holy Spirit's initial arrival in your spirit may be sudden and powerful for some; yet on the other hand, for others, it may be gradual and gentle. In either case, the individual recognizes that something new is happening to them, something that involves more than their physical body.

This is often referred to in the Bible as the anointing. To anoint is to rub with oil. The practice of rubbing persons and objects with oil is described in the Bible as a ritual performed by priests and ordained by God. The purpose was to make the person and object proper and acceptable to God. In the biblical context, the act of rubbing with oil as prescribed by God is to anoint. When the oil had been placed on the person or object by the priest as prescribed by God, the combining of the oil with the act of the priest was referred to as the anointing.

Today, Jesus Christ performs the role of the priest, and the spiritual impulse coming from the Holy Spirit is the oil. Jesus Christ "rubs on you," or anoints you, with the spiritual impulse of the Holy Spirit. The result is that spiritual impulses that the Holy Spirit has received from Jesus Christ are transferred from the Holy Spirit to your spirit, and you are spiritually anointed. One of these impulses is the spirit of peace.

Jesus Christ, when referring to the Holy Spirit, states in John 16:14 and 15:

> **He shall glorify me: for he shall receive of mine, and shall shew it unto you**
> **All things that the Father hath are mine: therefore said I, that he shall take of mine, and shall shew it unto you.**

The Holy Spirit is therefore very important to you on your peace journey. In fact, His importance is essential in the transfer of the Spirit of Peace from Jesus Christ to you. This fact is often overlooked by those seeking peace. Jesus Christ said He would ask the Father to send the Holy Spirit to guide us in our search for truth, which is a search to know Jesus Christ who is the Truth. So the Holy Spirit has the responsibility to guide those who are willing to Jesus Christ and, ultimately, to peace.

Here is the revelation of a divine mystery; the Holy Spirit is the Spirit of Truth sent by Jesus Christ to guide us to the truth. The Holy Spirit sent by Jesus Christ, under the authority given to Him by God the Father, brings what Jesus Christ would have us know and become. By receiving what the Holy Spirit shares with us, we are guided into the full knowledge of the nature of Jesus Christ including the nature of peace. As you desire this commune with the Holy Spirit, He and Jesus Christ will make their presence known unto you. Therefore, ask and you shall receive peace.

Angels

You will also encounter angels. Angels are spiritual beings, some good, others evil. The good angels are assigned as ministering spirits sent to help each of us. Evil angels are also active in our life, tempting us to disobey God's commandment. As you grow in peace and learn to follow the leading of Jesus Christ and the Holy Spirit, you will learn how to distinguish the difference between the spiritual activity of good and evil angels and how to defeat them. Later in this book, in the sections **War and Spiritual Influences** and **Cause and Effect**, we discuss how evil spirits attempt to influence mankind and destroy their peace.

Your Self

Your Human Spirit

Your human spirit is that part of the human being that is transformed to allow divine peace to flow into the human soul and human body. Your human spirit has direct interaction with the spiritual realm and is the place of initial interaction of Jesus Christ and the Holy Spirit with you. It's that part of you that is "born again." It also is eventually to contain the Spirit of God the Father, Son, and Holy Spirit and is purposed to grow to the likeness and perfection of Christ. It contains the "**I AM**" that is to give spiritual leadership to your human soul and human body. It is to become eternal. It also houses our conscience that plays a major role in peace formation.

Your Human Soul

Your human soul is transformed by obedience to the guidance received from the human spirit. It has direct contact with the spiritual-soul realm and influences the human spirit and human body. It animates the physical body. It is in our human soul that we first experience the activities of our thinking, feeling, and willing. Later, these activities are awakened and developed in our human spirit. It differs from the physical body and is not dissolved by death. It gives spiritual leadership to our human body. It is intended to become transformed and eternal.

Your Human Body

Your human body houses our fleshly components. The human body has physical components that have direct contact with the physical realm and influences the human soul. These physical components, consisting of the sense organs, heart, brain, nerves, etc., combine to form us into one physical unit. The human body provides a container for our human soul and human spirit while we live on earth. These physical parts of man are used to contact the physical world through physical senses. Our physical components decay after the human soul and human spirit leave the human body.

Your Human Mind

Your human mind is that part of your being that is dispersed throughout your entire being. It interacts with and connects your human spirit, human soul, and human body together as one. It is the spiritual portion of your mind that is used by your "I AM." This is where the higher levels of divine-based thinking, feeling, and willing occur. The "I AM" is to use the mind to communicate divine-based thinking, feeling, and willing impulses to your human spirit, human soul, and human body to manage them.

Your I AM—Ego

Your **I AM** is the divine part of God, given by God to *every* human being. It is the unique part of each of us that is specifically ours and ours along. It separates us from other human beings, animals, plants, and minerals. It is what enables us to think and talk with God. It is what makes us an individual. No other person can claim your **I AM**. God has place a part of Himself in you, a seed that has the potential of becoming divine if you permit the Spirit of Christ to enter into and work on it. The influence of the Spirit of Christ on and within your **I AM** is to transform you into a new creation. This is referred to in the Bible as being "Born Again." The **I AM** you possessed at your birth is not to remain as it was when you were born but is designed to become changed to become like Jesus Christ.

In scientific, psychological terms what I refer to as the **I AM** is also called the ego, a term used to describe one's self-consciousness. So another way of describing our **I AM** is that part of us that is the seat of our self-consciousness. Our ego is the self-awareness that reveals that you exist as a being separate and distinct from all other beings in creation.

The **I AM** is housed in our human spirit and given the role of growing to eventually control it as well as our human soul and human body. It is that part of us that has been given the freedom to guide or not guide our entire being as God through Jesus Christ and the Holy Spirit directs.

Your **I AM** is to receive divine influences from God, through Jesus Christ and the Holy Spirit, so that it becomes perfected into the design intended for you at the beginning of your creation. The process is very complicated and requires most importantly that you recognize and understand that you are a creation of God intended to become more than you are when first created, and that you are born with potential that may or may not be realized. Your potential will only be realized when you permit and act in accordance with the influences of Jesus Christ and the Holy Spirit.

God's love for mankind is so great that He asked Christ to come unto earth to provide a way for mankind to be rescued from the path of inevitable destruction they were on by believing in and accepting the life-spirit that only comes from Christ.

As you learn and apply the spiritual disciplines taught by Jesus Christ, you can reach your perfection. This book is intended to assist you with your efforts. Please grasp the fact that you (your **I AM**, your spiritual self-consciousness) must become an active participant in reaching your divine destiny.

NOTE:

*In this book, the term **I AM** and the term **I** when referring to a specific spiritual part of our being describe the same spiritual organ.*

Christ Mount of Olives

Description of Meditation

The Role of Christian Meditation

Many Christians and nonbelievers have questions about meditation. They ask "what is meditation"? "Why would I want to meditate"? "How does one meditate"? Some are doubtful about meditation and fear it. To help us understand how scriptural and essential the use of meditation is in our spiritual life, I have included the following scriptures that show the use of meditation in the Bible. You should study them to discover how the practice of meditation has been described in the Bible.

Meditation Scriptures in the Bible

> **This book of the law shall not depart out of thy mouth; but thou shalt meditate therein day and night, that thou mayest observe to do according to all that is written therein: for then thou shalt make thy way prosperous, and then thou shalt have good success**
> **Joshua 1:8**

> **But his delight *is* in the law of the LORD; and in his law doth he meditate day and night**
> **Psalm 1:2**

> **When I remember thee upon my bed, *and* meditate on thee in the *night* watches**
> **Psalm 63:6**

> **I will meditate also of all thy work, and talk of thy doings**
> **Psalm 77:12.**

> **I will meditate in thy precepts, and have respect unto thy ways**
> **Psalm 119:15**

> **Princes also did sit *and* speak against me: *but* thy servant did meditate in thy statutes**
> **Psalm 119:23**

> **Meditate upon these things; give thyself wholly to them; that thy profiting may appear to all.**
> **Timothy 4:15**

From the scriptures listed above, one can discover that meditation was used as a means to grow closer to God and was profitable for those that did so.

Prayer

Prayer is also a vital part of Meditation. Prayer is talking to God. When you talk to God, be honest and sincere. Talk to God from your spirit. It is your spirit to His Spirit. It is spiritual conversation. One of the major principles you will learn in your peace development is to learn to pray as God would have you pray.

The following is a passage of scripture that describes what the Lord Jesus Christ taught about prayer. What you will note in this passage of scripture is that the Lord tells you not to use a lot of self-centered words when you pray. It is not what you think you should pray but what God wills for you to pray that is correct. Learn to pray God's thoughts, not your own. The Holy Spirit will give you God's thoughts to pray.

> **But when ye pray, use not vain repetitions, as the heathen *do*: for they think that they shall be heard for their much speaking. Be not ye therefore like unto them: for your Father knoweth what things ye have need of, before ye ask him. After this manner therefore pray ye:**

The Lord's Prayer

Our Father which art in heaven, Hallowed be thy name.
Thy kingdom come. Thy will be done in earth, as it is in heaven.
Give us this day our daily bread.
And forgive us our debts, as we forgive our debtors.
And lead us not into temptation, but deliver us from evil: For thine is the kingdom, and the power,
and the glory, forever. Amen.

God knows what you need even if you don't. Often, your view of your situation is wrong. You think you need one thing when in fact you need something else. God knows what you need at all times. The Lord's Prayer is like Christian meditation, a means to enter into the presence of God and to hear and pray the words God wants us to pray.

Prayer and Christian meditation work together. Starting out in prayer should end in meditation. And when we speak to God, we should develop the reverent courtesy and practice to afterward listen, as in meditation, to what God says in response to our prayer.

Effective prayer is discussing with God what God wants you to realize and listening to His confirmation that you understand what He wants of you at that moment. His confirmation will help you at that time to obtain what you need at that time. It may seem not to fit your current individual world view of the situation, but it will be God's eternal world view and where you currently fit in it. God's response will be what He wills is needful for you at that time. God knows what you need before you ask. As stated above:

> **But when ye pray, use not vain repetitions, as the heathen** *do*: **for they think that they shall be heard for their much speaking. Be not ye therefore like unto them: for your Father knoweth what things ye have need of, before ye ask him.**

As you grow spiritually, you will develop the confidence that your Father God knows what you need before you ask. You might now ask if God knows what you need before you ask then why ask?

For me to give you an answer to that question, let's look at and meditate on another passage of scripture from Romans 8:26–27:

> **Likewise the Spirit also helpeth our infirmities: for we know not what we should pray for as we ought: but the Spirit itself maketh intercession for us with groanings which cannot be uttered. And he that searcheth the hearts knoweth what** *is* **the mind of the Spirit, because he maketh intercession for the saints according to** *the will of* **God.**

Verse 26 describes that the Spirit, the Holy Spirit, wants to help you know about your "infirmities." Infirmities are defined as lack of strength or ability to obtain what you want or believe you need. The Holy Spirit, Jesus Christ, and God know what you lack.

The Holy Spirit is sent to help you with your need. The interaction of the Holy Spirit in our prayer life is such that when He becomes active in our spirit, His very presence in our spirit can cause us to realize we have so many shortcomings in so many areas that we are gripped with holy fear and trembling. At times, this fear and trembling are expressed by groans and tears. You examine yourself, and the Holy Spirit reveals what you should be. We utter groans because we realize we don't measure up. It is all right because the Holy Spirit knows you don't measure up. **You have to grow to know you don't measure up!** You must grow to know that the Thoughts you pray may not be the thoughts of God.

The Holy Spirit knows the thoughts and the will of God. As you pray, the Holy Spirit has the role of making intercessions for you by correcting your thoughts so that they become in agreement with God's will. But you must grow spiritually to come to know and pray the same thoughts that the Holy Spirit wants you to pray, thoughts that come from God. God's thoughts that are brought to you by the Holy Spirit must come to be your thoughts. Then you pray the thoughts brought to you by the Holy Spirit because the Holy Spirit knows the thoughts, the will of God. God's thoughts are God's will. As a result of praying (speaking) God's thoughts, you become a co-creator of God's will (plan) in your life and in the world.

Now back to the question, if God knows what you need before you ask, why do you have to ask? You have to ask because you have to knowingly decide you don't know and willfully seek from God what He says you need. The only way you will get from Him what you need is to develop communication with Jesus Christ and the Holy Spirit. This communication is developed when you meditate and pray and grow your own spirit to receive thoughts from Jesus Christ through the Holy Spirit and make them your own. We developed the ability to hear what the Holy Spirit tells us about what God would have us will in any situation. Will means to decide or choose. God wants us to grow to choose what He wills for us. Remember what Jesus Christ said to God the Father, in the Garden of Gethsemane:

> ***Saying, Father, if thou be willing, remove this cup from me: nevertheless, not my will but thine, be done.***
>
> *Luke 22:42*

Another reason you have to ask is because you are being trained. God, through Jesus Christ and the Holy Spirit, is training you to use your own spirit to know His will and choose to do it. As you learn to pray God's will, your prayer takes on creative power and bring in to being what God intends for you. God, through Jesus Christ and the Holy Spirit, is training you to seek God's will, to know God's presence in your life and speak God's word So that you become a co-creator with Him in your divine destiny.

God desires that you grow your spirit to be like Jesus Christ's spirit. You become totally obedient to God's will. This can only occur when you permit the Holy Spirit to dwell in you, and you listen and obey the thoughts the Holy Spirit gives you, just as Jesus Christ obeyed the thoughts the Holy Spirit gave Him while He was in the Garden of Gethsemane.

Let us again consider once more how Christian meditation works with prayer. As we grow in our ability to meditate, we will grow in our spiritual ability to pray as we ought. As we grow spiritually in our ability to meditate and pray as we ought, we grow in our ability to recognize the voice of the Holy Spirit. As we learn to recognize the voice of the Holy Spirit, we then more easily receive what God, through Jesus Christ and the Holy Spirit, wants us to hear.

Meditation is essential to effective prayer. As we listen to the voice of the Holy Spirit, we receive the Will of God. As we receive the Will of God, then, when we pray, we will pray ***God's will be done in earth as it is in heaven***.

The Bible

The Bible also is essential to meditation. The Bible is a collection of God-inspired books and as such is unique because its origin is from God. The Bible shows us God's interactions with man. Some people say that portions of the Bible are easier to understand than others, while others declare that the Bible is shrouded in mystery and symbolism, and others say that literal acts are expressed in it. Some say it is so difficult to understand that it has no relevance today. Regardless of the various views, consider for our purposes to develop peace that it is God's word. For me, the proposition I considered that the Bible is the Word of God, served to draw me to Him. If you will endeavor to search its pages to find peace, it will become a refreshing spring of knowledge and inspiration.

The Bible describes how man was created in the image of God. Man is God's created child. The Bible declares the good, wonder, and majesty of you as a part of the family of God. You must recognize your origin as beginning from God, the maker of all things. Be watchful that you be not deceived by the workings of Antichrist forces in your environment that want to blind you from recognizing your true God nature.

You will be asked to read and apply principles set forth in the Bible to develop your peace. The Bible will be an essential tool for you. Hidden in the words of the Bible is spiritual power. This is a mystery that becomes known to those who are diligent in their efforts to discover this power. This power works in you, and you grow to use this power in the world as you meditate upon these words, and they become a part of you. They nourish your spirit, soul, and body and increase the power of peace in you.

Your Peace Journal

Obtain a separate notebook, either bound or loose leaf, that you will use to record your experiences while on this journey toward peace. This will become your peace journal. The peace journal is essential for the journey. Use the peace journal to write down what you experience as you go through the meditation exercises. It will also serve to record what the Holy Spirit reveals to you as He guides you in your search for peace. It is important to record all your experiences, for it will help reinforce what you are learning and doing.

Gandhi meditating

It is essential as you develop peace to know how to meditate. So in this book I would like to share what I have learned over the years about meditation. Although there are many ways that are taught on how to meditate, I have practiced and taught simple meditation techniques that are adaptable to our current lifestyles. These are simple and straightforward and will help you get started. Let's begin by stating that meditation in the context we are using the term is simply to intentionally position your body, mind, soul, and spirit in a posture to receive communications from God, through Jesus Christ and the Holy Spirit.

To communicate, one has to share. When God, through Jesus Christ and the Holy Spirit, communicates, He shares His spirit with our spirit. God longs to and does share with us. We are able to receive what He shares when we open our spirit to Him. God is a spirit, so meditation starts as a spiritual activity. When we decide to meditate in the sense I am using the word, we decide to open our spirit to God and accept the idea that God will share His Spirit with our spirit. During meditation, we are spiritually receiving information from God as we open ourselves to Him. By the consistent and steady practice of meditation, we develop our ability to hear and understand when God communicates His will to us.

It is therefore important as you undertake your peace development that you believe the Word of God. God inspired the psalmist to say:

> **blessed is the man that walketh not in the counsel of the ungodly, nor standeth in the way of sinners, nor sitteth in the seat of the scornful. But his delight is in the law of the Lord; and in his law doth he MEDITATE day and night.**
>
> *Psalm 1:1–2*

You start in meditation with the belief that God exists, and that He desires to reward, bless, and talk to you. God has always talked to man. He has in the past; He does today. In fact, He has talked to you! Many have heard the Spirit of God and not recognized it was God or either discounted what they heard.

My intention is to help you, beginning today, to develop your ability to hear and follow the Spirit of God that dwells within you. The voice of the Lord comes from within you. Avoid accepting spiritual voices from outside you. TEST AND CONFIRM ALL SPIRITUAL MESSAGES WITH THE BIBLE AND CHRISTIAN TEACHINGS.

> **And the sheep follow him: for they know his voice.**
>
> *John 10:4*

It is not difficult to meditate. To start your meditation, find a quiet place where you may be alone. It's there you will meditate. This should be a preferred place where there is solitude and stillness. The place will "feel" or seem right to you.

Before starting your meditation, examine the thoughts in your mind and stop thinking about unkind feelings or thoughts toward yourself or others. Imagine you are in the presence of the Lord Jesus Christ. Imagine the most respectful and holiest attitude you can. Some people will wash their bodies prior to starting meditation. This is not necessary. Just follow your own conscience. You should do what your conscience tells you is necessary to be in a state of holiness before the Lord.

Now you are ready to begin. You may sit in a straight-back chair or lie on your back on the bed or floor. Start by reading a scripture from the Bible or listening to uplifting music. Chose to meditate on a scripture, or an inspiring word like peace or joy or think of the sacred name Jesus Christ or music. If you chose music, select a song that creates a quiet and inspiring mood. Initially, avoid all external distractions. Later, external noises will not bother you.

Pray that God's love and light will protect you. Close your eyes, relax, take three deep breaths, and think on the scripture you read or the inspiring word, or name, or listen to the music you selected. Slowly let your external sensations fade away and become aware of your inner spirit. Begin to notice the thoughts that come to you. These are thoughts that may come from **inside or outside** your spirit. You gradually become aware that as you learn how to meditate, you develop the ability to recognize the differences and eventually whether or not the sources of the thoughts are good or evil. This will come as you grow in experience.

There are many voices that you can and will hear. Some are **inside** your spirit; others are **outside** your spirit. As you become aware of thoughts, know that they come from a source. All these thoughts or voices that you hear inside you come from some source. They may appear to be random thoughts; but they come either from your mind, your spirit, the Spirit of God, other spirits, other people, sources of good, sources of evil, etc. As you grow in your ability to meditate, you will develop the ability to distinguish the source of these thoughts— whether they are from you, from God, or from other sources, some of which are destructive Antichrist forces. **BE CAUTIOUS.**

> **There are, it may, so many kinds of voices in the world, and none of them is without signification.**
> *1 Corinthians 14:10*

Your spirit will receive messages from many spiritual beings. Don't be alarmed; be forearmed. I have news for you. **They have been around and talking to you for years; you just did not realize it**! In fact, many of these spirits have influenced you to do things contrary to the will of God without you realizing their presence. Read what was stated about this in 1 John 4, where it states that many spiritual influences are false and are enemies of Christ:

> **Beloved believe not every spirit, but try the sprits whether they are of God: because many false prophets are gone out into the world. Hereby know you the Spirit of God: Every spirit that confesseth that Jesus Christ is come in the flesh is of God: And every spirit that confesseth not that Jesus Christ is come in the flesh is not of God: and this is that spirit of Antichrist, whereof ye have heard that it should come; and even now already is it in the world.**
> **1 John 4:1–3**

Hence, we are told to test the spirits.

Over the years, as I have taught many how to meditate, I have noticed that some become fearful when they become aware that Antichrist spirits are present and are trying to hinder their spiritual development. I reminded them as I remind you that God has given His angels charge over you to keep you. The angels will assist you as you command these Antichrist spirits to cease their operations with you. So don't let these spirits slow down or hinder your peace development. A stage in your peace development consists of learning how to use the power God gives you to stop the activities of Antichrist spirits.

So you should examine the thoughts you receive during your meditation and **test** (the Bible says **try**) the spirit that brings them to ensure that the thoughts are in line with the Word of God, the Bible, and the spirits from which they come are of God. You should test the thoughts that come to you with the written Word of God and ask the spirit that comes to you to confess that Jesus Christ has come in the flesh. If the spirit refuses or gives a less-than-firm positive response, command that spirit to leave and continue with your meditation. You have the authority over these spirits, for Jesus Christ has given it to you.

> **Ye are of God, little children, and have overcome them: because greater is he (Jesus Christ) that is in you, than he (the devil) that is in the world.**
> **1 John 4:4**

Even after you initially confirm that the thoughts you receive are from God, if you still feel unsure, and many do at first, ask the Holy Spirit to give you a scriptural reference in the Bible upon which the information you are receiving is based. If you still are not satisfied with the first scriptural reference, ask for another scriptural reference and yet another if need be. The Bible states that by two or three witnesses shall a word be confirmed. So ask for two or three biblical references if you are unsure about the spirit voice and thoughts that you receive. It is my experience that the Holy Spirit does not mind being asked for biblical references if you are unsure. Realize that the Holy Spirit who is full of love and grace is observing and guiding you. He wants you to succeed and is a patient teacher and guide.

Listen to the thoughts that come. Check them with the scripture. They should be given to you in an uplifting and inspiring manner. Often in your meditation you will hear refrains of sacred music; these are also given to inspire and build you spiritually.

Keep this book and your peace journal close to you as you meditate. Record the word(s) and messages you receive in your peace journal. As you use the techniques described in this book, you will develop your ability to meditate more effectively and become more peaceful. As you hear, then you must act. Act upon what you receive from the Spirit of God. You only grow as you act on what you have received

Later in the section on Meditation Exercises, we have included a simple outline of these techniques. As you use the meditation outline, your experiences will increase to include many experiences that are not listed there.

Just remember that all divine experiences do not conflict with the Word of God. At times, they may appear to differ from the various translations and how they are currently interpreted, but as you follow Jesus Christ and the leading of the Holy Spirit, you will grow in the understanding of the divine truth. As your understanding of divine truth grows, so will your understanding of the divine truth within your meditation experiences.

A key first step in developing your ability to meditate is to believe; that is, be mentally persuaded that the Spirit of God will talk to you personally. Throughout history, the Spirit of God has talked to mankind. He does today, and He has talked to you. Many of you have heard and discounted what you heard. Our intention in this book is to assist you to begin today to develop your capacity and ability to hear, distinguish, and follow the Spirit of God's voice.

Eventually, as you continue to practice the techniques describe in the Christian Meditation Outline, you will be able to differentiate the source of the random thoughts you experience. You will notice that some are in line with God's written and spoken word; others are not. Also, your understanding of His word will change and appear new to you. You will also grow in the ability to distinguish God's thoughts from the thoughts of Antichrist spirits. You will also grow in the ability to distinguish God's thoughts from your own thoughts. This is good. It means your human spirit is growing in your ability to commune with the Spirit of God.

I want to continue to alert you, however, that at the beginning stage, some of the thoughts you receive are not always from God. Some are from Antichrist forces. Be alert and test the spirits (1 John 4:1–2), for all spirits are not of God.

We discussed this earlier, but it cannot be overemphasized. When you begin to hear a voice within you, ask the spirit that you hear, "do you confess that Jesus Christ has come in the flesh?" Any spirit that refuses to answer or answers in a less-than-scriptural way should be commanded to leave. Jesus Christ was tested by demonic spirits, and so will we be. His teaching and commandment to us in this regard is we will cast them out.

> **And these signs shall follow them that believe; In my name shall they cast out devils.**
> **Mark 16:17**

It is important to recognize that meditation is a way to hear from the Lord Jesus Christ and the Holy Spirit. By meditating, you develop your spiritual listening ability. As you develop this ability, you will become more certain of His direction and will for you. It is important that you record what you receive in your peace development, and that you continue to learn how to distinguish the Lord's voice. Jesus Christ declares, **"My sheep know my voice and a stranger they will not follow."** By the way, to hear means to receive the word and obey it. Keep your Bible and your peace journal close to you as you meditate. Record what the Spirit of God says to you.

Bible

Meditation and Your Thinking

Your encounters with life start as an infant. These encounters include a wide variety of sounds, smells, people, objects, and events that the larger world presents to you. Your individual world is built using these encounters. These encounters with the world have no prearranged sequence or order to them. It becomes your responsibility to make sense of them by putting them in some kind of order. You do this by using the experiences you have had in your smaller individual world. Indeed, your entire life is spent attempting to construct harmony out of these two worlds. One is your smaller individual world, and the other is the larger world that includes all the people, nature, objects, etc., that surround you. Some have called this "creating your own view of the world." This becomes the world as you see it. As you grow older, this becomes the world view you use to judge all your encounters. **When we are a child, we assume the position that we are the center of both of these world views; all things that are external to us are less important than us**. The process you use to construct this world view is your ***thinking***.

One of the major processes that occur when you think is your "naming of things"; that is, you associate concepts and ideas with sensations and experiences you have then give them name(s) or combinations of names. Then you sort or give order to these names by deciding how they fit together with other sensations and experiences you have had. This is done to give meaning to the new and previous sensations. In other words, you attempt to fit all your experiences together in a harmonious whole.

Our memory is one function we possess that assists us with this task. The healthy development of one's memory is important, for our memory is the internal source where our experiences are stored and serve in the development of our knowledge. Memories are developed when we convert sensations into images. The more you become able to convert sensations into images, the more you will improve your memory. Be aware that images you develop may be true or false. Inherent in spiritual growth for all of us is the ability to seek God for the truth and rightness of the images we form. We all must grow in the recognition of godly images and the ability to remove those images that are not from God. You will learn more about this process later in this book.

When new sensations and experiences occur, you think about what you will "name" them, and if you have no previous memory with which to compare them, you think about how they may or may not fit with your world view. Depending on the outcome of this thinking process, you then give them a "name." If they are new and appear to fit, you give them a new name. If you decide they do not fit your world view, you reject them and exclaim, "I have never heard that before" and totally reject the new experiences as nonsensical because it does not fit your current world view.

The Lord intends for you to learn to hear His voice, receive His thoughts, and use them to create a larger world view—first, of who He would have you be; later, of what He expects of you; and finally, of how you fit in His larger creation. This involves learning new names and new truths. Correct thinking and the resulting thoughts are crucial to developing these new names and new truth so that you will become who the Lord intends you to become. What you think is who you end up becoming

As the Lord states in Jeremiah 29:11:

> **For I know the thoughts that I think toward you, saith the LORD, thoughts of peace, and not of evil, to give you an expected end.**

Thoughts are powerful spiritual impulses. The Lord is constantly sending thoughts to us to assist us to become who He would have us be. Thoughts also are broadcast out from us as well and impinge upon others as spiritual impulses that although unspoken may be sense by those who are spiritual sensitive enough to receive and interpret them.

In Matthew 9:4, we read:

> **And Jesus knowing their thoughts said, Wherefore think ye evil in your hearts?**

And in Luke 5:22, we read:

> **But when Jesus perceived their thoughts, he answering said unto them, What reason ye in your hearts?**

Some may think these comments strange, that your thoughts and reasoning may be sensed by others. Perhaps this is because they have never heard that thoughts can be transmitted from one person to another. Many believe that every thought they think and have in their mind is produced by them, but this is not the case. **Not all thoughts in your head are from you!**

The thoughts that you use in your thinking may be from a source other than you. They may be true or false, good or evil. They may be based on the real or unreal. Thoughts must be tested to determine if they are in line with what God intends. As you proceed on your peace journey, you will come to recognize thoughts that are not from you. In fact, it is important that you develop the ability in your meditation to identify thoughts that you produce from those you receive from the Holy Spirit or godly beings as well as identify those thoughts that come from Antichrist sources. You will learn as you progress in your meditation exercises to separate the godly thoughts from the ungodly ones.

Meditation—Recognizing True Thoughts

Another means of developing your thinking and thought ability is learning how to recognize true thoughts. Truth is a divine quality of Jesus Christ. Jesus Christ says He is the Truth, so a thought that is true has the divine quality of Jesus Christ in it. Since thoughts are transferable, the thoughts you receive from Jesus Christ are divine, true thoughts. The thoughts you receive from other sources may or may not be true.

There is one source of truth yet many aspects of it. The truth that Jesus Christ transmits to us is dependent upon our ability to receive it. We must grow in understanding to be able to receive it. So it is important to be flexible, humble, and open to various points of view in our search for truth and not be dogmatic in our attitudes in regard to it.

In other words, we must be open to thoughts from Jesus Christ that may seem to conflict with earlier thoughts. You see at the earlier time, your soul was not equipped to accept the later truth. What comes to mind is the following scripture in Acts 10:10–20 in regard to Peter, one of Jesus Christ's disciples, who was confronted with new aspects of truth.

> **And he (Peter) became very hungry, and would have eaten: but while they made ready, he fell into a trance, And saw heaven opened, and a certain vessel descending unto him, as it had been a great sheet knit at the four corners, and let down to the earth: Wherein were all manner of fourfooted beasts of the earth, and wild beasts, and creeping things, and fowls of the air.**
>
> **And there came a voice to him, Rise, Peter; kill and eat. But Peter said, Not so, Lord; for I have never eaten any thing that is common or unclean. And the voice *spake* unto him again the second time, What God hath cleansed, *that* call not thou common. This was done thrice: and the vessel was received up again into heaven.**
>
> **Now while Peter doubted in himself what this vision which he had seen should mean, behold, the men which were sent from Cornelius had made enquiry for Simon's house, and stood before the gate, And called, and asked whether Simon, which was surnamed Peter, were lodged there. While Peter thought on the vision, the Spirit said unto him, Behold, three men seek thee. Arise therefore, and get thee down, and go with them, doubting nothing: for I have sent them.**

Peter, being an orthodox Jew, did not mingle with non-Jews, but the Spirit was directing him to do so. This was a new truth, and that is **the message of Jesus Christ is to be shared with non-Jews as well as with Jews.**

The appearance of truth to you is like the sparkles from a diamond. You see different aspects of a diamond with various colors, yet it is the same diamond, and so it is with the characteristics of truth. Truth shows itself in different ways from different views, but it comes from one source, Jesus Christ. It is very important for you to know this as you proceed on your peace journey. The information of Jesus Christ is to be shared with all in the various ways He would have it shared so that they would know Him.

As Jesus Christ says in John 14:6:

> **Jesus saith unto him, I am the way, the truth, and the life**

And also in John 8:31–32:

> **Then said Jesus to those Jews which believed on him, If ye continue in my word, *then* are ye my disciples indeed; And ye shall know the truth, and the truth shall make you free.**

So to know true thoughts is to know the thoughts that come from Jesus Christ. And to know the thoughts that come from Jesus Christ is to know the voice of Jesus Christ. As Jesus Christ also says in John 10:3–5:

> **To him (the Good Shepherd) the porter openeth; and the sheep hear his voice; and he calleth his own sheep by name, and leadeth them out. And when he putteth forth his own sheep, he goeth before them, and the sheep follow him: for they know his voice. And a stranger will they not follow, but will flee from him: for they know not the voice of strangers.**

This means that Jesus Christ's voice is recognized by those who chose to follow Him.

So as you develop your ability to recognize the source of thoughts, first get to know the voice of Jesus Christ. And just as the diamond shines forth with various aspects of color, so the Lord will transfer to you thoughts that contain various aspects of truth. Be diligent in recognizing His voice.

The Lord's thoughts are all consistent with His personality and character. Study the Bible and become familiar with the personality and character of the Lord. This knowledge will help you recognize the thoughts of the Lord. He will never send you thoughts that disagree with His word as written in the Bible

Meditation and Thought Voices

A thought has a voice as we have previously stated. You will come to recognize thoughts as voices speaking within you. I want to emphasize "within you." The Holy Spirit will guide you from within your spirit, not by external voices. Do not follow external voices. You will be guided from within your spirit. In John 14:16–17, Jesus, speaking of the Holy Spirit as the Comforter, says:

> **And I will pray the Father, and he shall give you another Comforter, that he may abide with you forever;** ***Even*** **the Spirit of truth; whom the world cannot receive, because it seeth him not, neither knoweth him: but ye know him; for he dwelleth "with you, and shall be in you."**

And in 1 John 4:12–13, we read:

> **No man hath seen God at any time. If we love one another, God dwelleth in us, and his love is perfected in us. Hereby know we that we dwell in him, and he in us because he hath given us of his Spirit.**

Do not listen to voices that come from unseen forces that speak to you from outside your spirit. Only listen for the voice of God from the Holy Spirit that dwells within you. Remember that even for voices that speak within you should be tested by asking them to confess Jesus Christ as Lord. If you are still uncertain, verify their message by two or three scriptural passages.

You have this constant, ongoing conversation within your mind, and it sounds like you talking to yourself. It sounds like what you think your voice sounds like to others. By the way, when you actually hear a recording of your voice, you are surprised to discover that the recording does not sound like the voice you hear in your "head."

Meditation and Your Thought Images

As you continue to develop your ability to distinguish the source of your thoughts and determine the truth of them, you will experience thought images within your soul and spirit. Thought images are spiritual images we see in our inner vision that are thoughts that have changed into picture form.

Just as a thought has a voice, it also may take on a picture form. You may have heard or recall the saying "a picture is worth a thousand words." So the words that create thoughts become images within in us.

Thought images may come to your soul and spirit at any time during your peace journey. Just as you should test thoughts for their truthfulness, so you also must test thought images for their truthfulness. The Holy Spirit will guide you in determining the truthfulness of these thought images.

Thought images may appear to you but may not be helpful for you. Let me illustrate with an example from your day-to-day life. You decide to go to the store to buy food. As you are on your way, you may see people, houses, cars, animals, etc., all become a part of your experience, but none may be helpful to you in getting to the store to buy the food. Since your guide is the Holy Spirit, He knows what is helpful in getting you to your destination, in this case to the store to buy food. The point is that you may experience thought images and be personally pleased that you are developing new spiritual abilities yet be alert. Always ask the Lord Jesus Christ through the Holy Spirit to tell you about the thought images you receive.

Meditation and God's Thoughts

I hope it is clear to you by now that peace comes from God through the Jesus Christ and the Holy Spirit to you. In order to have peace, you must acknowledge that peace comes to you embedded in godly thoughts. You must prepare yourself to receive God's thoughts into your thinking and apply them in your will. As recorded, this passage of scripture from Jeremiah 29:11 says:

For I know the thoughts that I think toward you, saith the LORD, thoughts of peace, and not of evil, to give you an expected end.

These words were spoken by the Lord God to Jeremiah (God's prophet) and sent to people in captivity, which were without hope. You should note that the Lord says He thinks thoughts toward the people. This indicates that His thoughts are transferrable from Him to the people. His thoughts travel from Him to those He thinks them *toward*. This may seem strange to some but is in line with our discussion that thought travels from one person to another and may be directional.

The Lord God's words are as true today as they were then. He still thinks thoughts toward all who seek Him. The thoughts are thoughts of peace and not evil. They are thoughts that if accepted and made your thoughts will give you peace and enable you to reach the expected end God has for you and your life.

A close examination of the passage clearly shows that God's thoughts are transmitted to those who look to Him for help. As you seek for peace in your life, know that God is aware of your search and is sending thoughts of peace to you.

Meditation and Your Feelings

One of the exciting and thrilling things about life is the feelings and passions we experience. The joy, happiness, and pleasure that occur in our encounters in the world motivate us to desire life and seek to experience it to its fullest. These are all positive, and we grow to love them. As new born babes, we explore all that is around us to learn more about things. This desire to learn, to know, leads us to recognize that the joy, happiness, and pleasure we love come with a price. For we rapidly discover that joy is often turned to sorrow, happiness may becomes sadness, and pleasure may turn into pain. These negative feelings we grow to hate.

Feelings come with great variety and play a major role in our life. They come from encounters we have with the world around us and from within our self. Some we accept and use to influence our world view, others we reject and refuse to include in our World View. It is only later that we learn that although the causes of feelings may be positive or negative and may be external or internal, we experience them nevertheless. We learn that both must somehow be considered in our world view.

The world is good for it provides the environment in which we develop our human spirit, human soul, and human body to become divine. As we learn to depend totally upon God, we become divine. It is a process of trial and error based primarily upon obedience to God's word. As the scripture states when describing the development of Jesus:

Though he were a Son, yet learned he obedience by the things which he suffered.
Hebrews 5:8

We struggle with the uncertainties of life that cause a wide variety of feelings. We must learn to think and understand these uncertainties and the feelings they cause. As we grow, we will grow to feel as God feels about them. Then we will possess God's world view about them and how they relate to us.

Meditation and God's Feelings

God is the creator of the world. His view of the world is that it is worthy of His love. For it is written in the Bible that:

For God so loved the world, that he gave his only begotten Son, that whosoever believeth in him should not perish, but have everlasting life.
John 3:16

God's feeling toward the world is captured in the above verse and indicates that His attitude is demonstrated by giving His Son to the world to ensure everlasting life for those who believe in Him.

But it is not God only that is involved in the world but Jesus Christ and us. We are included in the "*whosoever.*" We are to believe in Jesus Christ, and we are to have the same feelings toward the world that God has. We are to grow to love it. With all its perceived shortfalls and failings, we are to grow to love the world.

These feelings we experience are God-given ways to perfect us to learn to have the same feelings toward the world that He has. His love is manifested by the gift of His son Jesus Christ, who He gave that those in the world might receive the benefit of everlasting life. So the feelings that may seem negative as well as those that seem positive are both a part of the plan God has for us while in the world.

All are intended to lead us of our own free will to the proper relationship with God and our fellow man. Jesus Christ came to teach this because we don't know. We have been given free will to decide for our self, but it is a decision that must be based upon divine truth that we must be taught and must understand. The ultimate feeling we must possess is love. Jesus Christ came to teach us the law of love.

Meditation and the Law of Love

> **And Jesus answered him, The first of all the commandments is, Hear, O Israel; The Lord our God is one Lord: And thou shall love the Lord thy God with all thy heart and with all thy soul, and with all thy mind, and with all thy strength: this is the first commandment. And the second is like, namely this, Thou shalt love thy neighbour as thyself. There is none other commandment greater than these.**
>
> **Mark 12:29–31**

The lesson we learn is that God acts based on His love. The manifestation of that love was to give. God's love caused Him to give. The manifestation of His love and the subsequent love that emanated from Jesus Christ on earth is called compassion. Compassion is the act of love as manifested on earth. It is demonstrated as living toward others as God would have you live.

We are to love God and our neighbors. However, we must learn how to do this. We are born with the *capacity* to love, but we must develop the *ability* to love. As we learn to follow Jesus Christ and the leading of the Holy Spirit, we will learn how to think about the feelings we experience as Jesus Christ would have us think about them and respond to them as Jesus Christ would have us respond, thereby developing the *ability* to love.

We are to love God with our total being. Jesus further describes how this is done:

> **If ye love me, keep my commandments.**
>
> **John 14:15**

Meditation and Your Will

Willing is the act of putting your thinking and feeling into motion. Although you may **think** something and **feel** something, it is only when you **will** the thing you **think** and **feel** that the process becomes complete. When you will, you choose. Your **will** choice is first a spiritual action that becomes a spiritual manifestation. When you perform a physical act as a result of your **will** choice, the choice becomes a physical manifestation.

Willing is that action that is individually yours. Your will has direct impact on your life. As a result of what you will, you determine whether you are becoming what God wants you to become. You move toward your divine destiny or not based upon your will.

Willing is influenced by your thinking and feeling and as such is subject to the uncertainties present in them. The challenges we face is how to grow in right thinking and right feeling so that we make right choices and act as God would have us act.

Our will is the organ in our being that is best aligned with what is pleasing to us. It is what our heart desires. For this reason, in the Bible, the heart and will are often used synonymously:

> **When thou saidst, Seek ye my face; my <u>heart</u> said unto thee, Thy face, LORD, <u>will</u> I seek.**
>
> **Psalm 27:8**

> **The LORD *is* my strength and my shield; my <u>heart</u> trusted in him, and I am helped: therefore my <u>heart</u> greatly rejoiceth; and with my song <u>will</u> I praise him**
>
> **Psalm 28:7**

As you grow in peace, you will come to realize that your peace greatly depends upon how you use your will, what choices you make. We are expected to freely choose to align our will with the will of God. We see this clearly stated in the Lord's Prayer. We are taught that the Father's **will** is to be done "on earth" as "in heaven."

The supreme expression of our love of God is obedience to His will. Jesus Christ states this in John 14:15, when He instructs His disciples and the same applies to us that:

> **If you love me keep my commandments.**
>
> **John 14:15**

And,

> **He that hath my commandments and keepeth them, he it is that loveth me: and he that loveth me shall be loved of my Father, and I will love him, and will manifest myself to him.**
>
> **John 14:21**

Meditation and God's Will

God's will should first be in our hearts. One challenge is to know God's will. We must be able to hear the voice of God through Christ and the Holy Spirit to know God's will. That is why the study of His written word in the Bible is vitally important to you, for you, as a result of studying His written word, begin to develop an increased sensitivity to the spirit of His spoken word that you receive in meditation. The spirit of His written and spoken word always agree.

As you learn to meditate on God's written word, your spiritual organs of hearing become developed, which heightens your spiritual sensitivity to the influx of His living word as spoken to you through the Holy Spirit and Jesus Christ.

God's word is His will. God's will is what He declares is right. His will is manifested to you and the world as His righteousness. So when one does God's will, one does what is righteous in God's sight. The more righteous acts one performs, the more righteous one becomes. God makes His will known to us to perfect us so that we become divine.

As you will discover in later sections of this book, the righteousness produced in us by doing God's will plays a major part in us developing peace. In fact, they are closely integrated with each other. When we do God's will, we increase the peace we experience. The opposite is also true: when we ignore or fail to do God's will, we lessen our peace and give the forces of evil opportunity to implant disease in us.

One significant spiritual benefit from doing God's will is you grow in the ability to know and understand current and future events that are and will occur in your life. Doing God's will opens one up to receive information about things that are developing in one's life. This information is given to enable one to grow more in the direction that God intends for us.

Lord is my Shepherd

Meditation and Your Peace Journey

As you set out on your peace journey, I thought it would be worthwhile to share with you one of the most assuring passages in the Bible, Psalm 23. It serves to clearly establish the role the Lord performs as our shepherd and our role as followers of Him.**Psalm 23**

> **The LORD is my shepherd; I shall not want.**
> **He maketh me to lie down in green pastures: he leadeth me beside the still waters.**
> **He restoreth my soul: he leadeth me in the paths of righteousness for his name's sake.**
> **Yea, though I walk through the valley of the shadow of death, I will fear no evil: for thou art with me; thy rod and thy staff they comfort me.**
> **Thou preparest a table before me in the presence of mine enemies: thou anointest my head with oil; my cup runneth over.**
> **Surely goodness and mercy shall follow me all the days of my life: and I will dwell in the house of the LORD forever.**
>
> **Psalm 23**

Is a classic biblical scripture that captures the essence of peace. It establishes the framework for anyone desiring to acquire peace. It is filled with restful and delightful images that are figures of physical settings and events intended to create spiritual effects that will recreate our spirit, soul, and body.

Verse 1: The Lord is my shepherd; I shall not want begins the process by declaring that the Lord is your shepherd. A shepherd performs many functions, the principle ones being to lead, protect, and sustain. This is the role of the Lord. This verse also defines your role, and that you are willing to follow the Lord in His role as the shepherd. It also declares a personal, individual ownership of the follower's role. "The Lord is my shepherd" indicates a willing decision as an individual to take ownership of the Lord as *my* shepherd.

Verse 1 also establishes another aspect of the relationship of the Lord as shepherd to the individual as follower or "sheep," and that the follower will not have to want or go lacking. Another way to look at this role, a more advance spiritual state I might add, is that the Lord will provide for us to such a degree that we will no longer have to concern ourselves with wanting (unfilled wish) for things because the Lord will take total and complete care of us, and His will for us becomes what we want. Our want will be the same as His will for us.

Verse 2: He maketh me to lie down in green pastures: he leadeth me beside the still waters. This verse has a sense of being compelled by the Lord to lie down or rest in a pleasant place of growth, a place well watered and full of growth.

The verse has a sense of the wisdom of the Lord being expressed as a force that wills us to rest in a state of abundance and plenty, and this rest is really a compulsion that arises from the action of His Spirit with our spirit. We will to rest in this state and recognize that we are surrounded by abundance and growth.

The latter part of this verse reinforces these images by highlighting that this place of rest is bounded by quietness expressed as still waters. Water is often used in the scripture to represent truth. The search for and acquisition of truth is often a struggle that includes turbulent times and painful experiences. With the Lord as our shepherd, we can avoid these turbulent times and painful experiences for He will guide us to where we can experience the truth in a way that will be peaceful and quiet.

Verse 3: He restoreth my soul: he leadeth me in the paths of righteousness for his name's sake. The restoring of the soul is an important truth. Many do not realize or recognize that the soul requires replenishing and regeneration. As goes the soul, so goes the body. A tired or depleted soul will be reflected in a diseased or sick body. The Lord's leading us in the path or way that is righteous or good and healthy.

Righteousness is the intended state of the soul, but when we use our soul in ways that are unrighteous, we experience the unintended effects, which result in disease and sickness, not because God wishes to punish us but as a lawful results of the untrue use of our spirit, soul. or body. The Lord as our Shepherd wants us to be of sound health, so He leads us in ways that are righteous for that is His very state of being and His followers enjoy the blessing of this same state by willfully following Him

Verse 4: Yea, though I walk through the valley of the shadow of death, I will fear no evil: for thou art with me; thy rod and thy staff they comfort me. I had the opportunity to visit Israel several years ago. I recalled being told by our guide that on the road that leads from Jerusalem to Jericho, there is a location on that road where bandits would wait for travelers and rob them and do them harm. That location, according to the guide, was known as the "valley of the shadow of death." Travelers were very fearful if they had to travel that road and sought protection when they had to travel it. It was a source of fear, and so this verse might be referring symbolically to times in our life when we have to go or undertake actions or make choices that we perceive could cause us harm.

With the Lord as our guide, even when we are led through situations that to us present dangers and harm, we need not fear for the Lord is guiding us through them. Not only is He guiding us through them, His rod (weapon and authority over all things) and staff (ability to rescue, support) assists us even if we wander away from His directed path or way.

Verse 5: Thou preparest a table before me in the presence of mine enemies: thou anointest my head with oil; my cup runneth over. This verse is amazing for it seems to imply an action by the Lord that is intended to embarrass those who oppose us. I don't think that is accurate. As one looks deeper at this verse, it seems it is intended more for the follower than for those who do evil to them. The verse gives a sense of assurance that even though some would attempt to do you worldly harm, have no fear, for the Lord will bless you and those who attempt to deprive you will be able to observe the blessing that the Lord bestows upon you. Not only will they observe your success, they will also recognize that the blessings are from the Lord because there is no observable means available to you that would account for the blessings. It is the result of supernatural intervention.

The spiritual presence of the Lord will be experienced by you and is overflowing in your life. This activity also will be observed by you and those who oppose you in your quest to follow the Lord. This revelation of blessing and divine presence will become more and more evident to you as well as to those who oppose you in following the Lord.

Verse 6: Surely goodness and mercy shall follow me all the days of my life: and I will dwell in the house of the LORD forever. Goodness and mercy are the qualities of the Lord's divine nature. These are also aspects of love. Love is good, and love and God are one. God is love, so the Lord is love. Mercy is granted by the Lord to those who follow Him. His Mercy is everlasting to everlasting. As a result of following the Lord, we dwell in His presence forever. The house of the Lord is more than a physical building. It is wherever He abides. If He abides in you, then you are the house of the Lord. Wherever the Lord leads me, I will abide.

Meditation Exercises

Let us begin the journey. Since meditation is so important in our search for peace, we will start with ninety (90) days of meditation exercises. These exercises will be the beginning, yet a vital part of your peace development. These exercises will be the departure point for the journey that will increase your peace. Meditation will open up new understandings and enable you to consider what is written in the remainder of this book with a deeper appreciation of yourself and the information revealed in it.

The Christian Meditation Outline that follows should be used as a guide until it becomes an integral part of your physical and spiritual life. Review it continually as a refresher to assist you. Please perform the meditation exercise for the next ninety (90) days. They are structured to help you become more proficient in your meditation discipline as you continue with the remainder of the book.

It is essential that you have a good foundation in meditation. So relax and enjoy this part of your peace journey. Just practice the meditation exercises one day at a time, starting with day 1 and ending with day 90. Follow the information given and record your experiences. Again, don't become discouraged or frustrated if it appears you are not hearing from the Lord. Just practice the meditation outline and record what comes to your mind. You will be able to sort these various thoughts out later. Just keep in mind that all thoughts that come to you may not be from the Lord and are to be **confirmed** by two or three scriptural references (witnesses) from the written Word of God. Later as your conscience matures you will become spiritually sensitive to the Lord's voice. But until then confirm what you hear with the written Word of God.

Christian Meditation Outline

(Listening to God)

Thou will keep him in perfect peace whose mind
Is stayed on thee because he trusteth in thee.
Isaiah 26:3

Position

1. Sit in straight-back chair with back straight and feet flat on the floor, or lie on the floor or bed.
2. Wear loose-fitting clothing.
3. Take three deep inhales and exhales.
4. Clear your mind of distractions by doing one of following:
    A. Read Bible verse(s); start with Isaiah 26:3.
        or
    B. Think of God, Jesus, light, love, pure, gentle, kind, peaceable things, listen to quiet music.
    C. Slowly relax and listen for the inward voice of the Holy Spirit (John 14:26; John 16:13–15).

Experiences That May Occur

1. Feel breeze on your face.
2. Feel stinging sensation around eyes (this indicates healing).
3. Feel sensations on head, hands, feet, back, total body (this is an inflow of the Holy Spirit's anointing).
4. See visions in your spirit.
5. Hear inward thoughts (voices). Test voices with 1 John 4:1–2; not all thoughts (voices) are of God.
6. Smell sweet fragrances (heavenly visitors).
7. See spiritual entity.

Purpose

1. Communion with God.
2. Attune to God through the Holy Spirit under the leadership of Jesus Christ.
3. Worship.
4. Know God's purpose for you.
5. Glorify God and yourself as God's creation.

When

1. Set specific time.
2. Start five minutes (morning or evening), then be led by the Holy Spirit as to time.

Where

1. Find a favorite place to start; the Holy Spirit will assist you.
2. Later, follow the total leading of the Holy Spirit.

Day 1

Spiritual Exercise No. 1

Meditation Scripture:

Thou will keep him in perfect peace whose mind
Is stayed on thee because he trusteth in thee.
Isaiah 26:3

Meditation Exercise:

Meditate on the meditation scripture. As thoughts, come listen to hear the voice of **Jesus Christ**. Record what you hear below.

Meditation Comments:

Meditation Assignment:
(This is to develop your obedience to do God's will.)

Date:

Ask the Lord what He would have you do.
Test the spirit.
Record what you heard below:

Do what the Lord asked you to do.
Record your actions below:

At the end of the day ask the Lord to tell you how well you did Today:

Meditation Exercises

Days	Meditation Exercise
1–10	Meditate on the scripture **Isaiah 26:3**. Follow the meditation outline.
11–20	Meditate on the name **Jesus Christ**. Follow the meditation outline.
21–30	Meditate on **23rd Psalm**. Follow the meditation outline.

Meditation Exercises

Days	Meditation Exercise
31–40	Meditate on the scripture **Isaiah 26:3**. Follow the meditation outline.
41–50	Meditate on the **Lord's Prayer**. Follow the meditation outline.
21–30	Meditate on **23rd Psalm**. Follow the Meditation Outline.

Meditation Exercises

Days	Meditation Exercise
61–70	Meditate on the scripture **Isaiah 26:3**. Follow the meditation outline.
71–80	Meditate on the **Lord's Prayer**. Follow the meditation outline.
81–90	Meditate on and memorize **Psalm 23**. Follow the meditation outline.

CONGRATULATIONS! You are on your way. Now be faithful to the leading of the Holy Spirit as you are guided to your divine destiny.

Plowing

Snake River, Burley, Idaho

Rainbow – double Niagara Falls

Peace A Divine Substance
Peace Definition

Peace in the Old Testament and New Testament

The word "peace" is used in the Old Testament of the Bible to describe a number of conditions. It is sometime used to describe "completeness," "soundness," "health," "prosperity," "quietness," "tranquility," and "freedom from war." The Hebrew word typically used to describe all of these conditions is ***shalom***.

Another word for peace that has a similar meaning as *shalom* but differs slightly in that it, like *shalom*, not only means "complete" but also means "to make ready" or "to perfect." That Hebrew word is ***shalem***.

Another usage of the Hebrew word for peace is its description of a covenant relationship with another individual based upon terms and agreement, real or implied. The Hebrew word used to describe this is ***shalam***. An important divine principle included in this word is the principle of covenant relationships. God's relationship with man is based upon a covenant of free will, free choice, by man. Man has been given the opportunity by God to accept Him or reject Him. Many divine principles are embedded in this covenant relationship, including eternal existence, salvation, prosperity, peace, etc. Not to accept God's covenant relationship is spiritual death. To accept God's covenant relationship is to live by His principles. We see this expressed by God in the following:

> **If my people which are called by my name, shall humble themselves, and pray, and seek my face, and turn from their wicked ways; then will I hear from heaven, and will forgive their sin, and will heal their land.**
>
> **2 Chronicles 7:14**

Peace as a covenant relationship principle is what I want to keep before you. Peace is foremost a spiritual covenant relationship. So when a covenant relationship of peace is established, at its core is a spiritual relationship. Any breaking of the terms of the agreement, by either of the parties, creates a broken spirit in both. This creates the need to make an act of repentance for breaking the covenant by the offending party and the need to forgive by the party that has been injured. Compensation, "as in making peace with another," is to pay them compensation to restore covenant relationships.

The compensation offered to mend the broken relationship established by the covenant is called a "peace offering." A "peace offering" is that compensation that is necessary to restore the covenant relationship to its original state, thereby restoring the peace. Without it, the state of peace within the two parties would remain broken. The word for this is ***shelem***.

I am reminded of a television episode I saw where two friends were discussing a situation where one of them had betrayed the trust of the other. This resulted in much anger and distrust on the part of the friend who had been betrayed. The guilty party admitted the error and wanted to make amends. The other party also wanted to restore their friendship. The betrayed friend asked the one who had betrayed him, "Where do you want it?" The other one said, "In the stomach." The betrayed friend gave him a solid blow to the stomach. They both then hugged and went about their way. The covenant relationship was restored. The two used the blow to the stomach as compensation for restoring the peace between them. Without it, the covenant relationship would have remained broken. This act was a ***shelem***.

I don't want to imply that one should hit another as the solution for restoring broken covenants or relationships; that would be ridiculous. But seriously, I do want you to consider that our peace is often lost when there are no offers of peace made on our part when we have wronged another, or when another has wronged us. This peace offering has to be agreed to by either or both parties to be of equal value to the damage caused by the wrong act and has within it humiliation and perhaps suffering on the part of the one causing the harm.

I think covenants of peace are a precondition of our birth. We come into the world to live with each other with implied covenants of peace. God intends for us all to get along. Even when there is no formal act of agreement, one is preordained by God. We are born to have universal and joint agreement of love for one another. At the birth of Jesus, the angels sang,

Glory to God in the highest, and on earth peace good will toward men,

Luke 2:14

Peace on earth toward men was proclaimed at the birth of Jesus. Jesus Christ is the Prince of Peace. And yet we may not experience peace because peace is only perfected when we allow the Spirit of Peace from Jesus Christ to transform our spirit to have goodwill toward men. To express it more plainly, God's will toward men. Goodwill is God's will, for Jesus Christ said "only God is good." Goodwill toward men is based solely upon us putting God first in all we do between Him and each other. Anything that interferes with us first following God's will, as it is expressed in loving God by doing His will and loving our neighbors as we love our self, will result in us experiencing a lack of peace.

Disobedience to God's will result in a lack of peace within us. Often we may say "I don't like that person," believing that there is something wrong with the person, when in fact there may be something amiss in both of us. Deep inside of both persons may be a state of broken peace. Unless we have spiritual awareness, we will not recognize this as such, but if we understand the working of the spirit of peace, we will take action to fix it.

Furthermore, when our relationship with God is broken, we will experience this same lack of peace. You see, the Lord in both cases is stirring up uneasiness within us. This is illustrated by Jesus Christ when He states:

Think not that I am come to send peace on earth, I came not to send peace. but a sword For I am come to set a man at variance against his father, and the daughter against her mother, and the daughter in law against her mother in law. And a man's foes shall be they of his own household. He that loveth father or mother more than me is not worthy of me: and he that loveth son or daughter more than me is not worthy of me. And he that taketh not his cross, and followeth after me, is not worthy of me. He that findeth his life shall lose it: and he that loseth his life for my sake shall find it.

Luke 12:51–53

This passage of scripture appears to be contradictory to what one might believe about the spirit of Jesus Christ, so let's discuss it. The presence of the spirit of Jesus Christ in us is preordained for each of us. It is required. When His spirit is present in one member of a family, it will cause discomfort in others who do not possess it. Jesus Christ is the one who stirs up uneasiness and the lack of peace in us and in others to let us know that the peace covenant between God and us is broken. We must accept the divine work of the Lord within us if we are to claim Him as our Lord. This work is a work of sacrifice, humiliation, and obedience that lets us know the times when our peace is lacking. This lack of peace may remain in us until death, but that is not God's divine design. God intends that peace becomes an eternal quality of our being.

We should develop an attitude of peace toward others even if they refuse our offers of peace. God stands ready through Jesus Christ at all times to restore broken peace. But first we must desire to restore peace between our self and God, then He, through Jesus Christ and the Holy Spirit, will guide us in how to restore peace with the other person(s). God, through Jesus Christ, is always willing to guide us in how to renew our peace. We have discussed earlier that when the covenant of peace has been broken, God commanded a peace offering. The form of the peace offering will be revealed to you by God, through Jesus Christ and the Holy Spirit.

Attempts to mend broken peace with other men, even if your peace offerings, as directed by God through Jesus Christ, are not always accepted. In such a case, when you make your peace offering, your responsibility to the covenant relationship has been met, and you can move on with your life, knowing you have held up your end of the covenant. For example, Jesus Christ, when He sent out disciples, gave them this instruction:

> And into whatsoever house ye enter, first say, Peace be to this house. If the son of peace be there, your peace shall rest upon it: if not, it shall turn to you again.
> And in the same house remain, eating and drinking such things as they give: for the labourer is worthy of his hire. Go not from house to house. And into whatsoever city ye enter, and they receive you, eat such things as are set before you: And heal the sick that are therein, and say unto them, The kingdom of God is come nigh unto you.
> But into whatsoever city ye enter, and they receive you not, go your ways out into the streets of the same, and say,
> Even the very dust of your city, which cleaveth on us, we do wipe off against you: notwithstanding be ye sure of this, that the kingdom of God is come nigh unto you.
>
> *Luke 10:5–11*

The conclusion of the matter is this: our peace is perfected when we follow God's word to do His will regardless of how others receive us.

As I have studied the subject of peace, I have come to sense that God is grieved when there is a lack of peace between me and another. It is similar to the grief that a parent feels when their child commits a misdeed. I recognize that I must do something to restore a right relationship with the other person(s). Therefore, I am required to offer to make amends with whosoever I offend. If they do not accept my God-directed offer or compensation, it does not matter. As a result of my attempt to make amends, my relationship with God is restored. If not, I remain in a broken relationship with that person and with God.

Then there is a meaning of peace that involves speech or communication. In this usage, the party or parties involve keep silent or are commanded to keep silent, to hush, or to hold their tongue. The Hebrew word used to describe this is *hacah*.

There is one Hebrew word that is translated as peace that intrigues me more than the others. It is the translation of peace that also means to plow, or to engrave, or to devise. The Hebrew word is *charash*. This meaning appears to be so different from our normal thinking and usage of the word "peace" that it prompts additional reflection about how it relates to peace.

Plowing is a work one performs to prepare the soil to receive seed for growth and harvest. It opens up and softens the soil so that the seed will be able to penetrate it and eventually become rooted. Those who farm the land know there are proper processes for planting seed that must be in keeping with the laws of nature that God has foreordained. The laws of nature are in place to assure a successful harvest.

Peace is sent from Jesus Christ to act like a plow as it affects our spirit, soul, and body, opening us up to Him, the Word of God, the seed of God, which contains the Truth of God. Jesus Christ is the Truth of God who, along with the Spirit of Truth, the Holy Spirit, assists us in forming peace in us by cleansing our mind of nontruths so that the Truth of God, from Jesus Christ, might be implanted in us.

Peace prepares us to receive God's word. Initially, this occurs in our human spirit and subsequently in our human soul and human body in that order. The area of our human spirit that experiences this activity initially is our mind and specifically the part of our mind known as our **conscience**. It is in our conscience that peace first begins to "plow" as it "breaks up" old altitudes and beliefs that we thought were true. This is a softening process that opens our mind to receive an inflow of the Word of God. The specific divine attributes of the Word of God that peace opens us up to is **truth** and then **righteousness**. As we receive and use these divine attributes, we prepare our spirit to receive God's love.

The conscience is an organ in our human spirit whose purpose is to guide our mind by influencing first the understanding then the will. Our understanding is where we have developed what we think to be "true," and in our will is where we have developed what we think is "right or good." When our conscience is opened by peace, truth and righteousness are implanted in it and grow to a point where we begin to recognize the voice of the Spirit of God, the Holy Spirit, in our conscience. The result is our conscience becomes transformed and possesses the same truth and righteousness that exist in Jesus Christ. Our conscience serves as a witness to what is revealed to us through the Holy Spirit, Jesus Christ, and God the Father. This knowledge perfects our conscience, which then serves as a sort of "judge" of what exist as our understanding and will. The conscience enables us to exercise our own individuality and not have to depend upon anyone else as we declare God's truth and righteousness.

As St. Paul stated:

> **I say the truth in Christ, I lie not, my conscience also bearing me witness in the Holy Ghost**
> **Romans 9:1**

St. Paul uses "I," "my," and "me" to emphasize that individually we grow in the use of our own conscience to know and do God's will.

The "plowing" of peace as it prepares our conscience creates much discomfort in it. This discomfort occurs not only in our conscience but also in our understanding and will. This is because the peace process digs up, separates, and reveals former "truths" in our understanding, which in fact are false, from the truths of God and former "choices of right or good" in our will, which in fact are evil from the righteousness of God.

These false "truths" and evil "choices of right or good" are like stone boulders that have become implanted in our mind and must be plowed up and remove to make room for the planting of the Word of God. The peace process requires us to use our will to remove these false "truths" and evil "rights or goods." This is personally painful.

One of the major challenges we face as we undergo this process is to develop our will to control our mind. This requires developing our mind to "be still." The control of our mind must be developed by us with the help of Jesus Christ and the Holy Spirit. Meditation, prayer, spiritual exercises, and our submission to the will of the Holy Spirit of God in our personal life is the way to develop control of our mind. You will learn more about this as you apply the exercises in the meditation section of this book.

Another usage of the word *charash* to define peace is to **engrave**. One might ask what engraving has to do with peace. The Hebrew word *charash* literally means to carve words into metal, wood, or stone. Is it possible that peace is somehow used to spiritually carve something into our spirit? The answer is yes. In Jeremiah 17:1, it is written:

> **The sin of Judah is written with a pen of iron, and with the point of a diamond: it is graven upon the table of their heart,**

The word *charash* is translated as *graven* in Jeremiah 17:1; it also is translated as *peace* in other scriptures. When we consider that peace is used to prepare our human spirit for the incoming Word of God, is it also possible that once our spirit is open, peace is also used to "carve" into us what God wants us to remember? I believe so.

God wants us to remember His commandments, whether it is about His truth, goodwill, or about the evil things we have done or could do that displease Him. When one carves something, he remove a portion of it original substance by cutting some of it away while at the same time changing its form to represent a new form. The Lord uses peace to change the form of our spirit by opening it up to recognize what we have done or might do that violates His Word of Truth.

It is at first difficult to imagine that peace would be used to do something like carving, which involves cutting open something. Peace is normally believed to be painless and gentle, but carving or cutting us will hurt. Could it be that peace like other spiritual qualities may have a pain-causing quality as they are being acquired? The use of the Hebrew word *charash* strongly suggests so. Peace, when used by the Lord to open us up to the entrance of His word, involves not only "plowing" but also "carving" in our spirit. This causes pain. This carving action precedes the imprinting of His divine qualities in our spirit and is intended to bring us to a place of repentance and finally spiritual perfection

The spiritual part of us where this godly operation first occurs is our conscience. Because our conscience is coupled with our understanding and will, it also occurs in our understanding and will but principally in our will. Our will is often referred to in the scriptures as our "heart." This engraving action is first felt in our will and later as one develops, in our physical heart. As stated in Ezekiel:

> **A new heart also will I give you, and a new spirit will I put within you: and I will take away the stony heart out of your flesh, and I will give you an heart of flesh. And I will put my spirit within you, and cause you to walk in my statutes, and ye shall keep my judgments, and do them.**
>
> *Ezekiel 26:26–27*

And,

> **Whereof the Holy Ghost also is a witness to us: for after that he had said before,**
> **This is the covenant that I will make with them after those days, saith the Lord, I will put my laws into their hearts, and in their minds will I write them; And their sins and iniquities will I remember no more.**
>
> *Hebrew 10:15–17*

The Lord spiritually affects our will so that we do His will. Our will affects our understanding, and our understanding affects our will. They both interact with each other. The understanding and will, which are coupled with our conscience, are prepared by the "plowing" and "carving" action of peace to receive the divine inflow of the Word of God.

The divine inflow of God's word initially causes imperceptible changes to occur in our spirit and soul. As the word grows, we become conscious of its effects on our spirit, soul, and body, particularly in our physical heart.

The Hebrew word *charash*, as a definition for peace, is also used in connection with the word "devise." To "devise" is defined as to imagine, to fabricate, to develop plans or schemes. These imaginings, fabrications, plans, or schemes may be either good or evil. The Lord warns that those who devise evil will suffer the consequences of their deeds, and those who devise good, their deeds will cause them to be blessed.

Just as in the Old Testament, the usage of the word "peace" in the New Testament is used to describe a number of conditions. These include "physical and soul salvation," "prosperity," "a state of individual and national tranquility," "happiness," "quietness," and "rest." The Greek word used to define these conditions is *eirene*.

Taken collectively, these New Testament usages for the word "peace" are similar in many ways to those used in the Old Testament. However, in the New Testament, there seems to be a stronger focus on the individual's existence in this world and after death. As described in Jesus's words in the book of John:

> **Let not your heart be troubled: ye believe in God, believe also in me. In my Father's house are many mansions: if it were not so, I would have told you. I go to prepare a place for you. And if I go and prepare a place for you, I will come again, and receive you unto myself; that where I am, there ye may be also.**
>
> *John 14:1–3*

And,

> **Peace I leave with you, my peace I give unto you: not as the world giveth, give I unto you. Let not your heart be troubled, neither let it be afraid.**
>
> *John 14:27*

These verses all point to the assurance of peace while in the world and in the world to come.

One characteristic that is noted in both the Old and New Testaments, yet appears to me to be emphasized more in the New Testament, is the responsibility placed upon the individual to practice the qualities of peace in pursuit of their own salvation. In the New Testament, we see this stated in the book of James:

> **Do not err, my beloved brethren. Every good gift and every perfect gift is from above, and cometh down from the Father of lights, with whom is no variableness, neither shadow of turning. Of his own will begat he us with the word of truth, that we should be a kind of firstfruits of his creatures. Wherefore, my beloved brethren, let every man be swift to hear, slow to speak, slow to wrath: For the wrath of man worketh not the righteousness of God. Wherefore lay apart all filthiness and superfluity of naughtiness, and receive with meekness the engrafted word, which is able to save your souls.**
>
> **James 1:16–21**

We are to be active participant with the Spirit of God by recognizing that the gift of the Word of God given to us and growing in us requires that we learn to hear from God, learn to control our speaking, and learn to control our anger. Our soul's salvation is dependent upon us having a meek spirit able to proper receive the word of truth from God, which only grows in the soil of peace.

Because there are similarities between Old and New Testament usages of the word "peace," it would be redundant to dwell further on their similarities in our discussion. However, one use of the word "peace" that I have delayed discussing so far is its usage in both the Old and New Testaments to describe the absence of "war" or "the state of national tranquility." In both the Hebrew and Greek, peace is used to describe the absence of war.

Many books have been written about war. Carl Von Clausewitz, a military theorist and author, wrote a wide-ranging and extensive treatise about war. The title of the often quoted book is ***On War***. He defines war this way: **"war therefore is an act of violence intended to compel our opponent to fulfil our will."** I believe this definition to be helpful in our discussion of peace. For as we have explored peace, we have noted that the **will** plays a vital role in the obtaining of peace. And that our **will** is representative of our heart. The heart is that part of us that houses our wants and desires.

War occurs, therefore, when what we will or want is denied us by another, whether that other is an individual or nation. A brief review of the history of mankind reveals that wars have been fought since the beginning of mankind's time on the earth. Research into the occurrences of war shows that mankind has been involved in the use of violence to resolve conflicts of will since the beginning of time. One book that gives an insightful view of this is a book by Lawrence H. Keeley. In his book *War Before Civilization*, he discusses the past history of warfare and shows that violence not peace has been the prevailing way mankind has resolved conflicts of will.

Even when we search the Bible, it is interesting to note that the first reference to the word *"war"* appears in Genesis 14:2:

> **That these made *war* with Bera king of Sodom, and with Birsha king of Gomorrah, Shinab king of Admah, and Shemeber king of Zeboiim, and the king of Bela, which is Zoar.**

However, conflicts appear in even earlier chapters. The conflict of will between Adam and Eve and God in the Garden of Eden is one. The conflict between Cain and Abel, which resulted in the killing of Abel, and the subsequent concern of Cain about harm coming to him from others are examples. These all point to the fact that conflicts between God and man and between man and man have existed for a long time. Whether you read these instances of conflict literally, figuratively, or symbolically, the presence of conflict has been with us since the early stages of mankind's existence on earth.

Having stated the above comments, one wonders if mankind's search for peace is realistic, and yet the angels announced at the birth of Jesus:

> **Glory to God in the highest, and on earth *peace* good will toward men**
> **Luke 2:14**

So it must be possible or the angels would not have proclaimed it. Jesus is called the Prince of peace. But even He states that :

> **And ye shall hear of *wars* and rumours of *wars*: see that ye be not troubled: for all these things must come to pass, but the end is not yet. For nation shall rise against nation, and kingdom against kingdom: and there shall be famines, and pestilences, and earthquakes, in divers places. All these are the beginning of sorrows**
> **Matthew 24:6–8**

So is there uncertainty even in the scriptures that peace between individuals and nations is possible? And what is the role of Jesus Christ when He states that wars are inevitable; and if this is so, why is there this deep yearning for peace? The answer I believe lies in the nature of the role of mankind on earth and the relationship of mankind with Jesus Christ.

I would have you consider that the earth is not a permanent place of residence for mankind. The earth shall pass away. For mankind, the earth serves as a temporary dwelling place, a training ground. The earth serves as a place of learning and development for mankind. One of the essential attributes that individuals are to acquire on earth is peace.

Mankind as individuals and nations must learn to use peace to resolve conflict. Those who do not will not move on to the next stage of their divine development intended for them by God. While on earth, individuals are to acquire peace from Jesus Christ and use it to resolve conflicts. When they are placed in leadership roles, they must learn to share their knowledge of how peace is acquired and how peace is to be used to resolve conflicts.

The search for peace as a preventative to war is the search for Jesus Christ. Until the spiritual nature of our being is considered in our search for peace, there will always be war. And until individuals and nations recognize their true nature and the true nature of Jesus Christ, the search for peace on earth through means other than through Jesus Christ will be in vain.

War is evil. It is insanity. Its instigators are not physical but spirituals forces. The spiritual forces of evil are the influencers that promote conflict between individuals and nations. The Bible states that:

> **Put on the whole armour of God, that ye may be able to stand against the wiles of the devil. For we wrestle not against flesh and blood, but against principalities, against powers, against the rulers of the darkness of this world, against spiritual wickedness in high *places*. Wherefore take unto you the whole armour of God, that ye may be able to withstand in the evil day, and having done all, to stand. Stand therefore, having your loins girt about with truth, and having on the breastplate of righteousness; And your feet shod with the preparation of the gospel of peace.**
> **Ephesians 6:11–15**

War fought between individuals and nations is war instigated by spiritual forces. Mankind was not created by God to be warlike. Our initial defenses against war include **truth**, **righteousness**, and **peace**. These three, **truth**, **righteousness**, and **peace**, are affected by our conscience. Our conscience is that spiritual organ that must be developed in us to enable us to decide what is true from what is false and what is right and good from what is wrong or evil. As stated above and is repeated here, Jesus Christ first sends His peace to help form and prepare our conscience to receive His word of truth and then His word of righteousness so that we become able to choose between what is true and right for our self.

The search for Jesus Christ and peace involves the search for knowledge. Mankind must learn the right way to avoid war, both as individuals and nations. The knowledge we seek is knowledge of physical and spiritual forces as they affect individuals and leaders of nations. Wars don't just happen in a vacuum; there are causes. As we discuss in the section on **War and Spiritual Influences** and in the section of **Cause and Effect**, conflicts between individuals and among nations are many times the result of spiritual forces working on and through the hearts of men.

In summary, the various definitions and usages of the word "peace" in both the Old and New Testaments are intended to describe the state of a covenant relationship, which God intends to exist between mankind and Himself.

Peace among men involves divine force acting upon and through man's spiritual and physical nature to form in him a proper dwelling place for the Holy Spirit, Jesus Christ, and God the Father. Then mankind with their guidance, will be able to choose for themself what is truth and righteousness, for without these, there can be no peace.

Let me leave you with these thoughts from the works of Emanuel Swedenborg. In his book, *The Heavenly Arcana*, he describes peace as follows:

> **Peace is a state of perfection. A state of peace is a state of the Lord's kingdom; in that state the Lord's celestial and spiritual things are as in their morning and in their spring; for peace is like the dawn in the early morning, and in their spring in the springtime. The dawn and the spring cause all things that then meet the senses to be full of joy and gladness; every object draws an affection from the general one of the dawn and of the springtime. So is it with the state of peace in the Lord's kingdom; in the state of peace all celestial and spiritual things are as in their morning or springtide flower and smile, that is, in their happiness itself. So does the state of peace affect everything, for the Lord is peace itself.**
>
> **When a man is in the combats of temptations, he is by turns gifted by the Lord with a state of peace, and is thus refreshed.**

And,

> **What the tranquility of peace of the external man on the cessation of combat, when he is no longer disturbed by evil desires and false suggestions is, can only be known to those who are acquainted with the state of peace. This state is so delightful, as to exceed every idea of delight; it is not only a cessation of combat, but it is life proceeding from interior peace, and affecting the external man in such a manner as cannot be described; the truths of faith, and the good affections of love, which derive their life from the delight of peace then comes into existence.**

And,

> **To have peace is to rest. When spiritual things are being appropriated to the natural man, those things recede which belong to desire for evil and persuasion of falsity, thus which induce unrest; and those approach which belong to the affection of good and of truth, consequently those things which cause peace; for all unrest is from evil and falsity, and all peace is from good and truth.**

Ancient of Days

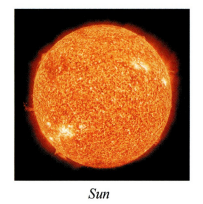
Sun

Milky Way Spiral

Full Moon

Earth

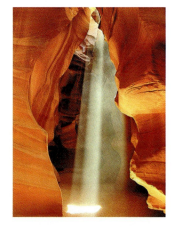
USA Antelope Canyon

Cause and Effect Discussion

The desire to make sense of our world creates a need in us to know about our surroundings and its effect upon us. This desire to know is evident in all of us. From infants to mature adults, the pursuit of knowledge is evident. This desire is often seen in the need to discover the causes of things that happen in our lives. We walk along a road and hear a crashing noise behind us and look around to see what caused it. We see a bright light and wonder what it means. The quest for what caused these and other things is a part of each of us.

Scholars, philosophers, theologians, and others have sought to describe the many phenomena of life—their causes and effects. They then place them into various categories and systems in order to make sense of them. These efforts have added greatly to mankind's knowledge of his world. and although many of these efforts have proven helpful for a time, much of this knowledge has been replaced with newer and more plausible discoveries.

I propose for your consideration, as we discuss peace, that the pursuit to know the causes of peace in our life will be found as we seek to know Christ who is the source of peace. This is not to suggest, as you will see in the discussion that follows, that Christ is the only source of what we experience in life. It is to suggest that He is the original cause of *life* with its various derivatives, one that is peace.

I have taken as a starting point for our discussion a simple thought that appears over and over again in the history of mankind's search for knowledge. ***That is, for every <u>effect, there is a cause</u>. Stated another way, there is a <u>cause for every effect</u>.*** (See the diagram below.)

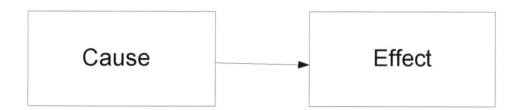

Another way of looking at **cause** is to define it as **reason**, or where there are multiple **causes**, we shall define them as multiple **reasons** for an **effect**. An **effect** would be the resulting outcome of a **cause(s) or reason(s)**. As we continue our discussion on cause and effect, I ask you to keep in mind that when we seek the cause of an effect, we are broadening our search to more than just the cause but to know the ***reason*** behind the cause. As mankind has grown in knowledge, he has discovered that behind a cause often is a reason, some of which are evident to the physical senses, and others for which the physical senses are not equipped to perceive. Some physical causes may require sophisticated instruments to perceive them. Spiritual causes cannot be perceived physically even with sophisticated instruments; but only through spiritual senses. Spiritual causes or reasons can only be perceived by spiritual senses. But more about this later.

God, through Christ, is the cause of divine life. In the discussion that follows, we shall describe how this life is also influenced by many other causes some good, others that are evil.

> GOD THE FATHER AND
> CHRIST THE SON
> DIVINE LIFE

God the Father, who is the source of divine life, is the original *cause*. He creates *effects* that are divine. God the Father has granted the authority to give divine life to Jesus Christ who in turns gives divine life to those who are deemed worthy by Him. Jesus Christ is the Giver of Life. He gives life in all its diverse forms as He wills. There is divine life that is eternal and heavenly and earthly life that is created and ends. Created forms of life have a beginning and end. Divine life does not.

Various types of created forms of life are described in the Bible as heaven and earth. These forms of life are described as consisting of "kingdoms." Kingdom, by definition, means dominion or rule over and does not refer necessarily to a space or geographical location. Kingdom encompasses the authority to determine laws to which persons or objects are subject regardless of where they are in space or geographically located. The being that has the highest authority to set laws and enforce them in a kingdom, and over those in that kingdom is called the king or ruler or lord.

There exist many kingdoms, but we will focus only on three major kingdoms with their subdivision. We have labeled them the Kingdom of God, the Kingdom of Heaven, and the Kingdom of Earth. The Kingdom of God is divine and is ruled by God the Father. The Kingdom of God has authority over the kingdoms of heaven and the kingdoms of earth.

The kingdoms of heaven are created and subject to the divine rules of God the Father through Jesus Christ and further subdivided into three levels. (St. Paul the apostle describes an experience of a person who visited the third level of heaven in 2 Corinthians 12:2–4):

> **I knew a man in Christ above fourteen years ago, (whether in the body, I cannot tell; or whether out of the body, I cannot tell: God knoweth;) such an one caught up to the third heaven. And I knew such a man, (whether in the body, or out of the body, I cannot tell: God knoweth;) How that he was caught up into paradise, and heard unspeakable words, which it is not lawful for a man to utter.**

The Old Testament of the Bible alludes to three heavens, the immediate atmosphere above the earth, the area of the planets and stars, and an area called paradise where the angels of God dwell.

Other historical writings, including the ***Apocalypse of Moses***, the ***Book of the Secrets of Enoch***, and fragments of ***Coptic historical literature***, include references to the various levels of heaven.

Emanuel Swedenborg describes levels of heaven in his book *Heaven and Its Wonders and Hell*. It is on the basis of the writings of St. Paul the apostle, Emanuel Swedenborg, and various other historical writings that our discussion references three levels of heaven and establishes that heaven has divisions with it.

The Kingdoms of Earth are created and subject to the Kingdoms of Heaven and the divine rule of God through Jesus Christ and is subdivided into the Human Kingdom, Animal Kingdom, Plant Kingdom, and Mineral Kingdom.

The kingdom of earth is further distinguished into a kingdom under the earth. This refers to the supersensible beings that affect the elements of the earth from within the earth. These elemental beings manifest through these elements and through them have impact within the subkingdoms of the earth and upon the earth.

The kingdoms of heaven and earth were all created by God through Jesus Christ, with life that is particular for each, all with fixed duration. They are not eternal. The following is a list of the kingdoms:

NAME	MANIFESTED LIFE
Kingdom Of God Father-Son-Holy Spirit	Divine Beings - Eternal
Kingdom Of Heaven a. First b. Second c. Third	Spiritual – Created - Godly Beings - Ungodly Beings
Kingdom Of Earth a. Human b. Animal c. Plant d. Mineral	Spiritual and Physical – Created - Mankind - Animal - Plant - Mineral - Demonic Beings

Kingdom Under the Earth	Spiritual and Physical – Created
	- Supersensible Beings
	  - Fire
	  - Air
	  - Water
	  - Earth

The life in each of the kingdoms comes from God and operates within the prescribed laws and boundaries established by God. All created life has the capability to become divine but only as God determines. God the Father has given Jesus Christ the right to exercise this determination over the kingdoms of heaven, earth, and under the earth.

When we consider **cause and effect**, I ask you to accept the proposition that since the life in each of the kingdoms comes from sources outside of them and since the Kingdom of God is the source of *all* power, then the power that **causes effects** in the kingdoms of heaven, in earth, and under the earth comes from the Kingdom of God. The divine life that comes from the Kingdom of God therefore is intended to cause effects that lead to divine life.

Life in the kingdoms of heaven and earth affect each other. Spiritual and physical life interpenetrates each other. So what happens in one affects the others. Physical life will cause effects in spiritual life, and spiritual life will cause effects in physical life in ways established or permitted by Jesus Christ.

You will note that the kingdoms of heaven consist of both godly and what we have labeled ungodly beings. These are spiritual beings often referred to as "angels," some of which are obedient to the laws of God and others that are not. The question of how "lawful angels" and "unlawful angels" could exist or yet be tolerated by God has puzzled mankind for centuries.

One view described in early religious text and as seen in the actions of Jesus Christ that makes sense to me is that they are permitted by God to exist for a reason. Their existence being for the purpose of helping develop and grow man's divine and spiritual nature by tempting or "testing" him. As Jesus Christ and the Holy Spirit assist mankind to become divine, these unlawful angels are permitted to oppose mankind. The good or benefit derived from this opposition is that man's understanding of truth and his will to do good are transformed and strengthened.

This testing is necessary if mankind is to become what God intends. This testing or what is sometimes called temptation comes in the form of external spiritual and physical hindrances in man's external environment and internal being. One of mankind's major adversaries is often referred to as the "devil" or Satan. An example of the devil's tricks is seen in his encounter with Jesus Christ as described in the Bible in Luke 4:1–13:

> **And Jesus being full of the Holy Ghost returned from Jordan, and was led by the Spirit into the wilderness, Being forty days tempted of the devil. And in those days he did eat nothing: and when they were ended, he afterward hungered. And the devil said unto him, If thou be the Son of God, command this stone that it be made bread. And Jesus answered him, saying, It is written, That man shall not live by bread alone, but by every word of God.**
>
> **And the devil, taking him up into an high mountain, shewed unto him all the kingdoms of the world in a moment of time. And the devil said unto him, All this power will I give thee, and the glory of them: for that is delivered unto me; and to whomsoever I will I give it.**
> **If thou therefore wilt worship me, all shall be thine. And Jesus answered and said unto him, Get thee behind me, <u>Satan</u> for it is written, Thou shalt worship the Lord thy God, and him only shalt thou serve.**
>
> **And he brought him to Jerusalem, and set him on a pinnacle of the temple, and said unto him, If thou be the Son of God, cast thyself down from hence: For it is written, He shall give his angels charge over thee, to keep thee: And in their hands they shall bear thee up, lest at any time thou dash thy foot against a stone. And Jesus answering said unto him, It is said, Thou shalt not tempt the Lord thy God.**
>
> **And when the devil had ended all the temptation, he departed from him for a season.**

As stated, these "ungodly angels" have exerted influence in the kingdom of heaven and in both of the earth kingdoms. In fact, these "ungodly angels" are organized into a spiritual hierarchy, with a ruler who, as we noted above, has been given the name Satan as well as the devil and is sometimes mentioned or portrayed as a dragon. He is the lord over these "ungodly angels" who wage war against the angels of God and mankind. In Revelation 12:7–8, we read:

> **And there was war in heaven: Michael and his angels fought against the dragon; and the dragon fought and his angels, And prevailed not; neither was their place found any more in heaven. And the great dragon was cast out, that old serpent, called the Devil and Satan, which deceiveth the whole world: he was cast out into the earth, and his angels were cast out with him.**

Satan or the Devil has authority to tempt mankind in spiritual and physical life until the time of Satan's judgment as described in Revelation 20:10:

> **And the devil that deceived them was cast into the lake of fire and brimstone, where the beast and the false prophet are, and shall be tormented day and night forever and ever.**

The kingdom under the earth refers to forces who exist under the earth yet have influence both under the surface of and upon the earth. These include the forces we refer to as the forces of nature. In the Bible, Jesus Christ also has been given power over this kingdom:

> **Wherefore God also hath highly exalted him, and given him a name which is above every name: That at the name of Jesus every knee should bow, of *things* in heaven, and *things* in earth, and *things* under the earth;**
>
> **Philippians 2:9–10**

Jesus Christ has power over the beings and power that rule the forces of nature:

> **And there arose a great storm of wind and the waves beat into the ship, so that it was now full. And he was in the hinder part of the ship, asleep on a pillow: and they awake him, and say unto**

him, Master, carest thou not that we perish? And he arose, and rebuked the wind, and said unto the sea, Peace, be still. And the wind ceased, and there was a great calm. And he said unto them, Why are ye so fearful? how is it that ye have no faith? And they feared exceedingly, and said one to another, What manner of man is this, that even the wind and the sea obey him?

Mark 4:37–41

Now let us delve deeper in our discussion of cause and effects as it relates to peace.

In the *beginning*, God created the *heaven* and the *earth*.

Genesis 1:1

```
┌─────────────────────────┐
│     KINGDOM OF GOD      │
└───────────┬─────────────┘
            ▼
┌─────────────────────────┐
│   KINGDOMS OF HEAVEN    │
└───────────┬─────────────┘
            ▼
┌─────────────────────────┐
│   KINGDOMS OF EARTH     │
│      - ON EARTH         │
│      -UNDER THE EARTH   │
└─────────────────────────┘
```

Out of the Kingdom of God was created the kingdoms of heaven and then the kingdoms of earth (they consisted of the kingdom on the earth and the kingdom under the earth). Jesus Christ, also referred to in the Bible as the Word is a co-creator with God the Father of the kingdoms of heaven and the kingdoms of earth:

> **In the beginning was the Word, and the Word was with God, and the Word was God.**
> **The same was in the beginning with God. All things were made by him; and without him was not anything made that was made. In him was life; and the life was the light of men.**
>
> **John 1:1–4**

The kingdoms of heaven and earth affect each other. Jesus Christ describes an aspect of how this works when He stated to His disciples that actions on earth can cause effects in heaven:

> **And I will give unto thee the keys (powers and authority) of the kingdom of heaven and whatsoever thou shalt bind on earth shall be bound in heaven: and whatsoever thou shalt loose on earth shall be loosed in heaven.**
>
> **Matthew 16:19**

The kingdoms of heaven and the kingdom of earth are created kingdoms with fixed durations; they shall pass away. The Kingdom of God is eternal.

> **Heaven and Earth shall pass away, but my words shall not pass away.**
>
> **Matthew 24:35**

These kingdoms are subject to the authority of Jesus Christ as given by God the Father.

> **And Jesus came and spake unto them, saying. All power is given unto me in heaven and in earth.**
>
> **Matthew 28:18**

And,

> **Wherefore God also hath highly exalted him, and given him a name which is above every name: That at the name of Jesus every knee should bow, of *things* in heaven, and *things* in earth, and *things* under the earth; And *that* every tongue should confess that Jesus Christ *is* Lord, to the glory of God the Father.**
>
> **Philippians 2:9–10**

As stated earlier, "ungodly angels" exist in the kingdoms of heaven in their own subkingdom. Although "ungodly angels" exist in the kingdoms of heaven and affect and exist in the kingdoms of earth, they are subject to the rules of the Kingdom of God as administered by Jesus Christ. As Jesus said:

> **Every kingdom divided against itself is brought to desolation; and a house *divided* against a house falleth. If Satan also be divided against himself, how shall his kingdom stand? because ye say that I cast out devils through Beelzebub. And if I by Beelzebub cast out devils, by whom do your sons cast *them* out? therefore shall they be your judges. But if I with the finger of God cast out devils, no doubt the <u>kingdom of God</u> is come upon you.**
>
> **Luke 11:17–20**

Actions that occur on earth have effects in heaven, and actions that occur in heaven have effects on earth. Having stated that, let us begin to view just how the processes of **cause and effect** interactions in the kingdoms of God, heaven, and earth as they relate to peace.

Earlier we proposed that for every **effect, there is a cause**. That is, every **cause results in an effect**. To this proposition, I would add several others. A cause (except in what may truly be accidental) is always preceded by reason or purpose and has a goal or objective. The reason is the purpose. The cause is the parent. The effect is the offspring. The end result is the goal. The effect generated by a cause may in turn be the cause for another and different effect(s). And finally, that there is always—where reason or purpose is involved—an ultimate goal. In ideal situations, the ultimate goal is predetermined in the reason or purpose. Learn to look for hidden and unrevealed reasons or purposes in physical events. Recognize also that many of the visible results or effects of causes may not be the real end goal or expectation. As you grow in spiritual sensitivity, you will grow in this knowledge.

Everything God does is divine, eternal, and good. Divine purpose is in all His design. His design has within it divine life that causes effects intended to achieve a divine end. So out of the Kingdom of God come causes that are expected to manifest the divine ends designed by God. These causes are divine life processes that take the form of "seeds" that, when planted and grown to maturity under the right conditions, create the fruit that is predetermine within the "seeds." Peace is a fruit expected to grow from divine life.

The growth of peace within man is based upon the interactions of the Kingdom of God within the kingdoms of heaven and earth. Divine life, which obeys the laws of God, although experienced in various ways, works in harmony with the laws of each of the other kingdoms. The laws of the Kingdom of God are divine laws and infinite. The laws of the kingdom of heaven are spiritual laws, but are finite. The laws of the kingdom of earth are physicals laws and also finite. While the divine laws of God are superior to the other laws, the other laws are permitted to work within the boundaries of their kingdoms.

Man, as a created being, is to work in harmony within the boundaries of all these laws. When he does not, he suffers. These sufferings are not intended to destroy man but to warn him that his disobedience is harmful to him. The ultimate result of disobedience is eternal death. The ultimate result of obedience is divine life that is the life of God. As Jesus said:

> **My sheep hear my voice, and I know them, and they follow me:**
> **And I give unto them eternal life; and they shall never perish, neither shall any *man* pluck them out of my hand.**
>
> **John 10:27–28**

God's ultimate purpose and end is good. However, as we discussed, within the kingdoms of heaven and earth exist beings whose role is to hinder and stop the influences of good in the affairs of mankind. You might recall that we proposed that these ungodly beings tempt and test man in order to help him grow in divine knowledge, understanding, and willpower.

Jesus Christ came into the created world, that is into the kingdoms of heaven and earth, that mankind could be saved or redeemed from the effects of these ungodly beings. Jesus Christ was sent as a "cause" to "effect" those kingdoms so that they would be reconciled and become perfected, which is God's ultimate objective for them.

Man is to become perfect like Christ. He is to become perfected. As it is written in Ephesians:

> **And he gave some, apostles; and some, prophets; and some, evangelists; and some, pastors and teachers; For the perfecting of the saints, for the work of the ministry, for the edifying of the body of Christ: Till we all come in the unity of the faith, and of the knowledge of the Son of God, unto a <u>perfect man</u>, unto the measure of the stature of the fulness of Christ:**
>
> **Ephesians 4:11–13**

One of the qualities that exist within the "fullness of Christ" is perfect peace. Christ has been sent so that mankind might obtain perfect peace. This coincides with the primary cause for the presence of Christ in the kingdoms of earth, and that is that mankind might have an opportunity to receive divine life. Divine life is an everlasting life of perfect peace. Mankind as a created being, does not have perfect peace or eternal life at birth. Perfect peace contains divine life, which can only be obtained through Christ. So Christ came into the world as a "cause" to have an "effect" on mankind that would result in mankind obtaining everlasting or divine life.

> **For God so loved the world, that he gave his only begotten Son, that whosoever believeth in him should not perish, but have everlasting life. For God sent not his Son into the world to condemn the world; but that the world through him might be saved.**
>
> **John 3:16–17**

Before proceeding further on our journey to discover the role that **cause and effect** play in our search for peace, I want to emphasize again that there are both known and unknown causes that affect us every day. Most of us proceed with our lives without giving much thought to the causes of events in our life and deal primarily with their effects. But this is changing especially in the world of commerce.

More and more, the business world has realized that inferior products and services result in fewer sales, and that there are causes for this, some of them known and others unknown. Consequently, now, more time is being spent in industry to improve the quality of production and service through efforts to connect causes and effects. Cause and effect as a logical, systematic process has been lifted out of the lofty halls of philosophical dialogue and has emerged to become a technique used in industry and the practical affairs of the world to determine why things happen as they do and change traditional processes into new ones that will cause desired effects.

Kaoru Ishikawa, a Japanese university professor and management expert in quality improvement processes, developed in the 1960s a way to display how various causes could create consequential effects in the production of products and service. His work was based upon earlier work of W. Edwards Deming and J. M. Juran. These men did extensive research and developed tools to lessen defects and enhance the quality of industrial products and the delivery of service to consumers. Their combined work resulted in the development of what was called "quality circles," where individuals gathered to discover the causes of effects in products and services and what actions should be taken to lessen the causes of identified defects and increase the causes of quality. These techniques later were used by quality improvement teams and in continuous improvement management efforts.

I propose that in our search for ways to achieve peace, that "peace quality circles" be established to research how to achieve peace among people and nations. This would be an ongoing process including experts from a wide range of fields. They would gather to determine what would cause peace in all aspects of our individual, local communities, national and international lives and recommend tools, plans, actions, measurements. and corrective procedures that could be use to achieve peace.

Dr. Ishikawa developed a way to display the various causes and ultimate effect of those causes. Later, this came to be known as the *Ishikawa Diagram*. Below is a simple but typical example of what an *Ishikawa Diagram* looks like:

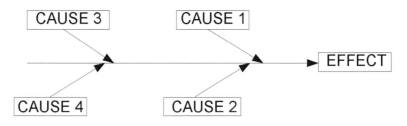

The center line is referred to as the "BACKBONE"

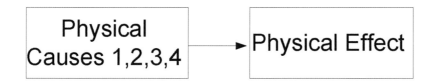

The "backbone" represents the accumulated processes that incorporate all the known causes that result in the effect. The effect is the result of causes 1, 2, 3, and 4. (Typically, the assumption is made that physical effects are solely determined by physical causes. But as we shall discuss a little later, this is not totally true. Unseen spiritual causes also contribute to physical effects. In the *Ishikawa Diagram* processes, however, only physical causes are consider. I have chosen to introduce the *Ishikawa Diagram* process to illustrate a way of thinking about the occurrences we experience in the world.)

As more causes are identified. they are added to the diagram until the list is finalized. The intent of the *Ishikawa Diagram* process is to identify all causes over time and if required correct them until the desired quality effect is achieved.

In our pursuit of perfect peace, we are influenced by causes from the Kingdom of God, kingdoms of heaven, of earth, and of under the earth, which ultimately affects our spirit, soul, and body and our activities in the physical and spiritual worlds. The role of the causes from the Kingdom of God is intended to perfect us to become divine. Causes from the kingdoms of heaven, of earth, and of under the earth may help or hindering us from becoming divine. By us understanding which is which and overcoming those that hinder us, we become perfected. By overcoming evil, we grow in the knowledge of truth in our understanding and the growth of righteousness in the use of our will to become more like Jesus Christ.

In the diagram that follows, the interactions of these causes and effects are generally displayed. The main point I want you to grasp is that mankind must have interactions with the kingdoms, their causes and effects, in order to become perfected and divine. The kingdoms operate according to specific principles, unique to them yet within the divine design they all operate in harmony.

There are many principles that are in operation, but we will only discuss a few. The principle we are currently discussing is the **divine principle of cause and effect**. Although we may only be aware of physical effects, we must grow to recognize unseen spiritual forces affecting us as well.

The **divine principle of cause and effect**, which is unique for each of us, involves our interaction with forces that may cause good or evil effects. We must learn to identify both the effect and their respective causes. Then we must eliminate and prevent the evil forces, through the help of Jesus Christ, from affecting us (**resist the devil and he will flee from you; James 4:7**). When we incorporate the good forces into our spirit, soul, and body, we will become what God expected us to become when we were first created (**Be ye therefore perfect even as your Father which is in heaven is perfect; Matthew 5:48**).

In our search for peace, we will learn to understand what causes peace and what prevents peace. We also will learn that peace while given by Jesus Christ to those who believe in Him will not abide in us if we do not continually live in truth and righteousness. We also learn that our thoughts and feelings must be guided by us through the help of the Lord, or else we will never receive nor maintain our peace.

One insight that has proven vital for me is the recognition that on the path to spiritual perfection, one must learn to disconnect thoughts created by physical and spiritual causes from feelings and willing. When what we think, feel, and will is based solely upon what we sense from physical and spiritual causes, we become "slaves" to external and internal influences. We must grow to recognize not only the sources and reasons for causes but also their associated effects and their end goals. Ultimately, we must grow to identify the **divine** influences and act based upon them only. This is only possible through the assistance of Christ. This requires wisdom, which only comes from Him.

Come to understand that eternity is a quality of the life of God and is given to us through Christ. So the divine design was in the "beginning" in Christ, and our "end" divine destiny is His to give. The life that Christ gives is our beginning and our desired end. In the Bible, He states that He is Alpha and Omega. In Him is embodied the beginning or reason or purpose and the end or expected objective.

> **I am Alpha and Omega the beginning and the end. I will give unto him that is athirst of the fountain of the water of life freely**.
>
> **Revelation 21:6**

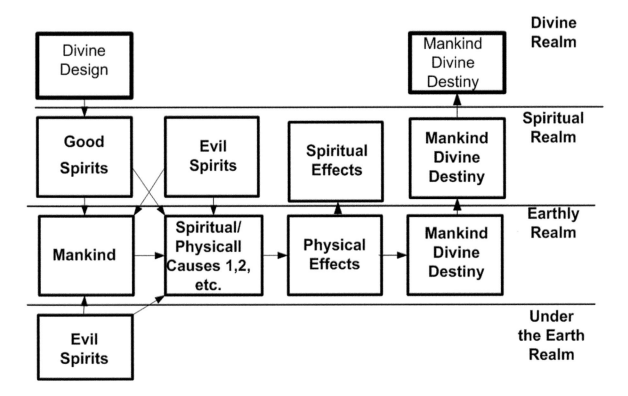

Study and meditate upon the above diagram. Develop an image of it as an environment in which you live. Expand your sense of awareness of the seen and unseen beings and processes that cause effects in your life. Please recognize that this is an ever-flowing interaction of physical and spiritual forces in your personal life and in your environment, which will affect the outcome of your eternal destiny.

In the diagram is depicted the following, starting at the top left:

The **divine design** at the top left is a box intended to depict what God purposes for mankind, individually and collectively. It contains the creative aims of God. Within these aims are the divine forces, features, functions, forms, processes, and all the creative beings, including mankind, their characteristics, etc., that lead to mankind's divine destiny.

Good spirits are spiritual beings that obediently perform God's will with mankind and in the spiritual and physical world. They cause influences in mankind that lead to God's intended effect.

Evil spirits are demonic beings such as Satan that hinder the performance of God's will. They war against good spirits, against mankind, and against God's will in the heaven, earth, and under the earth. Their perceived purpose is to kill, steal, and destroy mankind's divine destiny, but wisdom reveals that they serve to introduce free will and choice in mankind.

Mankind includes you and all of humanity. It represents each of us individually and collectively. Mankind is influenced by divine, spiritual, and physical causes that create godly and ungodly effects. Freedom of choice is provided to us by God. We must learn to recognize and choose what God wills us to choose, or else we will also cause evil effects in the world. We must take a special interest in assisting all of humanity to gain this knowledge and its role in our and their pursuit of peace. It is not enough to gain peace for our self and not help others to do the same.

Spiritual and physical causes are actions of Christ, the Holy Spirits, good spirits and evil spirits, and human beings in the physical and spiritual worlds.

Spiritual and physical effects are the spiritual and physical effects of Christ, the Holy Spirits, good spirits and evil spirits, and human beings in the physical and spiritual worlds.

Mankind's divine destiny is the expected outcome of all these interactions. Mankind is to become what God through Christ purposed for man at his creation. Mankind is to acquire divine qualities that will permit him to function as a divine being in the divine realm, in the spiritual realm, in the earthly realm, and in the realm under the earth.

Again, it may seem strange to some that evil spirits play a role in our destiny, but they do. They present resistance to the working of God's power in us, but as we exercise God's will, we grow in strength and perfection in the use of His power. This prepares us for existing in godly endeavors in this world and in worlds to come.

I will repeat that in order to achieve this destiny, it is important for us to grow in the knowledge of the causes that create effects in our lives, causes that are not only physical but are also spiritual. This knowledge serves as the basis for decisions and actions we will make in life. We are to participate in life with godly understanding and will, working with God, in order to achieve our own salvation. As it is written:

> **Wherefore, my beloved, as ye have always obeyed, not as in my presence only, but now much more in my absence, work out your own salvation with fear and trembling. For it is God which worketh in you both to will and to do of *his* good pleasure.**
>
> **Philippians 2:12–13**

Each of us is expected to work out our own salvation using the knowledge we acquire. Knowing God's will, we are expected to freely choose to do it. When we do this, we achieve the goal He has set for each of us at the beginning of our creation.

Our growth to peace requires we mature in the knowledge of who we are in the world. That knowledge includes our understanding of the various effects on and in our lives. As we have discussed, these effects come from multiple causes from the various physical and spiritual kingdoms that surround us. Our knowledge of the many influences from these kingdoms might appear a daunting task, but the need is there nevertheless. God the Father, God the Son, and God the Holy Spirit are present to help us know them.

God has created us also with capabilities to deal with these influences. Christ and the Holy Spirit are standing ready to guide us in what to do. God the Father placed in us a desire to know and understand the truth of things. He also has given us freedom to choose what to do about what we know and understand. Christ and the Holy Spirit are come to guide us to our right relationship with the Him.

A key principle is the principle of sowing and reaping. Sowing and reaping involves seeds and formative forces. Seeds reproduce fruit with seeds like itself. Formative forces influence seeds so that they produce fruit and more seeds. These formative forces are causes. Divine life exists in divine seed that has been acted upon by divine formative forces. Divine attributes are manifested in the fruit of these interactions.

Therefore, it is the interactions of divine formative forces within and upon the divine seed within us that will affect us in such a way as to causes us to become, under the right conditions, divine. The "I AM" seed (our unique God-given self) that is within us has the potential for divine life. Under the influence of Jesus Christ and the guidance of the Holy Spirit, we can grow to become divine. This seed has all the potential divine attributes that are to grow within us. Peace is one potential this seed possesses.

As we grow in understanding, we come to realize that there are both seen and unseen forces at work in our world. In the above diagrams describing the various kingdoms, their causes, and their effects, we come to recognize that physical and spiritual causes operate in our lives. Also, we learn that reasons or purposes precede causes, and we learn that effects may become causes that ultimately result in a final goal and outcome. The final outcome when ***perfected*** existed in the original purpose. I want to point out to you the emphasis on the word **"*perfected*."** For if not ***perfected***, the final outcome will not be obtained. Let me illustrate. The seed has within it the expected outcome, the fruit. The purpose for creating the seed is to achieve the fruit. When the seed is first seen, the purpose is not visible. It is only after the fruit appears and examined that the purposes becomes revealed. So it is with our lives.

Therefore, it becomes important to us to become knowledgeable of the fruit of our lives, to understand what we are becoming, and to take actions to achieve perfection. This ability is given to us as we learn to develop our thinking ability to know causes, effects, as well as reasons and intended outcomes. Furthermore, we learn to identify visible and invisible causes and their sources, some that are good and others that are evil.

As you proceed to the next sections, we will discuss **divine truth and divine righteousness** and more about how they relate to **divine peace**. We will also explore more about how your physical, mental, and spiritual capabilities are to be developed to enable you to reach the spiritual perfection and divinity God intends.

Peace Dove

Divine Truth and Divine Righteousness—An Overview

It might be beneficial if we spent a little more time talking about God's creative processes before proceeding to discuss more of the complexities of **divine truth** and **divine righteousness**. God's creative processes start with a design stage, then a formation stage, then an indwelling stage, and lastly an action stage. He determined the design of our being and gave forms to our bodies and organs with capacities and capabilities. Afterward, He transfers spiritual and physical content into them and gives us freedom and power to activate them. Forms in our spiritual and physical bodies and organs with their capacities are created to receive attributes transmitted into them from God. We are to use them to do His will.

Before we get into a more detail discussion of this, I would like to review a few things with you. Christ came into the world to demonstrate and teach how mankind can reach his divine destiny. He taught what was needful but declared that there was more and that the Holy Spirit would be dispatched by God the Father to assist Him in teaching mankind even more about his divine destiny. Jesus Christ said to His disciples:

> **I have yet many things to say unto you, but ye cannot bear them now.**
> **Howbeit when he, the Spirit of truth, is come, he will guide you into all truth: for he shall not speak of himself; but whatsoever he shall hear, that shall he speak: and he will shew you things to come. He shall glorify me: for he shall receive of mine, and shall shew it unto you.**
> **John 16:12–14**

Later, we see where St. Paul writes that not only the Spirit but many believers are also called to assist with this effort:

> **And he gave some, apostles; and some, prophets; and some, evangelists; and some, pastors and teachers; For the perfecting of the saints, for the work of the ministry, for the edifying of the body of Christ: Till we all come in the unity of the faith, and of the knowledge of the Son of God, unto a perfect man, unto the measure of the stature of the fulness of Christ:**
> **Ephesians 4:11–13**

To reach this perfection requires receiving the infilling of the Christ Spirit and continual growth of our human spirit, human soul, and human body. This growth comes as a direct result of our obedience to guidance of the Christ Spirit.

We are sent into the earth to become more than what we are when we are born. Adam and Eve, when they were created, were "naked." This does not mean that they had no clothes. It means that they were yet to be clothed with the spiritual qualities that were expected to come forth in and through them. Qualities like love, truth, wisdom, righteousness, goodness, long-suffering, and meekness, all the qualities that are called the Fruit of the Spirit.

Adam and Eve were created "very good" yet not perfect. This is clear in that they were vulnerable to be led astray by the devil. Their desire to become wise by eating the fruit of the tree of good and evil shows that they believed they were lacking in wisdom, hence were vulnerable to the serpent's influence. They went so far as to defy God and accept help from a deceptive source because of this perceived lack.

They were not what they were created to become. When we are born, we are not what we are created to become. Our divine destiny is only achieved as we accept and follow the guidance of Jesus Christ and the Holy Spirit and become workers with Him in the transformation of our human spirit, human soul, and human body.

> **But as many as received him, to them gave the power to become the children of God, *even* to them that believe on his name:**
> **John 1:12**

Our birth on earth is just the beginning of our journey with God, and this journey will only be successful if we achieve the goal set before us—a goal that I sense is visible as a pattern in God's creation if one only knows where and how to look. The pattern I speak of is seen in the growth of trees on earth that result in "fruit" and "seed."

To help illustrate this, let's look at the growth of fruit trees. The fruit tree comes from a seed, which goes into the soil and produces a root system. The root system takes nutrients and water from the soil. The nutrients and water are used to produce the tree trunk, which grows and produces branches. The branches produce leaves. The leaves receive light from the sun, which shines down on them and carbon dioxide from the air that surrounds them. The tree converts the light from the sun into a form of energy that it combines with the carbon dioxide that it extracts from the air. The energy and other organic compounds that result from these combinations travel up and down throughout the body of the tree, increasing it in size and height while at the same time ultimately producing fruit. The fruit is then used by humans and other creatures for food and as replenishment to the soil to be reused by the tree in the next round of its growth cycle. The fruit produced is completely dissimilar to the tree in appearance and function, although without the tree it would not exist.

The growth processes within us is in some ways similar, but more complicated. For in addition to the growth of our physical body forms from seed, we have spiritual body forms that grow from spiritual seed as well. Our spiritual body forms, starting with our "I AM," are to be "born again" of the formative Spirit of Christ. Our "born again" spiritual body forms grow within our physical body forms and begin a process of new spiritual interactions in them as well. We receive nutrients from the earth that nourishes our physical body and keeps it alive. These include food, oxygen, water, sunlight, etc. The spiritual seed that is planted within our physical body likewise obtains worldly substances (sensations, thoughts, feelings, knowledge, etc.) as well as new spiritual substances from God through Jesus Christ and the Holy Spirit. These divine substances, along with worldly substances, are used by us to help us grow spiritual fruit. These worldly substances subsequently go through a process within us that converts what is appropriate for us to become transformed into what God desires for us and enables us to produce spiritual fruit within our spiritual and physical bodies.

The physical body houses what is needful for us to produce physical fruit in the earth . . . be fruitful and replenish the earth is a commandment given by God . . . but more importantly, it serves as the soil for our spiritual seed to enable each of us to also produce spiritual fruit that is used by our spiritual and physical bodies. Just as the fruit from the tree is eaten by others and falls to the earth and replenishes the soil, so does the fruit of our spirit become absorbed in our physical bodies, replenishes our soul, and spiritualizes our human body. I want to emphasize and have you recognize that each of us is expected to participate in the production of spiritual fruit within our spirit, which we use to become divine and are commanded to give to others and present to God through Jesus Christ to be used as He wills.

Each of us is to become the fruit of the earth spoken of in the Bible. Our presence on earth is not random, but purposeful. We are each individuals purposed to become a child of God. We possess a human body, a human soul, and a human spirit—all with multiple features, functions, and forms that enable each of us to produce spiritual fruit. We are to become the fruit spoken of in scripture:

> **Be patient therefore, brethren, unto the coming of the Lord. Behold, the husbandman waiteth for the precious fruit of the earth and hath long patience for it, until he receive the early and latter rain.**
>
> **James 5:7**

And,

> **But the fruit of the Spirit is love, joy, peace, longsuffering, gentleness, goodness, faith, Meekness, temperance: against such there is no law.**
>
> **Gal. 5:22–23**

And,

> **For the fruit of the Spirit *is* in all goodness and righteousness and truth;**
>
> **Ephesians 5:9**

Therefore, like the fruit tree, we are on earth to obtain from the earth that which is needful to enable us to become the children of God. Hence, the physical world is necessary: the water, air, sunlight, animals, other physical and spiritual beings, etc., in fact, all the creation and what it offers mankind is necessary. But the expected outcome of all our physical encounters is not physical results only but spiritual ones. We are each to use what we learn in the world to become spiritual fruit, which we share with others as well as to be harvested by God and used as He wills.

All the divine attributes mentioned in the Bible will also become attributes of our spirit when we become perfected. In earlier portions of this book, we have often referred to peace and righteousness without calling them "divine." I am sure many of you noticed that the use of "divine" began to appear later. This was done to highlight the fact that our use of these terms starts out with a common meaning of them that is later changed into a meaning that refers to their spiritual nature, and the term "divine" is used to indicate this fact. As we go forward in our discussion, we have recognized that fact, and when discussing the peace, truth, and righteousness that come from God, Jesus Christ, and the Holy Spirit, we prefaced them with the word "divine."

Divine peace plays a primary role in attaining divine attributes and so does divine truth and divine righteousness. So the following discussion will spotlight the role divine peace plays with divine truth and divine righteousness in helping us reach our final goal of becoming divine.

We will discuss how these three interact with each other to bring this about. Keep in mind that mankind has been given a major opportunity to determine what type of spirit he becomes. Mankind is a co-creator of their own destiny. In the growth processes involving mankind, mankind can choose to obey God or not. The growth processes in other parts of the creation, such as the growth of trees, cannot. Therefore, it is exciting that when we obey God, we become a co-creator with Him in the spiritual fruit we become; this includes obtaining knowledge of all God's physical and spiritual creation.

IBM Super Computer

Space Walk

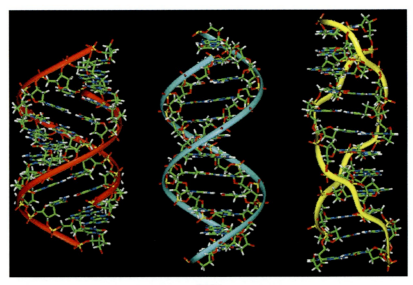
DNA

Mankind's discoveries and applications of what is learned from what God has created in the world teach us the wonderful attributes of God. As God presents Himself to us in seen and unseen phenomena, we are challenged to apply our knowledge as God wills in all the world in which we exist.

That part of us that has been given this ability is our "I AM," which dwells in our human spirit. It is also known as the ego. The "I AM" has been formed in us to contain the love of God. It is the "I AM" that becomes "born again." It also experiences all that goes on with our human spirit, soul. and body. The "I AM" learns to transform the worldly extracts into divine truth and divine righteousness by submitting to the directions of Jesus Christ through the guidance of the Holy Spirit.

In what follows, we will explore this in more detail. First, we will look at divine truth. Then we will look at divine righteousness. We have discussed divine peace in much detail in earlier sections of the book. So in this section, we will show how divine peace working within our human spirit and mind is an integral part of divine truth and divine righteousness. We will also discuss the fundamental role that grace and faith play in our development as spiritual fruit.

God has given Jesus Christ ruling power over the kingdom of heaven and the kingdom of the earth and the kingdom under the earth. He is assisted by the Holy Spirit, the Spirit of Truth, in this effort. As it is written:

> **Wherefore God also hath highly exalted him, and given him a name which is above every name: That at the name of Jesus every knee should bow, of** *things* **in heaven, and** *things* **in earth, and** *things* **under the earth; And** *that* **every tongue should confess that Jesus Christ** *is* **Lord, to the glory of God the Father.**
> **Philippians 2:9–11**

And,

> **Howbeit when he, the Spirit of truth, is come, he will guide you into all truth: for he shall not speak of himself; but whatsoever he shall hear,** *that* **shall he speak: and he will shew you things to come. He shall glorify me: for he shall receive of mine, and shall shew** *it* **unto you. All things that the Father hath are mine: therefore said I, that he shall take of mine, and shall shew** *it* **unto you.**
> **John 16:13–15**

And,

> **Now there are diversities of gifts, but the same Spirit** (spiritual gifts are received from Jesus Christ by the Holy Spirit and imparted unto believers). **And there are differences of administrations, but the same Lord** (Jesus Christ is in charge).
> **And there are diversities of operations, but it is the same God which worketh all in all** (God determines what the gifts do and how they operate).
> **1 Corinthians 12:4–5**

God has also given us grace as a free bonus gift. Grace is a divine substance that opens up the path to the other divine gifts. It is given from God to make it possible for mankind to receive all that Jesus Christ has to offer. Grace is a formative force given as an expression of God's love and desire for mankind to return unto Him. It affects our "I AM" and consequently our total being.

Without grace, none of the divine attributes we will discuss would be available to us. Grace facilitates the formation of our faith. It later assists with the acquisition of all the divine attributes of God. We would have no access to God, Jesus Christ, or the Holy Spirit without the Spirit of grace being given to us. For this, we must be eternally grateful. Please keep this in mind as we proceed further in our discussion of divine peace, divine truth, and divine righteousness.

God, Jesus Christ, the Holy Spirit, and our spirit, soul, and body all have roles in our journey to become divine. Because it involves so many parts, I realize a further explanation would be helpful. Since these relationships are not simple I ask you to be patient yet persistent as we proceed with them.

The Trinity

God the Father, Jesus Christ working with the Holy Spirit, sends forth spiritual power and substance to man's *mind* to create a spiritual organ called **understanding**, another spiritual organ called **conscience**, and another spiritual organ called **will** (there is much more involved in the perfecting of our human spirit, human soul, and human body, but these spiritual organs are the ones that concern us at this point in our discussion). At the appropriate time during the forming of these organs, divine truth, divine peace, and divine righteousness are sent forth from Jesus Christ to be implanted in them and to assist the individual to become divine.

The spirit of a man, starting with his mind, is given the responsibility to guide all his being. That part of the spirit that is given this role is the "I AM," sometimes called the ego or self. When a man refers to himself as "I AM," he refers to his spirit ego and self.

This "I AM" is that part of you that experiences all you experience in the world and grows to comprehend your being as separate from other beings and objects in the world. This "I AM" is continually attempting to discover meaning from all it experiences and where it fits in the midst of the other beings and objects it senses in its world. It uses thinking, feeling, and the thoughts produced from them to construct its place in its world of experiences. The "I AM" uses all the various parts of the physical body, soul, and spirit to become what God intends them to be.

Knowledge of my "I AM" grows when I began to view external things as "not me" and when I come to view myself as "I AM." Knowledge of the "I AM" is the knowledge that I exist as a subject, and things external to me are objects. Ironically, I later must also grow to recognize parts of my being as objects. When I grow to realize parts of myself as objects as well as my "I AM" as subject, I am on the first step to spiritual maturity.

There remains a caution with this growth, even though it must occur if we are to become what God would have us be. That caution is as I recognize myself as "I AM," I may become so selfish that I become dangerous and destructive to myself and others.

The "I AM" in us uses our mind. Our mind is a spiritual form created by divine creative forces. Divine creative forces create spiritual and physical features, functions, and forms as we explained. Our mind is a spiritual form consisting of other subforms, the principle ones being our understanding, will, and conscience.

The mind is our organ of thinking. It is with our mind that our "I AM" generates thoughts and feelings and choices. When we say "I think," "I feel," or "I choose," we are describing products of our mind.

The mind uses the understanding (which houses divine truth) and the will (which houses righteousness) to accomplish its role in interacting with all parts of our spiritual and physical body. The mind though not physical, uses physical forms such as our brain, nerves, muscles, etc., to accomplish its role in our physical body.

It is with our understanding that we develop our mind to see or know the truth. Our understanding and hence our mind is dependent upon the knowledge of truth. Unfortunately, for most of us, the truth that is initially used to develop our understanding is dependent totally upon physical sense knowledge obtained by our five senses.

Our five-sense knowledge is limited. For example, there are objects in our physical and spiritual world that we are not able to see or hear because of our inability as human to see certain light frequencies or hear certain sound frequencies. As a result, the "truth" we develop based upon this knowledge is in turn limited. When we use this limited knowledge to develop our understanding, our understanding is also limited. That is why the scriptures tell us to "lean not on our own understanding" but to acknowledge divine understanding that comes from God through Jesus Christ and the Holy Spirit. For what we see and hear with our physical eyes and ears, when it is the sole basis for developing our understanding, results in a limited understanding.

If we seek to perfect the truth and understanding we obtain from the use of our five senses, it is necessary to seek the help and guidance of Jesus Christ and the Holy Spirit. As the scripture also states:

> **Jesus saith unto him, I am the way, the truth, and the life: no man cometh unto the Father, but by me.**
> *John 14:6*

And Jesus Christ when referring to the Holy Spirit said:,

> **Howbeit when he, the Spirit, of truth is come, he will guide you into all truth for he shall not speak of himself; but whatsoever he shall hear, that shall he speak: and he will shew you things to come. He shall glorify me: for he shall receive of mine, and shall shew it unto you.**
> *John 16:13–14*

This *all truth* spoken of above indicates that there is more truth than that obtained through use of our five senses only, and that Jesus Christ and the Holy Spirit will help us obtain it.

As you develop your thinking and feeling ability, your "I AM" consciousness grows, and you become aware of your sensations and resulting thoughts and how they interact to form images, ideas, concepts, names, memories, and beliefs. Eventually, you develop the ability to examine these memories and beliefs and form self-truth about your world and all that exist in it.

Self-truths then become content of our **understanding**. However, we must eventually discover that our understanding is limited if it relies solely on our own self-truths. When we discover that self-truths are limited and discover that there are higher truths, we eventually learn that our self-truths can be perfected by receiving divine truth from Christ. If we open our understanding to receive divine truth from Him, we will expand our **understanding** and perfect our **conscience** and **wil**l so that we grow in peace.

Man's understanding, conscience, and will are suborgans of his mind. As we stated earlier, the understanding serves as a receptacle for divine truth. The conscience serves as a receptacle for peace, and the will serves as a receptacle for righteousness. These three organs of the mind serve together as an inner voice to guide the individual to what Christ calls good and right and what results in peace. As is stated in Psalm 85:10:

Mercy (goodness) and truth are met together; righteousness and peace have kissed each other.

It might be helpful to view the mind as a spiritual representation of our physical brain. As our brain guides our physical body and has extended itself throughout our physical body by forming nerve fibers and nerve plexus that send and receives impulses throughout our physical body, so the mind has extended itself through a mental network that transmits thoughts and feelings that permeate our entire spirit, soul, and body.

Thoughts and feelings are products of our thinking. It is through our thinking that these thoughts and feelings affect us. They affect what we think about faith and love, truth and righteousness, our beliefs, our memories, the ideas, concepts, images, and names we attached to sensations we experience in the physical world.

Thoughts and feelings are spiritual objects and are tangible. But not all the thoughts and feelings you experience are created by you. Thoughts and feelings from other beings are experienced by us. We must learn to view them as such and become able to distinguish thoughts and feelings we create from those created by other beings that affect us. And learn not to take ownership of thoughts and feelings from other beings without first understanding them and deciding if they are of Christ are not. We learn as we grown to divine maturity to manage our thoughts and feelings as directed by Christ.

I am often amazed at the actions of otherwise moral and upstanding persons who are caught doing a petty crime like shoplifting a small item from a department store. Immediately, I recognize that they were influence by a thought and feeling that otherwise they would not create but have received from an external being and taken ownership of them as their own. As a result, they committed the crime that if they were "in their right mind" they would not commit.

Many years ago, while teaching a Bible class, I made the statement "every thought you have in your mind is not yours." There were stares of disbelief, and one person strongly disagreed, saying that every thought they had was their own. Shortly thereafter, this particular person was shopping in a grocery store. They were near the cheese section and heard a voice say to them, "pick up that cheese and put it in your purse and walk out the store no one will notice." The voice was so audible and clear they looked around to see who said it. They did not see anyone. Of course, they did not touch the cheese and immediately left the store. They related the story to me afterward. From that moment on, they realize that invisible beings are capable of transmitting thoughts to them and became watchful of their thoughts and feelings.

It is in our mind that divine attributes from Christ meet knowledge we have gained from our experiences (sensations) in the world. Our experiences go through a complicated process before becoming knowledge in our mind. First, we become aware of a sensation that then becomes an idea, concept, image, and we give it a name. These all are stored in our memory where we then form them into beliefs. Beliefs then become established as self-truth. Prior to our belief and following of Christ, this limited truth is used to form our understanding. When one comes to believe that Christ is who He says He is, then faith (a divine attribute) is received from Christ. Faith opens the door of our mind to the reception of divine truth, and transformation begins in the mind where our previous understanding based on limited truth is transformed into what Christ would have us understand about our physical experiences (sensations).

The identical process happens with righteousness, except self-righteousness is also formed from our beliefs. It is not the divine righteousness of Christ but is what we feel is right for us. Prior to our belief in Christ, this self-righteousness is used to form our will. When one comes to believe in Christ, love (a divine attribute along with faith) is received from Christ. Love opens the door of our mind to the reception of the divine righteousness of Christ. This divine righteousness then becomes the content of our will and is used to guide our actions.

Our divine destiny requires we look to Christ for what we think and do. Our growth to this destiny requires we develop our spirit, soul, and body by the use of thoughts and feelings that are in agreement with Christ.

This starts with what Jesus Christ calls "born again." Our new birth changes our view of the world and the physical sensations and encounters we have. Our mind becomes transformed, and yet we still have the freedom to learn through the acquisition of knowledge what things and events mean. We give them names. We learn to remember and keep the ones that Christ would have us keep and discard the others. We learn about our self and others. We learn that some things we think are true, while others are not, and we learn some things we think are right are not, even though we might feel pleasure from them. We learn some things that are pleasurable at first turn out to be painful.

We learn that the source of truth is Christ, and we learn that the right action (divine righteousness) is what He would have each of us do. As a result of this knowledge, we obtain peace and joy.

The conscience, when we permit it to become formed through the influx of peace from Christ, serves as a judge of what is true and right in our mind. When the conscience becomes formed, we recognize, when we think untruths, that it sets off an inner alarm to warn us, and when we think unrighteousness, it also sets off an inner alarm. The conscience also bears witness when we are in divine truth and divine righteousness by transmitting a sense of joy within.

We then no longer have to rely on another to tell us what is true and right in God's sight because we will know for ourselves. God, through Christ, has put us in charge of our own destiny, and we need no man to tell us what is true and right. We will know for ourselves. As it is written:

> **For this is the covenant that I will make with the house of Israel after those days, saith the Lord; I will put my laws into their mind, and write them in their hearts: and I will be to them a God, and they shall be to me a people: And they shall not teach every man his neighbour, and every man his brother, saying, Know the Lord: for all shall know me, from the least to the greatest.**
> **Hebrew 8:10–11**

As you continue on your peace journey, recognize that you have been given responsibility to use your capacities and abilities under the guidance of Jesus Christ to reach your divine destiny of peace. It would be helpful to know that the path has seven challenges all along the way. They are:

1. Body sensations may be limited because of impairment or injury.
2. Ideas, concepts, images, and names you form may be incorrect because of faulty sensations and limited experience.
3. Memory may be incomplete or distorted or both because of poor reasoning and recall.
4. Beliefs based upon incomplete or distorted memory will be in error.
5. Self-truths and self-righteousness based on faulty beliefs will be wrong.
6. Faith may never be received from Christ because of lack of belief in Him.
7. Understanding and will formed from erroneous memories, beliefs, self-truth, and self-righteousness will hinder growth to perfection.

Each of the above seven challenges are sources for strife and tension, which will impede if not prevent the achievement of peace. Therefore, it becomes vital for us to learn to be patient, humble, good listeners, open to changing our opinions when divine truth is revealed, flexible, and gracious to others whenever we encounter disagreements and conflict. Especially this is true in the use of names and words we hear and speak.

Sacred Heart of Jesus Christ

The Search for Divine Truth

Divine truth must be acquired by us if we are to live in peace. As you have seen in our cause and effect discussion, there are multiple sources that cause multiple effects. Physical and spiritual causes result in physical and spiritual effects, some good, some evil. It is our personal responsibility, with the assistance of Christ, to learn how to identify these sources, causes, and their effects then respond to them as Christ intends. We learn to do this as we learn the divine truth about experiences that occur in our life and what Christ would have us do about them. We are born to learn to distinguish between those things that are of God and those things that are not. Jesus Christ stresses the importance of acquiring the truth for one's self.

And ye shall know the truth, and the truth shall make you free

John 8:32

To know the truth is vital in our personal journey for peace. Truth when known leads to peace. Truth is personal because it is individually acquired. Because it is personal, it is also limited. Much of its limitation for each individual is because of the individual's physical and spiritual makeup and their environment. However, we must learn to overcome these limitations if we are to obtain the peace we seek. We must learn that truth has divine aspects as well as physical and spiritual ones. Christ teaches this through His word. Through the use of our intellect and **faith**, we prepare our understanding to receive divine truth from Christ. I want to emphasize that it is impossible to obtain divine truth from the intellect alone.

Let us begin at the beginning. Our birth into the kingdom of the earth is the culmination of causes or actions that occurred well before our birth occurred. God, Christ, the angels, and our fore parents, all have played a role in our existence. The moment of our birth is not even an event we remember. If asked to testify to our birth in a court of law, we would present evidence that is "hearsay" for although we participated in it, our participation has been told to us by others. The only verification of the birth is our existence. We accept our birth on what some call "faith"; that is, our birth is **evidence of something not physically seen by us**.

Our birth is a fact of our very existence, and yet we cannot declare with certainty that we remember it. We come to know who we are and objects in our world through experiences. These experiences are based upon physical sensations acquired by our physical sense organs from external and internal objects. But what these all mean eludes us at time, and their meaning is often told to us by other.

Thus, our world is based upon our own experiences of objects and events and what we are told by others about the objects and events that we experience. Some of these experiences are physical; others are spiritual. As we grow in age and in the use of our senses, we become aware of another inherited ability, the ability to think. Our physical sense organs and the use of our thinking ability working together assist us in determining if what we experience is true.

The accuracy of what we physically sense is also determined by the health of the physical sense organs and the soundness of our thinking. Yet these along are not enough to reach divine truth. As stated earlier, divine truth is a spiritual substance that is imparted to us by Christ. It resides in our understanding and is imparted into it after our understanding has become open to divine input from Christ. Divine truth is a spiritual substance and power that gets placed in our understanding by Christ after we have received faith from Him and used that faith to receive divine truth. The challenge we face is how to develop our understanding through the use of our intellect and belief in Jesus Christ so that we can receive divine truth. We get a glimpse of this in the following scripture from the Gospel of Mark:

> **And they reasoned among themselves, saying, It is because we have no bread. And when Jesus knew it, he saith unto them, Why reason ye, because ye have no bread? perceive ye not yet, neither understand? have ye your heart yet hardened? Having eyes, see ye not? and having ears, hear ye not? and do ye not remember. When I brake the five loaves among five thousand, how many baskets full of fragments took ye up? They say unto him, Twelve. And when the seven among four thousand, how many baskets full of fragments took ye up? And they said, Seven. And he said unto them, How is it that ye do not understand?**
>
> *Mark 8:16–21*

The disciples, in the above passage of scripture, in their use of human reasoning, failed to *perceive* or spiritually see the spiritual causes at work behind the physical effects of the feeding of the five and four thousands by Jesus and as a result *did not understand* its meaning. So are we often confronted with physical and spiritual happenings in our lives that we also do not perceive nor understand because our reasoning has not prepared us to receive divine truth.

Our understanding requires preparation for receiving the truth of Christ. This requires a change of our perceiving or spiritually seeing and our knowing the meaning (our understanding) of what we experience in our life in light of what Christ is doing. Also, a change of our hearing (our doing) and a change of our heart (our will) are required.

We consist of a human spirit, human soul, and human physical body—all with appropriate forms and subordinate parts. As stated in the section on Divine Preparation, God's creative processes consist of first preparing a form or body, within which He later infuses physical and spiritual substance(s). The form or body once constructed uses the substance(s) to sustain it and to fulfill its purpose. The form or body may consist of smaller subparts or organs that assist in the accomplishment of the larger purpose of the physical or spiritual systems and bodies. For example, our physical body consists of organs that receive proper substances to sustain them in performance of the larger purpose of sustaining the physical body. Our heart receives oxygen from our lungs, which it mixes with the blood and distributes this enriched blood to the entire body, which the body uses to sustain itself.

The same is true of our human soul and human spirit. Both consist of organs or forms that receive spiritual substances that are used to sustain the spiritual organs within them and enable them to perform the purposes assigned them by God.

The mind is one of these major spiritual organs. It is the command center for our thinking. Just as we possess physical organs such as our heart and lungs in our physical body, we also possess spiritual organs in our spiritual body. The mind is one such organ. And just as there are component parts to our heart such as the right and left atriums and right and left lobes in our lungs, so is our mind made up of component parts.

The understanding and will are two of these spiritual organs in our mind. And like the heart and lungs, there is a constant interchange of the contents of both the understanding and the will. Truth in the understanding is shared with righteousness in the will. Truth is derived from knowledge, and righteousness is derived from feelings. Choices that are products of the will are shared as acts with our human spirit, human soul, and human physical body. This is an ongoing activity of the mind, the result of which determines our ability to survive in the world.

Our mind is a magnificent spiritual thinking organ, and when developed as God intends, it leads us to our divine destiny. We see this in the scriptures as we are challenged to develop our mind to be like the mind of Jesus Christ:

> **Let this mind be in you, which was also in Christ Jesus:**
> *Philippians 2:5*

And,

> **And be not conformed to this world: but be ye transformed by the renewing of your mind, that ye may prove what is that good, and acceptable, and perfect, will of God.**
> *Romans 12:2*

We must learn how to do this. We must learn to know the truth and do the will of God. In order to know the truth about our world, we must develop our mind by using our thinking to develop our understanding so that we will recognize the divine truth in physical and spiritual encounters.

Just as in our earlier discussion about cause and effect, we see that we encounter causes from the various kingdoms in which we live. We must grow in the knowledge of the truth of these causes and their effects upon us and others. We also must learn to will God's wills so that we become the divine creations He intends.

> **Wherefore, my beloved, as ye have always obeyed, not as in my presence only, but now much more in my absence, work out your own salvation with fear and trembling.**
> **For it is God which worketh in you both to will and to do of his good pleasure.**
> **Philippians 2:12–13**

The way we develop our mind to receive divine truth is through meditation, study of the Word of God, and exercising our will as directed by Christ and the Holy Spirit. The Christian Meditation section of this book describes a way that has proven beneficial to countless believers.

The development of the mind is complex, not simple. It involves a progressive climb from our initial physical sense experiences as infants to the perception of divine truth and its working in our understanding as mature Christians. The divine design for us is to use physical knowledge and experiences gained through physical sense organs to develop our intellect and understanding to a point where it is ready to receive divine truth from Christ.

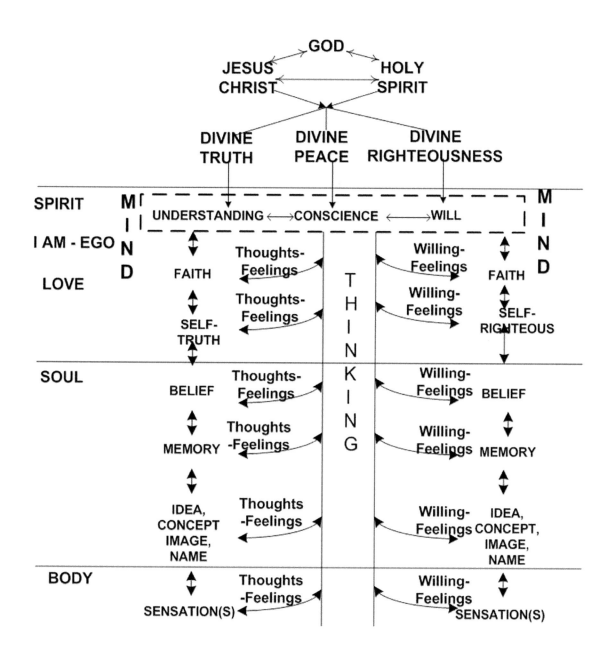

Divine Peace, Divine Truth, Divine Righteousness Diagram

The following should help explain the diagram shown above. In this section, our focus is on divine truth. We have discussed divine peace in an earlier section, and our discussion of divine righteousness will come later.

The diagram shows a progression from the sensing of an object in your physical environment to your final understanding of the object. This progression is greatly dependent upon your thinking and feeling ability, which creates thoughts and feelings about the object or event.

Through the use of your thinking and feeling ability, thoughts form in your consciousness to create ideas, concepts, images, names, memories, beliefs, self-truths, understanding, and faith for those who mentally persuade themselves to believe in Jesus Christ. Thoughts that are formed by our thinking move through our soul and spirit, eventually becoming the content of our understanding as personal self-truths.

The major challenge we face in obtaining correct understanding is learning to distinguish our personal self-truth from divine truth. This battle occurs in our understanding. Peace that comes from Jesus Christ assists us to win this battle. Peace helps our mind identify and remove those "boulders" or "rock" of untruth so that we might receive divine truth from the Holy Spirit, who is also called the Spirit of Truth, and Jesus Christ. Peace "softens" our understanding so that the Spirit of Truth, which is the Word of God, may become rooted in us (see peace definitions).

In the parable of the sower, Jesus explains the critical importance of the soil, the mind, and specifically the understanding, being prepared, to receive the seed of the Word of God.

> **Hear then the parable of the sower:**
> **When anyone hears the word of the kingdom and does not understand it, the evil one comes**
> **and snatches away what has been sown in his heart. This is what was sown along the path.**
> **As for what was sown on rocky ground, this is the one who hears the word and immediately**
> **receives it with joy, yet he has no root in himself, but endures for a while, and when tribulation**
> **or persecution arises on account of the word, immediately he falls away. As for what was sown**
> **among thorns, this is the one who hears the word, but the cares of the world and the deceitfulness**
> **of riches choke the word, and it proves unfruitful. As for what was sown on good soil, this is**
> **the one who hears the word and understands it. He indeed bears fruit and yields, in one case a**
> **hundredfold, in another sixty, and in another thirty.**
>
> *Matthew 13:18–23*

Our understanding plays a major role along with peace on the way to our divine destiny. As it is written:

> **Trust in the LORD with all thine heart; and lean not unto thine own understanding**
> **In all thy ways acknowledge him, and he shall direct thy paths.**
> **Be not wise in thine own eyes: fear the LORD, and depart from evil.**
> **It shall be health to thy navel, and marrow to thy bones.**
>
> *Proverbs 3:5–8*

Faith in Jesus Christ is required if we are to form divine understanding. Therefore, it is also essential in the search for divine truth. Faith is a spiritual substance that comes from Jesus Christ to us when we believe in Him. In the upward movement to understanding as shown in our illustration, **faith** is shown to come from **self-truth**, which proceeds from **belief** in a progression that starts with physical sensations. Physical sensations are processed by our thoughts and feelings to create names, images, concepts, ideas, and eventually memories. This process is what we call physical reasoning and is how we develop our intellect.

Our intellect is the spiritual process that ultimately creates our beliefs, but without faith, these beliefs are based on physical sense knowledge only and when stored in our understanding is limited. Physical sense knowledge is limited because it is missing divine input. When we apply faith, which is divine to what we have intellectually developed, we ascend to a higher intellectual level that permits the spiritual substance of divine truth to enter our thoughts and transform erroneous beliefs and self-truths into divine truth.

This comes from the faith relationship with Jesus Christ and the Holy Spirit. Jesus Christ and the Holy Spirit guide us as we ascend to understanding and truth. If Christ and the Holy Spirit are not present in our search, we will never reach truth, for truth is not intellectually derived but is spiritually perceived. Truth comes to us as a divine revelation. Jesus Christ is responsible for that revelation:

> **Jesus saith unto him, I am the way, the truth, and the life: no man cometh unto the Father, but by me.**
>
> *John 14:6*

And the Holy Spirit is the Spirit of truth. As Jesus declares:

> **And I will pray the Father, and he shall give you another Comforter, that he may abide with you forever; Even <u>the Spirit of truth</u>; whom the world cannot receive, because it seeth him not, neither knoweth him: but ye know him; for he dwelleth with you, and shall be in you.**
>
> *John 14:16–17*

And,

> **Howbeit when he, the Spirit of truth, is come, he will guide you into all truth: for he shall not speak of himself; but whatsoever he shall hear, that shall he speak: and he will shew you things to come. He shall glorify me: for he shall receive of mine, and shall shew it unto you.**
>
> *John 16:13–14*

<u>The Role of Our Mind</u>

It is essential that we learn to know the divine truth about the effects we experience in our world, individually and collectively. God has given us the capability to know this divine truth. He has given us our mind. The mind is a spiritual organ. It is our thinking command center. Just as we possess physical organs such as our heart and brain in our physical body, we also possess spiritual organs in our spiritual body. The mind is one such organ.

The major parts of our mind are our understanding, will, and conscience. These are also made up of subparts. Our understanding functions as a storehouse for truth, our will for righteousness, and our conscience for peace. Truth, righteousness, and peace are all spiritual substances that have functions in our mind and subsequently in our entire being. Just as blood and oxygen are freely exchanged between the heart and lungs and our entire physical body, so are truth, peace, and righteousness freely exchanged between our understanding, conscience, and will and our total being. To repeat, the contents of the understanding, conscience, and will, just like those of the heart and lungs, are constantly shared.

<u>I AM, Spirit Consciousness</u>

The I AM in the diagram represents your ego or spirit consciousness. It is a spiritual organ that has been formed in us to contain the love of God. The I AM is your self-consciousness. It is your individuality. It is that part of you that looks out of your being into your world. This I AM is that part of you that experiences all you experience in your world and grows to comprehend your being as separate from other beings and objects in that world. This I AM is continually attempting to discover meaning from all its experiences and to determine where it fits in the midst of the other beings and objects it senses in its world. It uses thinking, feeling, and willing to construct its place in its world of experiences. Your I AM has the responsibility to use the love of God to manage your physical body, soul, and spirit and to become what God intends you to become.

Knowledge of the I AM grows when you began to view external things as "not me," and when you come to view yourself as a unique, one-of-a-kind human being. Knowledge that you are unique is the knowledge that you exist as an individual "subject," and things external to you are "objects." Ironically, you later grow to recognize yourself also as an object.

When you grow to realize yourself as an object as well as a subject, you are established on the road to spiritual maturity. There remains a caution with this growth, even though it must occur if we are to become what God would have us be. That caution is as I recognize myself as I AM, I may become so selfish that I become dangerous and destructive to myself and others.

As you develop your thinking and feeling ability, your I AM consciousness grows and you become aware of your thoughts and how they interact with sensations to form ideas, concepts, names, memories, beliefs, and self-truths. Eventually, you develop the ability to examine these ideas, concepts, names, memories, beliefs, and self-truths about your world and all that exist in it. Your self-truths come to make up your understanding about your world. However, you must eventually discover that your understanding is limited if it relies solely on your own self-truths. When you discover that self-truths are limited and discover that there are higher truths, you will eventually learn that your self-truths can be perfected by Christ if you open your understanding to receive divine truth from Him. When you expand your understanding through divine truth, you grow in peace.

This growth to divine truth comes in eight stages.

First Step: Sensations, Thoughts-Feelings

The first step on the climb to divine truth begins with our physical senses and sensations of object or events in our physical world. These sensations create experiences whose meanings we attempt to understand. Our ultimate understanding of the meaning of worldly experiences depends to a great degree on the effectiveness of our senses. If our senses are limited, then the information we sense through them will be flawed, and thoughts based upon this flawed information will be inaccurate. Our thinking is intended to play a vital role in helping us to determine the accuracy of what we sense by our physical senses and the resulting thoughts and in helping us to become divine.

We must learn to use the physical senses correctly if our search for divine truth is to be successful because objects and events we experience in our physical world are essential to our understanding. We must learn that there may be aspects to physical experiences that might not be correctly sensed by our physical senses. There are spiritual aspects to physical experiences that are only perceived by spiritual senses. As you look at the picture below, what do you see? It is an illusion that shows both a young woman and an older woman. Which do you see? If you answer young woman, someone else might disagree and say an older woman. This is just a simple example that demonstrates that knowledge acquired through our five senses might cause us to see things differently than others. Knowledge based upon physical sensations along is limited.

Second Step: Ideas, Concepts, Images, Names, and Thoughts-Feelings

From our sensations, we produce ideas, concepts, images, and finally names. These all are derived from thoughts-feelings produced by the interactions of our thinking process and our physical sensations. Ideas, concepts, images, and names are thoughts uniquely created by each of us for our own use. And though we attempt to share these ideas, concepts, images, and names with other persons, it often becomes difficult at times because of the unique nature of our individual thinking process. We may create ideas, concepts, images, and names for objects that are totally different from the ideas, concepts, images, and names created by another individual. What one person calls a thing may not be what we call it. That is seen in the above illustration.

> **And out of the ground the LORD God formed every beast of the field, and every fowl of the air; and brought them unto Adam to see what he would call them: and whatsoever Adam called every living creature, that was the name thereof.**
>
> **Genesis 2:19**

God gave Adam the freedom to call every living creature. Yet God had already created them and, based upon earlier actions by God as described in the book of Genesis, had already named them. (**To name a thing is to define attributes and qualities about that thing. Names you give a things also determine what that thing subsequently means to you**). In the case of God, because He has all power, for Him to name a thing means He established true attributes, qualities, measures and boundaries for that thing.

For mankind to name a thing means to establish arbitrary attributes, qualities, measures, and boundaries for the thing we name. Indeed, in this case with Adam, the names Adam called the creatures meant that to Adam the living creatures then took on the attributes, qualities, measures, and boundaries Adam imposed not those established by God. (The same applies to each of us when we name or call a thing something out of our own thinking and not the thinking of God).

The implication in the scripture is that God has given to mankind the freedom to call things as mankind chooses and to give them the characteristics he thinks they should have, even though these may not be what God had already established for them.

This naming by Adam has the effect of limiting *living creatures* to a state of *living* that in Adam's mind may be different than that given them by God. Mankind, when he does not call things what God calls them, will always limit the original creation of God, and thus, mankind will live within a limited world view and a false view of the world, although it may appear to mankind to be truth.

In the scripture cited above, God does not tell Adam what to call or name the living creatures brought to Adam. This is an example of the freedom given to mankind. This is completely different from the earlier occurrences in Genesis where God called and named things Himself.

God is seen in the biblical scriptures to interact with many individuals in efforts to guide them to their divine destiny by permitting the freedom to choose for themselves. During the course of His interactions with them and this freedom, we find a transformation within them that result in a change of their nature and characteristics. This transformation necessitates a change of their name. For example, Abram name is changed to Abraham, Sarai becomes Sarah, Jacob becomes Israel, and Saul becomes Paul. All these had names changed because their spirit, soul, and physical bodies have progressed and become transformed by their interactions with God, and a change is required to their names.

Divine truth entered our understanding to change it into what God through Jesus Christ wants it to be. Our understanding and resulting thoughts then change our ideas, concepts, images, names, memories, beliefs, self-truths, and faith to become what God intends. When this occurs, our nature is changed by God, and we get a new name.

> **Because thou hast kept the word of my patience, I also will keep thee from the hour of temptation, which shall come upon all the world, to try them that dwell upon the earth. Behold, I come quickly: hold that fast which thou hast, that no man take thy crown. Him that overcometh will I make a pillar in the temple of my God, and he shall go no more out: and I will write upon him the name of my God, and the name of the city of my God, which is new Jerusalem, which cometh down out of heaven from my God: and I will write upon him my new name.**
>
> **Revelations 3:10–12**

The path to our divine destiny is filled with freedom. This freedom in seen in the opportunities we have to name things and hence to make choices even if they are poor choices. We have been given this freedom so that we will come to the knowledge that right choices are those God would have us make. God choices are divine choices and are filled with eternal life. Choices without God in them are not eternal and doomed to die.

Another result of the freedom each man has to name things has been the creation of great confusion in our language and in our attempts to communicate with and understand each other. This we will learn is a result of demonic influence, which is permitted to test us. Although the world of objects we live in is common to all, the ideas, concepts, names, and images we create to describe them may not be common. Because of this, great confusion and turmoil has arisen in the history of mankind. The solution is to seek the true nature of names and images and the resulting words we use when we communicate with each other.

If we but paused to realize that others may sense things differently than we, then we would attempt to listen to and observe more intently what others say and recognize that there may be differences that should be identified and resolve so that true communication could occur. Listening and observing with an attitude of peace will result in peace.

Third Step: Memory and Thoughts-Feelings

Ideas, concepts, images, and names create by our thinking interact with thoughts and feeling to produce memories. Memories are stored in us for later use. We don't remember all our experiences, but the intensity of physical sensations appear to play a role in the duration of our memories. Often, only fragments of experiences are remembered, and missing portions of experiences are sometimes "filled in" with things that did not occur. Over time, many of these "filled-in" memories take on the form of actual memories, while the actual ones fade away into the "sea of forgetfulness." This too is a cause of much confusion, mistaken communication, and lack of peace.

Fourth Step: Belief and Thoughts-Feelings

It is from out of our memories that we produce our beliefs. Through the use of our thinking process, we use thoughts-feelings to assemble the various memories we possess into what we call beliefs. Beliefs are persuasions derived from previous memories that help us determine the meaning of our worldly experiences. Beliefs may be of short or long duration. Nevertheless, they represent thoughts that are not *directly* related to external sensation. Beliefs are personal creations usually derived from ***memories*** of prior physical experiences. As described above, these memories may or may not be based on truth. Yet it is in the area of our beliefs that divine development starts. Our beliefs eventually must become what God would have us believe. They must be based upon His word. To help with this, we must first believe in Jesus Christ. Our belief in Jesus Christ opens the door to the receiving of **faith** from Him. Faith is the divine spiritual substance that comes from Jesus Christ that enables us to understand things and objects as God understands them.

Faith, when we use it, serves as a springboard that permits us to leap up and over false beliefs we formed from physical sensations into the spiritual world of divine revelation and divine truth. Then our beliefs began to be changed into what God through Jesus Christ and the Holy Spirit would have them be.

Don't be indecisive about beliefs based upon faith. Be diligent in the forming of them for it is through faith-based beliefs that our intellect is properly developed, and we acquire correct intelligence about our world and our role in it. Mankind must develop and acquire this intelligence about the physical world because what we learn through physical experiences help teach us about God's divine nature and processes.

Fifth Step: Self-Truths and Thoughts-Feelings

Self-truths are beliefs that have become for the individual "the way things are." They represent standards by which the individual conducts their life. One of the weaknesses of self-truth is that we may expect others to use our self-truths as standards in the conduct of their life.

As we discussed earlier, we start with a consciousness of the world based on physical sense knowledge. This knowledge is limited. From this physical sense knowledge, we develop self-truths that conform to our view of the world but are not divine truth. As our world expands, so do our self-truths. If we are to grow in divine truth, we must be flexible, humble, not hardheaded, hardhearted, or stiff-neck but open to more truths as they are revealed.

Sixth Step: Faith and Thought-Feelings

We mentioned **faith** in step 4 because it is closely tied to belief. But faith is more than belief. As we stated, it is a divine substance with attributes and power that comes from Christ to all who have developed a belief in Him. In the Bible, it is described in Romans 4:16–17:

> **Therefore *it is* of *faith,* that it might be by grace; to the end the promise might be sure to all the seed; not to that only which is of the law, but to that also which is of the faith of Abraham; who is the father of us all, (As it is written, I have made thee a father of many nations,) before him whom he believed, *even* God, who quickeneth the dead, and calleth those things which be not as though they were.**

Faith is a spiritual power that is granted by God to those who like Abraham believe in Him. They are given supernatural power to become a co-creator with God as was the case with Adam in Genesis 2:19, where Adam was permitted by God to call every living creature, as you might recall the following scripture:

> **And out of the ground the LORD God formed every beast of the field, and every fowl of the air; and brought *them* unto Adam to see what he would call them: and whatsoever Adam called every living creature, that *was* the name thereof.**

The key to what I want you to see is that ***calleth*** or ***to call*** denotes the ability to confer particular qualities and or quantities to things. Like Adam and then Abraham, we who receive faith from God through Jesus Christ are empowered to become a co-creator with God and Jesus Christ in the formation of things; that is, to give them **names**, which means to give them qualities that determine what they mean.

Faith is important to us if we are to correctly develop our understanding for it is through the giving of the correct names to things that we gain correct understanding and, ultimately, divine truth. For by faith we have the power to change our thinking and thoughts into what Christ would have them become. Faith is received from Jesus Christ as a result of our believing that Jesus Christ is the Way to Truth.

Faith is "evidence of things not seen"; that is, it is evidence acquired by spiritual means not through physical senses. Faith is acquired by spiritual organs and is called *perception*. Faith is *perceived spiritual knowledge* that is transferred from Jesus Christ to us through spiritual organs, which we develop in our spirit and soul by meditation, belief in the Word of God, and right actions.

Spiritual knowledge is perceived and transferred. The word "perceived" is used to denote that we become aware of spiritual knowledge by way of spiritual senses as opposed to physical knowledge, which we acquire through physical senses. This spiritual knowledge has power to affect spiritual and physical things and objects. If we only use physical-sense knowledge to determine our self-truths, we will limit the growth of our understanding because physical-sense knowledge is limited. Physical knowledge must be combined with spiritual knowledge to gain true understanding. And true understanding is required if we are to receive divine truth from Jesus Christ and the Holy Spirit.

Faith is a divine power from God that is given to each person that believes in Him to achieve God's purpose. The process is like this. The person **believes** in God and Jesus Christ; as a result, they **receive** from them faith into their **understanding** where it helps purify their self-truth and convert it into divine truth. Meanwhile, because of the person's **beliefs**, faith is also **received** into their **will** where it helps purify their self-righteousness and convert it into divine righteousness.

Divine truth is then united with **divine righteousness** in their **will** where the person of their own **free will** performs actions that affect themselves, other beings, and or objects as commanded by God through Jesus Christ.

Seventh Step: Understanding and Divine Truth

Understanding, as stated before, is a spiritual organ in the mind. We are to use our mind in the perfecting of our understanding for it is the spiritual organ where divine truth is ultimately housed. The understanding exchanges its truth with other components of our mind, human spirit, human soul, and human body. Our I AM helps us accurately interpret what we previously thought was true (what we have labeled in our discussion as self-truth). The understanding is the ultimate destination for all our truths, whether they are self-truths and limited or divine truths and eternal.

What starts as physical sensations will interact with our thinking and feelings and eventually if combined with faith will end up as divine truths in our understanding. The Bible states:

> **Trust in the LORD with all thine heart; and lean not unto thine own understanding**
> **In all thy ways acknowledge him, and he shall direct thy paths.**
> *Proverbs 3:5–6*

And,

> **But he that received seed into the good ground is he that heareth the word, and understandeth it;**
> **which also beareth fruit, and bringeth forth, some an hundredfold, some sixty, some thirty.**
> **Matthew 13:23**

The understanding is developed through our thinking process. If the individual acknowledges through belief in Jesus Christ that there is a truth higher than their self-truth derived from physical sensations, they receive the spiritual gift of faith from Him, and they become open to receiving divine truth. Divine truth, once acknowledged by the individual, is then used by the understanding in subsequent thinking and thought formation processes to bring one's ideas, concepts, memories, images, names, and beliefs to an alignment with divine truth.

We are born with the potential to receive divine truth. We do not possess it at birth. We grow to know it as we believe the Word of God. Divine truth exists in all aspects of our worldly experiences. Their purposes, causes, processes, effects, durations, expected outcomes, what we should know, how we should respond, etc., are all present in our world. Perceiving the divine truth in these things frees our heart from worry and creates in us His peace.

Jesus Christ said:

> **Then said Jesus to those Jews which believed on him, If ye continue in my word, then are ye my disciples indeed; And ye shall know the truth and the truth shall make you free.**
> **John 8:31–32**

And,

> **But the hour cometh, and now is, when the true worshippers shall worship the Father in spirit and in truth for the Father seeketh such to worship him. God *is* a Spirit and they that worship him must worship *him* in spirit and truth.**
> **John 4:23–24**

Five-sense knowledge and truth is limited but expands as we seek divine truth from Christ. We grow in divine truth as we expand our physical and spiritual experiences. As the circle of our experiences expands, so does our knowledge of physical and spiritual truth.

I liken spiritual growth, in divine truth, to being lifted up successively to a higher and higher level of divine truth as through a funnel. This lifting occurs as if one was in a spiral. This enables one to see aspects of truth from a 360 degree view. Each level reveals more divine truth. Even when we have reached the level where we have received what we believe is the ultimate in divine truth, know that there are still higher levels. As our knowledge expands, the opportunity for more truth expands and so on. Divine truth is eternal and far exceeds our ability to comprehend it.

The following is a story about the great scientist Dr. George Washington Carver, who did wondrous work with the peanut and other plants that might serve to illustrate this point. Dr. Carver tells the story of his relationship with God. As recorded in the story, Dr. Carver asked God questions about the purpose of the universe and was told his mind could not understand the scope of the answer and to ask a question about something his mind could understand. So he asked about the purpose of man and was again told by God that he was still asking something he could not properly comprehend. Then he asked God what more could he do with all the peanuts that were growing in the fields around him. Then God told him that he was now asking a question about something for which his mind could understand the answer. As a result, he was ultimately taught by God how to create many products from the peanut. They included face powder, printer's ink, butter, shampoo, soaps, dyes, instant coffee, and many more helpful products. As a result of the products he created, the world was blessed, he became world famous, and social progress was gained.

As we end this section of our discussion about peace, it might be helpful to mention that divine truths, like all of God's gifts, are given by measure with boundaries. The following illustration of what I call a truth funnel might serve to show this:

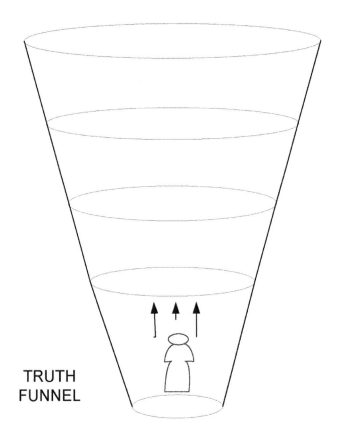

TRUTH FUNNEL

Divine Truths: Measure and Boundaries

Divine truths, like all divine attributes, are transmitted to man by measures with boundaries. That is, they come by measure and cover only as much of God's creation as He reveals to you at any given time. From the creation of heaven and earth to the length of life, to the construction of the body, soul, and spirit, in nature, in the seasons of the year, in the universe, etc., in all His creations, God uses measures and boundaries.

God's use of measures and boundaries is seen even in His granting of spiritual gifts to believers for their growth to Christian perfection. We read the following in the New Testament:

> **For I say, through the grace given unto me, to every man that is among you,**
> **not to think of himself more highly than he ought to think; but to think soberly,**
> **according as God hath dealt to every man the <u>measure of faith</u>.**
> **Romans 12:3**

And concerning boundaries, we see a direct statement of this in the book of Job, where God counsels Job on his understanding of the reality of boundaries in God's creation:

> **Then the LORD answered Job out of the whirlwind, and said,**
> **Who is this that darkeneth counsel by words without knowledge?**
> **Gird up now thy loins like a man; for I will demand of thee, and answer thou me.**
> **Where wast thou when I laid the foundations of the earth? declare, if thou hast**
> **understanding. Who hath laid the measures thereof, if thou knowest? or who hath**
> **stretched the line upon it? Whereupon are the foundations thereof fastened? or who**
> **laid the corner stone thereof; When the morning stars sang together, and all the sons of**
> **God shouted for joy? Or who shut up the sea with doors, when it brake forth, as if it had**
> **issued out of the womb? When I made the cloud the garment thereof, and thick darkness**

> **a swaddlingband for it, And brake up for it my decreed place, and set bars and doors, And said, Hitherto shalt thou come, but no further: and here shall thy proud waves be stayed?**
>
> **Job 38:1–11**

Man is not equipped to understand the deep mysteries of God's creation without learning them from Him. Man increases in spiritual knowledge as he becomes obedient to Christ and follows the leadings of the Holy Spirit. As it is written:

> **Then said Jesus to those Jews which believed on him, If ye continue in my word, then are ye my disciples indeed; And ye shall know the truth, and the truth shall make you free.**
>
> **John:31–32**

And,

> **Howbeit when he the Spirit of truth is come, he will guide you into all truth: for he shall not speak of himself; but whatsoever he shall hear, that shall he speak: and he will shew you things to come.**
>
> **John 16:13**

None of us will ever know all the divine truth about any of God's creation nor about things we experience in the world. We are given by Christ only that portion of divine truth that is good for us at the current time. We must learn to live in the "now." We are given the divine truth that is sufficient for us today. I think this is because He wants us to realize that we need Him and each other and that a godly life is a life lived in community. Our role is to share the divine truth we have with each other and to seek the divine truth they have in order that we benefit for the good of all. We must learn to live in community and to share.

When it comes to seeking for the divine truth of a matter, it is always helpful to seek insights from other godly and wise counselors. As it is written:

> **The way of a fool is right in his own eyes: but he that hearkeneth unto counsel is wise.**
>
> **Proverbs 12:15**

DIVINE ATTRIBUTES

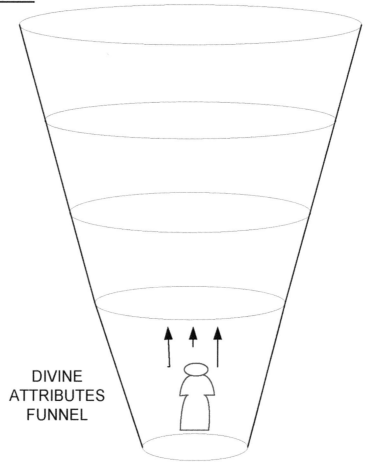

I might add that just as divine truth, when imparted unto us by Jesus Christ and the Holy Spirit, has measures and boundaries, so do all divine attributes.

Peace, **righteousness**, **truth**, **love**, **faith**, **goodness**, **gentleness**, **meekness**, **temperance**, **long-suffering**, and **joy** all are acquired by measure with boundaries and can be viewed as if one is rising up through a funnel. We never acquire all the aspects nor the magnitude of divine attributes, for they are attributes of God and as such are infinite. So as you grow in divine attributes, there is more to know about them and more ways to use them in the service of God. So be humble and be patient with yourself and others.

Peace Dove

Sacred Heart of Jesus Christ

Eagle

Hunger and Thirst after Divine Righteousness

Blessed *are* they which do hunger and thirst after righteousness: for they shall be filled.
                                                                    Matthew 5:6

In the discussion about **divine truth**, we touched upon the various steps in the growth to **understanding** and **divine truth**. The diagram below also depicts the stages of growth to **divine truth** but focuses primarily on the stages of upward growth to our **will** and **divine righteousness**. These are depicted on the right-hand side of the diagram. In this discussion, please note that the word "<u>Will</u>" is sometimes highlighted in bold and capitalized to indicate it as a spiritual organ not an action or choice.

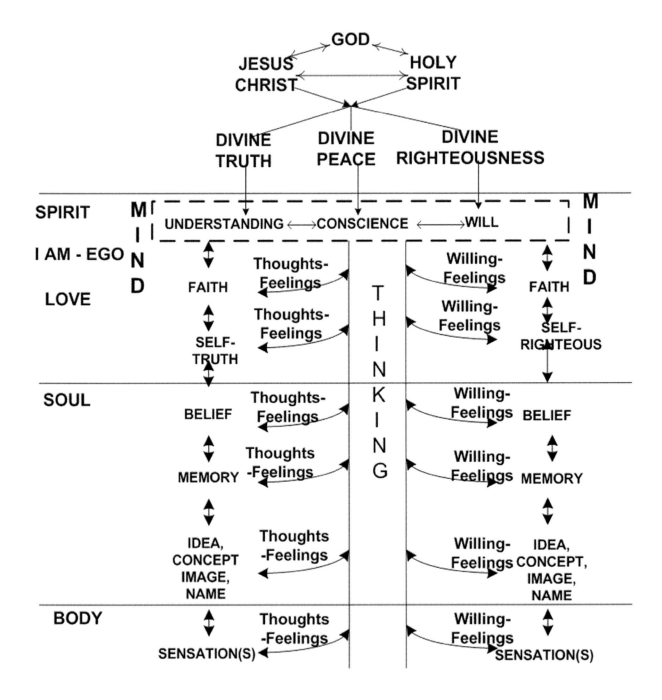

Divine righteousness is also divine substance that is imparted to the mind of our spirit by God, through Jesus Christ and the Holy Spirit. The mind, although centered in our spirit, spreads throughout our entire being. So our mind is active in our spirit, soul, and physical body. It assists us in choosing what is right. The right act is what God would have us choose and do when making a choice. Our choices are first decided in our mind in the area of our **Will.**

Our **Will** is where our desires, likes, and dislike are formed from the range of feelings that influence us. Our feelings likewise are influenced by the choices we make with our **Will**. There is a constant interaction between our feelings and our **Will**, which eventually produce what we know as **choice**. We must learn to use the righteousness of God to guide our feelings and our **Will** to help us select the **choice** God would have us make.

Divine righteousness reveals how to act as God would have us act in any given situation. It would be as if God Himself had made the act. Each choice we make is judged by God. When we act as God would act, we are said to be justified or just. So divine righteousness, at its core, is a state of being judged by God to be in agreement with God's will.

Our conscience, when filled with divine peace, serves as a witness to us that the choices we make are in agreement with the choices God would have us make. When we act contrary to God's choices for us, our conscience sends a spiritual impulse that warns us that we are in error. This interaction is a self-correcting mechanism that God has placed in us to help us know the right things to do without having to depend upon someone else to correct us.

This all happens so that our "I AM," or ego, is formed then develops and grows to perfection as it uses our **Will** and righteousness as well as divine truth from our understanding and divine peace from our conscience. These are required to transform our human spirit, human soul, and human body. The "I AM" is formed to contain the love of God. As the "I AM" uses the love of God, to respond to the divine peace, divine truth, and divine righteousness, it receives from God, through Jesus Christ and the Holy Spirit, it grows in the measure of divine peace, divine truth, and divine righteousness it contains.

First Step: Sensation, Willing-Feelings

Growth in divine righteousness, like growth in divine truth, begins with the recognition of sensations from experiences in our physical world. Although we may recognize these physical world experiences, we go further and attempt to determine their meaning and understanding. Our ultimate understanding of the meaning of worldly experiences is influenced to a great degree by how we feel about what we sense. If what we sense is distorted by our feelings, then the meaning and subsequent understanding will be inaccurate.

The physical body is not intended to be immortal, but it is vital in the development of our "I AM," which is intended to be immortal. Our "I AM" grows to become conscious of itself in relationship to God's physically manifested creation. If the "I AM" acts in error in the physical manifested creation such acts are reflected back in the physical body and physical creation as sickness, disease, famine, plagues, etc.

The effects of erroneous acts of the "I AM" are reflected back to the "I AM." They travel through our physical body sensations and eventually reach our understanding and our **Will**. There they serve to transform the self-truth in our understanding and the self-righteousness in our **Will**, if we are receptive, to divine truth and divine righteousness.

It is through this process, that is through our experiencing the effect of our acts on and within the manifested physical creation, that the "I AM" learns how to correctly response to physical sensations. The "I AM" is trained in the ways of God's love by exercising the love it receives from God to guide the physical body, human soul, and human spirit to use God's will to response to physical sensations. When this is done correctly, the conscience (divine peace) reacts with a spirit of joy.

The survival needs or desires of the physical body under the influence of the physical senses at times overwhelm our "I AM" and rather than acting in accordance with the love given it by God the "I AM" follows the desires of the physical body. There is a constant, ongoing struggle between our "I AM" and our physical body. We know this first hand when it comes to hunger and thirst. For example, sometimes the physical body's demand for food and drink will cause one to consume damaging food and drink to satisfy hunger and thirst needs.

Jesus Christ used the following statement to illustrate that just as physical needs compel us to satisfy them, so should spiritual needs as well. Blessed ("God filled") will be those who spiritually seek after righteousness like one who is hungry and thirsty.

> **Blessed *are* they which do hunger and thirst after righteousness: for they shall be filled.**
> **Matthew 5:6**

This brings us to the point in our discussion where we are confronted with the reality that each of us must work out our own salvation. With the help of Jesus Christ and the Holy Spirit, we each are responsible for managing our physical body so that the righteousness of God rules in it as well as in our human spirit and human souls. Our "I AM" with the help of God, through Jesus Christ and the Holy Spirit, must do this. My "I AM" must learn through my love of God to use divine righteousness to guide my hands, my feet, my speech, my taste, my eyes, my smell, my hearing, and my entire being so that what they experience is correctly perceived and the deeds performed as a result of those experiences are in total alignment with God's will. For what I do with my being is what I ultimately become.

Second Step: Ideas, Concept, Image, Name, and Willing-Feelings

Our thinking process form ideas, concepts, images, names, and memories from physical sensations and experiences in our world. Our thinking processes at the same time connect our **Will** (choices) and feelings to these experiences and sensations. This gives our ideas, concepts, images, names, and memories the unique characteristic of being our own. When we attempt to share these ideas, concepts, images, names, and memories with others, it frequently becomes difficult to get agreement with them because our ideas, concepts, images, names, and memories differ from theirs. These differences are often the cause of great misunderstanding of how we and others see the world.

 God has given man tremendous freedom of choice. Let's look at the following biblical passage:

> **And out of the ground the LORD God formed every beast of the field and every fowl of the air; and brought them unto Adam to see what he would call them: and whatsoever Adam called every living creature, that was the name thereof.**
> **Genesis 2:19**

Just as in the earlier discussion about divine truth, God gave Adam the freedom to name things he saw in his world. To name a thing is to choose to define attributes and qualities about that thing, and the names you give things are influenced by the feelings the things stimulate in you. These choices and feelings are often arbitrary and flawed by inaccurate sense knowledge not founded on the choices of God. So we are given the freedom to name things as we see them, but these names are often inaccurate and may conflict with what God intends.

In our discussion about the thinking process, we pointed out that thoughts are transferrable. Thoughts are transmitted like radio waves. The following verse, spoken by the Lord, applies to all of us. He transmits thoughts to us. What we think also goes forth to others.

> **For I know the thoughts that I think toward you, saith the LORD, thoughts of peace, and not of evil, to give you an expected end.**
> **Jeremiah 29:11**

Individuals may receive thoughts and be influenced by them. The same thing is true of feelings since feelings are made up of thoughts. Feelings are also transmitted and may influence others. It becomes important in our growth to spiritual maturity to develop the ability to distinguish the origin of thoughts and feelings that influence us and only heed those that come from God through Jesus Christ and the Holy Spirit. **<u>Not all thoughts in your mind are from God or from you! Many of your thoughts are from other sources and false.</u>**

The path to our divine destiny is filled with freedom. This freedom is seen in the opportunities we have to name things and hence to make choices even if they are poor choices. We have been given this freedom so that we will come to the knowledge of how to identify and choose the God choices. The right choices are those God would have us make. God choices are divine choices and filled with eternal life. Choices without God in them are not eternal and are doomed to die.

<u>Third Step:</u>   <u>Memory and Willing-Feelings</u>

Ideas, concepts, images, names, willing, and feelings that come from physical experiences are ingredients for our memories. Memories contain all of these to some degree, and they are stored in us for later use. We don't remember all the physical experiences that initiated our memories, but the intensity of our **feelings** and our **Will** (choices), which we use when forming memories, appears to play a role in their duration. Often, only fragments of memories are remembered, and missing portions are often "filled in" with things that did not occur. Over time, many of these "filled-in" memories take on the form of actual memories, while the actual ones fade away into the "sea of forgetfulness." Nevertheless, the resulting feelings, if intense, associated with those memories may last a lifetime. When the memories are recalled, the feelings also are triggered.

<u>Fourth Step:</u>   <u>Beliefs and Willing-Feelings</u>

Our beliefs are formed out of our memories. Through the use of our thinking process, we assemble the various memories we possess into what we call "beliefs." Beliefs are persuasions derived from memories. Beliefs help us give meaning to worldly experiences. However, I want to point out that our **beliefs are not based solely upon our current memories but also upon new thinking influenced by new willing and feelings. New thoughts about our beliefs are continuously confronting us to be accepted or rejected.** We are constantly challenged to determine which beliefs are true and which are false. Our world view will be determined by our choices. If our beliefs are not transformed by thinking derived from divine peace, divine truth, and divine righteousness, our beliefs will continue to be false.

Beliefs are an area for great disharmony among mankind. For it is from our beliefs that we initially form the contents of our **Will**.

<u>Fifth Step:</u>   <u>Self-Righteousness and Willing-Feelings</u>

Self-righteousness is formed from our beliefs. Self-righteousness is the point of view one takes about the world and how they will conduct their life in it. One of the difficulties with self-righteousness as with self-truth is that other individuals have established their own self-righteousness, and each individual believes their standard of self-righteousness is the correct one.

In our discussion about divine truth, we pointed out that basing our knowledge of the world solely on our senses will cause us to have a limited, if not false, knowledge of the world. From this, we can say that if we use sense knowledge only to build up our beliefs of what is right in the world, our view of the world will be limited, if not false. If we are courageous, this will bring us to the point where we realize that more information is needed.

When we realize more information about our world is needed, if we are a seeker of truth and righteousness, we will seek this information from a reliable source who knows more about the world and how we fit in it. What better source than from the Creator of the world? That is, God and His Son Jesus Christ. Without our interaction with them, our view of the world will be limited. To expand our knowledge of our world and place our self-righteousness on a sound basis, we have to establish contact with God the Father of all creation. To contact God, we must go through Jesus Christ:

> **Jesus saith unto him, I am the way, the truth, and the life: no man cometh unto the Father, but by me.**
>
> John 14:6

So through our contact with Jesus Christ, we have access to God. As our access to God is open through Jesus Christ, our knowledge of the world becomes transformed into what is true knowledge, and our self-righteousness expands to recognize the divine righteousness that comes from Jesus Christ. The state of our spirit, soul, and physical body becomes open to the power of Jesus Christ. Our beliefs become transformed by the entrance of divine truth from the Holy Spirit. Then through the grace of God, we receive from Jesus Christ another divine substance called **Faith**.

Sixth Step: Faith and Willing-Feelings

Faith is a divine attribute and power that comes from Christ to all who believe in Him. Faith is important to us if we are to correctly develop our knowledge of divine righteousness and the role it plays in the correct operation of our **Will** and thus our feelings. For it is by operating our **Will** correctly that we receive divine righteousness from Jesus Christ and transform our feelings. The power to change our feelings into what Christ wills only come through our receiving and following the promptings of the divine righteousness of Jesus Christ. This occurs because the divine formative substance faith is received from Jesus Christ after we believe in Him. Faith begins a work in us that prepares us to receive the divine righteousness of Jesus Christ. Divine righteousness subsequently transforms our previous "self-righteousness" into the divine righteousness of Jesus Christ.

Seventh Step: Righteousness and Will

It is in our **Will** where self-righteousness is first housed. As we have stated before, our self-righteousness must be changed to become the divine righteousness of God. This is an ongoing process of transformation because our initial self-righteousness is based on our physical senses only and is not divine and is inaccurate.

The "I AM," or ego, is the divine being of the individual, not the **Will**. The "I AM," or ego, is to manage this transformation of the **Will** so that the individual becomes what God intends. Your "I AM" is to manage your understanding, **Will**, and mind.

Strong resistance to a change of our understanding, **Will** and mind comes from physical sense-based beliefs, self-truth, and self-righteousness that are viewed as vital to the survival of the individual. The **Will** contains selected beliefs we have stored up over our lifetime as self-righteousness. We view them as true and vital to our survival. Any change is considered as a threat to our survival. We are created with an innate instinct to survival. We know this as self-preservation. The selected beliefs that we develop in life and house in our **Will** are considered necessary for the preservation of our ego, or "I AM."

When we are born, we are born with a desire to survive, yet we have a need to depend upon others to teach us how to do so. Our **Will** is formed initially by what we learn from our parents, family, others, and the environment in which we live. During our early years, we imitate others; and also because we depend upon others for our survival, we adopt their attitudes and ways.

Much of what we are taught and what we learned are traditions and social mores passed down from generation to generations. These include religious, political, racial prejudices, and beliefs, many of which are considered vital to our survival. They are considered vital and right and are saved as contents of our **Will** and mind. We resist changes to them. This resistance may be viewed as necessary in order to survive, especially if a change threatens valued beliefs.

Acts of violence are often the results when changes are seen as threats to a **Will** intent on preserving itself. Attempts to change religious, political, racial prejudices, etc., often fail because they are experienced as attempts to destroy the very essence of the individual.

How does this come about? The physiological and psychological needs of a person are satisfied when external and internal forces provide "food". Jesus used the same analogy in the above scripture when He stated, "blessed are they which do hunger and thirst after righteousness: for they shall be filled". Beliefs, self-truth, and self-righteousness serve the function of food to our understanding and **Will**. Beliefs, self-truth, and self-righteousness are initially provided to us from others. In others words, we learn from external sources initially as we grow. So what we physically see, hear, and experience from external sources become the "food" with which our self-truths, self-righteousness, and understanding and **Will** are formed. If we are taught to dislike or hate other religions or political parties or persons as we grow from infancy to adulthood, that hate becomes the "food" that forms our **Will** and consequently builds our self-preservation and survival.

If our desire and feelings for acceptances by those who provide us this "food" are reinforced, then our **Will** is strengthened by their "food." Our **Will** begins to use these beliefs, self-truths, and self-righteousness as its own and uses them to shape the survival instincts of our "I AM," or self.

To become like Christ requires understanding this and transforming our beliefs, self-truths, and self-righteousness into the beliefs, divine truths, and divine righteousness of Jesus Christ. This is what Jesus Christ means when He says we must be "born again." To do this, we must recognize that our "I AM," or ego, must "be born again." Our love of God must take control of our **Will** and mind and must become strong enough to overcome the resistance of our **Will** and mind to the power of Jesus Christ and the Holy Spirit. This occurs when we, through grace and faith, believe in Jesus Christ, study His words, and learn to hear from Him through the working of the Holy Spirit in our spirit and then obey what He directs. Again, meditation, prayer, Bible study, and obedient actions are required. Obedient actions are righteous actions; they are actions that come from a **Will** that agrees with the will of God.

Our **Will** is an amazing spiritual organ and is comprised of a tremendous spiritual power and strength with influence upon the actions of our spirit, soul, and body yet is resistant to change. Because of this, it is a difficult task to manage and develop it into what it is to become. Our "I AM" has the challenge of doing just that. The only way this is possible is through the help of Jesus Christ and the Holy Spirit. We cannot do it alone. We must be taught and learn that the divine process of accomplishing this is through faith in Jesus Christ.

Our "I AM" must increase in strength so that it can manage the transformation of our understanding, our **Will**, and our mind. This transformation involves the implanting of divine peace, divine truth, and divine righteousness in our human spirit, human soul, and human body.

The "I AM" has the role of harmonizing this growth in divine peace, divine truth, and divine righteousness so that they all act as one. The harmonizing unity of the three flows throughout our entire being as one, bringing under captive the workings of our human spirit, human soul, and human body to the will of God through Jesus Christ and Holy Spirit.

The role our mind, understanding, and **Will** is to play in our growth to becoming divine is expressed in the following scripture:

Let this mind be in you, which was also in Christ Jesus: Who, being in the form of God, thought it not robbery to be equal with God: But made himself of no reputation, and took upon him the form of a servant, and was made in the likeness of men: And being found in fashion as a man, he humbled himself, and became obedient unto death, even the death of the cross. Wherefore God also hath highly exalted him, and given him a name which is above every name: That at the name of Jesus every knee should bow, of things in heaven, and things in earth, and things under the earth; And that every tongue should confess that Jesus Christ is Lord, to the glory of God the Father. Wherefore, my beloved, as ye have always obeyed, not as in my presence only, but now much more in my absence, <u>work out your own salvation with fear and trembling. For it is God which worketh in you both to will and to do of his good pleasure.</u>

Philippians 2:5–13

DIVINE PEACE APPLIED

Afro-American Freedom Monument

Susan B. Anthony

President Johnson signing Civil Rights Bill

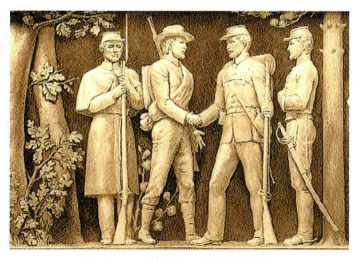

Peace accord End of U.S. Civil War

Customs, Changes, Conflicts and Courage

Customs are typically the results of beliefs from older generations and or social practices that are formed from these beliefs and subsequently handed down from generation to generation. They become accepted practices by individuals and social groups for which the reason for the practices are often forgotten.

Some of you may have heard the story of the family that gathered during the holidays for a family dinner. There were four generations gathered, the mother and father, their daughter and her grandmother, and the great grandmother along with other family members. The mother was preparing a beef roast and proceeded to cut off both ends of the roast before putting it in the pan and then into the oven.

Her daughter notice what she was doing and asked her, "Mother, why did you cut off both ends of the roast?" The mother answered, "Well, that's the way you cook a roast. You cut off both ends first. Ask your grandmother. She will tell you. I learned by watching her." The daughter then asked the grandmother, "Grandmother, why is it necessary to cut off both ends of the roast before cooking it?" The grandmother said, "That's the way I cooked a roast and learned it from my mother. Ask your great-grandmother. She will tell you." The young girl then asked the great-grandmother. "Granny, why is it necessary to cut off both ends of the roast before cooking it?" The great-grandmother smiled and said, "Well, child, it isn't necessary if you have a cooking pan bigger enough to hold the roast. When I used to cook a beef roast, I had to cut off both ends because the cooking pan I used was too small for the roast, so I cut off both ends so it would fit."

What the great-grandmother had started eventually became a family custom and practice. This family custom eventually became what I call a "self-truth" to her descendants. Some customs are not as innocent. Customs that exist within nations, social classes, races, religious, political groups, and individuals are much more complex and often become so ingrained that they create conflict. And yet, within each of these groups, these customs often become beliefs and customs which must change with the times

The world is in a constant state of change. These changing world conditions required that groups and individual change. Especially this is seen among religious and political groups. In religious and political groups, established beliefs become doctrines, which over time harden into dogma that resists the need for change. As a result, conflicts appear, peace is threatened, and strife is often the result.

Change presents new life experiences. New experiences challenge our beliefs. However, challenges to our beliefs, which have become "self-truths," are hard to accept. Sometimes we resist to the point of experiencing conflict within our self and between our self and others. New experiences are a part of life. In order to grow to the level of understanding divine truth, we must be flexible and open to deal with new experiences in a Christ-centered way. As it is written:

> **Therefore if any man be in Christ, he is a new creature: old things are passed away; behold <u>all things are become new</u>.**
> **2 Corinthians 5:17**

And,

> **And he that sat upon the throne said, Behold, <u>*I make all things new*</u>. And he said unto me, Write: for these words are true and faithful. And he said unto me, It is done. I am Alpha and Omega, the beginning and the end. I will give unto him that is athirst of the fountain of the water of life freely. He that overcometh shall inherit all things; and I will be his God, and he shall be my son.**
> **Revelations 21:5–7**

To grow in peace, one must become willing to adopt new things. We must be open to change, flexible, humble, and compliant to the truth and will of God, through Jesus Christ and the Holy Spirit. When changes of beliefs and "self-truths" become necessary, we must learn to accept them in a spirit of peace.

Our former beliefs and "self-truths" are transformed by new experiences and new revelations from Jesus Christ. These new experiences and new revelations are often physical and spiritual tests that require we change our beliefs and "self-truths." Many of these changes are physically and spiritually painful. Nevertheless, they are necessary to transform us.

Some of the new experiences and revelations come as tests to determine what we have already been taught. Others are critical and life-changing applications. What I mean is some tests are given us as training exercises to prepare us for later experiences that have impact on our present and future life as well as the present and future lives of others.

Let me illustrate. Jesus was led by the Spirit into the wilderness where He was tested by the devil. Jesus was tested with three different test, each of which He met successfully. He used the power that was placed into Him by the Holy Spirit to do the will of God His father. But these were tests or training exercises.

It was during the events of His ordeal in the Garden of Gethsemane, crucifixion and resurrection that the power He experienced and exhibited in the wilderness was used in critical life-changing applications for Him and for others. For what Jesus learned in the wilderness by overcoming His agony was applied by Jesus during His trial, crucifixion, and resurrection. As a result, He successfully completed His mission and received His reward, for all power in the heavens, on earth, and under the earth was given to Him, and He prepared the way for all who believe in Him to have access to eternal life.

We must learn to recognize the difference between training exercises (tests) in our life that are meaningful yet not critical. It is the same as practicing for a game of basketball and the actual game. In one, you are developing skills; in the other, you are applying skills you have practiced. Both require learning to hear and follow the instructions of your coach and trainer so you develop skills that enable you to win the game.

In our day-to-day activities, we are faced with experiences that challenge our knowledge and application of God's will concerning peace. Many of these activities are developmental. Through them, we learn to apply peace. We are successful at times. At other times, we are not. But there will come times and situations when for the good of our present and future life and the lives of others, we **must be successful**. This requires courage such as we see in the emerging movement of women across the globe in their pursuit of peace. One example of this is the "Pray the Devil Back to Hell" movement of the women of Liberia.

Nobel Peace laureate Leymah Gbowee, 39, was awarded the Nobel Peace for her efforts in mobilizing the women of Liberia to use prayer and protest to end civil strife in that country.

Courage is always required. History has taught us that courage and righteous sacrifice on the part of individuals and people have always been required for divine goals such as peace to be reached.

As we accept and apply divine truth from Jesus Christ, we experience peace. The process does not end there. This new truth will continue to be tested by Satan until he determines he cannot defeat us. This testing may last in some form throughout our lifetime. However, with every test, we grow stronger in divine understanding (truth), divine will (righteousness), power, and divine peace.

Once we decided to accept Jesus Christ as our Lord, we undergo attacks and conflicts. Please remember that the Lord, the Holy Spirit, and your angels are there ready to help in every instance. But also remember that there are things they will do and things we must do. An important thing we must do is develop our courage to do what is required of us by God to do His will.

As we learn, we grow in ways to maintain our peace regardless of the conflicts. As we recognize these satanic tests, we become skilled in the application of peace and grow in our trust of Jesus Christ in every situation we encounter and as a result develop our courage.

War in Heaven

St. Michael fallen angels

Crusades

The Storming of Fort Wagner – U.S. Civil War

Peace Dove

World War II – Kamikazes Raid

Nuclear Explosion

President Obama Peace Prize

War and Spiritual Influences

Finally, my brethren, be strong in the Lord, and in the power of his might.
Put on the whole armour of God, that ye may be able to stand against the wiles of the devil. For we wrestle not against flesh and blood, but against principalities, against powers, against the rulers of the darkness of this world, against spiritual wickedness in high places. Wherefore take unto you the whole armour of God, that ye may be able to withstand in the evil day, and having done all, to stand. Stand therefore, having your loins girt about with truth, and having on the breastplate of righteousness; And your feet shod with the preparation of the gospel of peace.
Ephesians 6:10–15

In modern times, many books have been written about the causes of war between nations. The principal accepted causes include the following:

1. Political ambition of nations' leaders
2. Personal rivalry and revenge of individuals
3. Economic gain
4. Territorial gain
5. Racial hatred
6. Religion

These causes are natural physical causes involving human beings. Few, if any, references are made to spiritual influences as causes of war. Yet the ancient history of many cultures reveals the influences of spiritual beings, the "gods," in the affairs of mankind, especially as it relates to war. In the past, Oriental, Indian, Persian, Egyptian, Grecian, Roman, Hebrew, Islamic, and other cultures sought direct involvement of their "gods" in the affairs of their lives, especially in times of war.

As mankind has become more materialistic and more prone to favor science, spiritual influences have been ignored. The realm of the spirit has become virtually nonexistent in the affairs of mankind. Mankind's ability to kill larger and larger numbers of other men has also increased as his love of material things and reliance on science and ignorance of our spiritual relationships to each other has increased. Yet the Bible is very clear that the interaction of mankind with spiritual forces should not be ignored.

In the passage of scripture cited above and the subsequent verses that follow, St. Paul informs the Ephesians and us that evil spiritual beings are involved in the dangers they confront in their lives. He mentions specifically, "***Principalities, powers, rulers of the darkness of this world, spiritual wickedness in high places***." All these refer to demonic spirits that are organized into a spiritual hierarchy to oppose the will and purposes of God, Jesus Christ, and the divine destiny of mankind. Opposing these evil spiritual beings are spiritual beings that are loyal to Jesus Christ. These good spiritual beings are involved in assisting mankind to resist the powers of the evil spiritual beings. Both the good and evil spiritual beings are also given the title of "angels."

Dionysius the Areopagite, a follower of St. Paul mentioned in Acts 17:34 of the Bible, knew of these angels and either wrote about them or revealed to his followers their nature; and his followers wrote about them. In a publication credited to Dionysius, known as ***The Celestial Hierarchy***, a listing of three choirs or groups of angels are described. Each choir is said to consist of three categories of these good angels. The categories in the first choir are called Seraphim, Cherubim, and Thrones; the categories in the second choir are called Dominions, Virtues, and Powers; and the categories in the third choir are called Principalities, Archangels, and Angels. These are angels who do God's will under the leadership of Christ.

Opposing the good angels as we mentioned are other angels that have rebelled against God, who are also organized in choirs directly opposed to the angels loyal to God. Early Christian and other cultures describe hierarchies of evil angels that are organized under a power known in Christian theology as Satan, or the devil. It is this group of evil angels that St. Paul describes when instructing the Ephesians about their spiritual enemies.

Not only does St. Paul mention this evil hierarchy; he also points out that they use *wiles* to achieve their evil purposes. Another translation of this word *"wiles"* is *"methods."* The devil uses methods against mankind, which sometimes causes mankind to war among each other.

What a heartbreaking picture this makes when we come to realize that our warring with each other is in fact caused by evil spiritual beings manipulating us into destroying each other. Mankind does not realize as a species that we are being manipulated by evil spirits to destroy ourselves.

There is a passage of biblical scripture, though it may seem hard to believe by some, that may shed light on this subject. In Genesis 6:1–5 of the Bible, a very unusual relationship of the sons of God and the daughters of man is depicted. It reads as follows:

> **And it came to pass, when men began to multiply on the face of the earth, and daughters were born unto them, That the sons of God saw the daughters of men that they *were* fair; and they took them wives of all which they chose. And the LORD said, My spirit shall not always strive with man, for that he also *is* flesh: yet his days shall be an hundred and twenty years. There were giants in the earth in those days; and also after that, when the sons of God came in unto the daughters of men, and they bear *children* to them, the same *became mighty men* which *were* of old, men of renown. And GOD saw that the wickedness of man *was* great in the earth, and *that* every imagination of the thoughts of his heart *was* only evil continually.**
> **Genesis 6:1–5**

There is an expanded record of this scripture in a little-known book, the ***Book of Enoch***. The *Book of Enoch* is not a canonized or a recognized source by many religious Christian denominations. However, it is by the Ethiopian Church and is mentioned in fragments from the Dead Sea Scrolls, as well as in several Greek and Aramaic sources. It is also mentioned in Hebrew mystical writings.

The author of this book, Enoch, is mentioned in the Bible in the book of Genesis as well as in the book of Hebrew. He is identified as the great-grandfather of Noah and is described as being of such a holy nature that he did not experience death but was translated into heaven because he pleased God. As it is written:

> **By faith Enoch was translated that he should not see death; and was not found, because God had translated him: for before his translation he had this testimony, that he pleased God.**
> **Hebrew 11:5**

The *Book of Enoch* describes encounters of certain rebellious ones of the sons of God (angelic beings) with mankind, and the outcomes are disastrous. These angelic beings taught mankind how to make weapons of warfare; they taught them the use of enchantments and all kinds of magical arts and evil practices that led to ungodliness and horrible acts of terror and human slaughter.

The word that is translated ***"mighty"*** and ***"men of renown"*** is also translated by other sources as ***"warrior"*** or ***"giant"***. These words refer to beings who indulged in warfare. These were beings of great statute, which often appear in myths and children stories as fearsome creatures. In the account described in the *Book of Enoch*, these giants went on to destroy men, beast, birds, fish, and each other. Their offspring are referred to in the Bible as Nephilim. The giant Goliath, whose battle with David is described in the book of 1 Samuel in the Bible, is viewed to be a distant descendent of the Nephilim. I believe it is from the influence of these angelic beings and there off springs that the earth became filled with the violence of war.

In the *Book of Enoch*, the original human offspring of these rebellious sons of God were eventually destroyed by each other and by a great flood. The Bible states that many of these wayward angels are finally bound with "chains of darkness" until a time of final judgment. Other sources suggest that a certain percentage of these rebellious sons of God were permitted to remain as adversaries of mankind.

These early biblical accounts and occurrences would lead one to believe that the influences that causes war among mankind springs from the interactions of evil spiritual beings with mankind. Spiritual beings influenced mankind to fight and kill each other.

What is referred to in historical mythological records and labeled as fantasy is in many cases fact based on real occurrences. What the mythology of many cultures portrays in symbolic forms as fables are real wars and interactions of good and evil spiritual beings with mankind. These evil spiritual beings continue to have warlike interactions with mankind even today and have caused great harm.

In the following, which is a continuation of the above biblical scripture, we read God's displeasure with the results of this relationship:

> **And GOD saw that the wickedness of man *was* great in the earth, and *that* every imagination of the thoughts of his heart *was* only evil continually.**
> **And it repented the LORD that he had made man on the earth, and it grieved him at his heart.**
> **And the LORD said, I will destroy man whom I have created from the face of the earth; both man, and beast, and the creeping thing, and the fowls of the air; for it repenteth me that I have made them.**
>
> **Genesis 6:5–7**

Unfortunately, these warlike interactions of evil spiritual beings with mankind were allowed to continue. If the purpose of their continual existence, as some have suggested, is to serve as adversaries for mankind, they should not be ignored. Are they involved in wars on earth? I believe so. The principal cause of war is the direct and indirect influence of demonic beings within mankind and mankind's ignorance of them. War is insanity. Especially this is true of the deceptive and misplaced use of honor, courage, and patriotism by leaders to inflict death, rape, and destruction upon others and to spend enormous sums of money to fight wars. Rational reasoning can draw only one conclusion: war is insanity.

Jesus Christ states:

> **The thief cometh not, but for to steal, and to kill, and to destroy: I am come that they might have life, and that they might have *it* more abundantly.**
>
> **John 10:10**

Christ in the above passage is describing war. Wars incite acts of killing, stealing, and destroying of lives and properties. War is Antichrist behavior. Until mankind considers evil spiritual influences as contributors to war, and until mankind uses the guidance given us by Jesus Christ to resolve conflicts of will without violence, wars will continue.

As a point for more discussion on this matter, let's consider the definition of "war" given by General Carl Von Clausewitz, who wrote an often referenced book titled ***ON WAR***. In it, he describes war as follows: "**war therefore is an act of violence intended to compel our opponent to fulfil *our will*.**" I might add that the ultimate aim is the total destruction of the opponent. If we accept that *our will* is a key factor in whether one goes to war and recognize that the real enemies who wants us to go to war are evil spiritual beings and other human beings influenced by evil spiritual beings, then perhaps we could develop a greater understand of the role **our will** plays in what we do and learn how to strongly resist the influences of these evil spiritual beings upon **our will**.

When we first find our self in a conflict of **will** with another individual, we should immediately recognize that the next step could be an act of violence against the other individual. The act of violence may be spiritual or physical by us or them. The act may stem from an internal thought or feeling. The act may be a spoken word or a physical act. All manifested by a resulting choice of our will. If we accept that war is a conflict of will that leads to violence, we can see how war may exist among individuals, groups, communities, and nations but can be avoid if we rightly control our **will**.

We should therefore study what strategies and tactics these evil spiritual beings use to manipulate our will to cause us to use our will to perform acts of violence. Then we should develop counter strategies and tactics to combat and defeat them. These are necessary for interactions among individuals, groups, communities, and nations.

This is a reasonable task. Mankind is capable of developing countermeasures to the evil influences of these spirits if only we sought the guidance of Jesus Christ and the Holy Spirit. The Bible points out that evil spirits use strategies and tactics that include what are called **wiles, devices, and snares**:

1. The **wiles** of the devil:

Wiles are methods the devil uses to compel us to do his **will**. It is beyond the scope of this book to expand in great detail about these wiles, but demonic methods are many yet identifiable and can be defeated. It is hoped that these may be discussed in more detail in a future work, God willing. However, I can briefly state that the Bible does instruct us to:

> *Put on the whole armour of God, that ye may be able to stand against <u>the wiles of the devil</u>.*
> *Ephesians 6:11*

What is the "**whole armour of God**" and how to "**put on the whole armour of God**" must be understood and taught in the context of contemporary life if mankind is to withstand the methods evil spirits use to attack mankind. Ephesians 6:14–18 of the Bible is a start in understanding what we should do:

> <u>**Stand therefore, having your loins girt about with truth, and having on the breastplate of righteousness;**</u>
> <u>**And your feet shod with the preparation of the gospel of peace;**</u>
> <u>**Above all, taking the shield of faith, wherewith ye shall be able to quench all the fiery darts of the wicked.**</u>
> <u>**And take the helmet of salvation, and the sword of the Spirit, which is the word of God:**</u>
> <u>**Praying always with all prayer and supplication in the Spirit, and watching thereunto with all perseverance and supplication for all saints;**</u>

These scriptures require further study if they are to be understood by our current culture. Please meditate on them and record what the Spirit reveals about what they mean for you. As you understand and act properly on what the Spirit reveals about the methods the devil uses to affect you and what you should do in response, you will grow in peace.

The devil attacks us with specific and general methods. We all must grow to understand which attacks are specific and only applies to us and which attacks are general and applies to all human beings. We will come to discover that they both have patterns that are often repeated. This knowledge will prove helpful in the combat to defeat and overcome personal devilish attacks and in how to be of assistance to others in attacks upon human beings in general.

2. Satan (or the devil) uses **devices**:

Devices are thoughts of the mind. Satan's strategy is to use satanic power in ways to place thoughts in our minds that will cause us to use our **will** in ways that do his **will**.

> **Lest <u>Satan</u> should get an advantage of us: for we are not ignorant of his <u>*devices.*</u>**
> **2 Corinthians 2:11**

The proper use of our mind and our thoughts are essential. Godly development of both under the guidance of Jesus Christ and the Holy Spirit are areas of vital importance. This calls for immediate and future research and application if mankind is not to be taken advantage of and defeated by Satan.

3. The devil uses **snare**:

Snare is a trap or noose that captures us and binds us to or in something so that another entity may control what we do. The Bible tells what we should do in response to a **snare**:

> **And the servant of the Lord must not strive; but be gentle unto all *men*, apt to teach, patient, In meekness instructing those that oppose themselves; if God peradventure will give them repentance to the acknowledging of the truth; And *that* they may recover themselves out of the <u>*snare*</u> of the <u>devil</u>, who are taken captive by him at his will.**
>
> 2 Timothy 2:24–26

And (the person referred to as casting out devils is Jesus Christ)

> **And he was casting out a devil, and it was dumb. And it came to pass, when the devil was gone out, the dumb spake; and the people wondered.**
> **But some of them said, He casteth out devils through Beelzebub the chief of the devils. And others, tempting *him*, sought of him a sign from heaven.**
> **But he, knowing their thoughts, said unto them, Every kingdom divided against itself is brought to desolation; and a house *divided* against a house falleth. If Satan also be divided against himself, how shall his kingdom stand? because ye say that I cast out devils through Beelzebub. And if I by Beelzebub cast out devils, by whom do your sons cast *them* out? therefore shall they be your judges.**
> **But if I with the finger of God cast out devils, no doubt the kingdom of God is come upon you.**
>
> Luke 11:14–20

Then we note the importance of peace:

> **When a strong man armed keepeth his palace, his goods are in <u>*peace:*</u>**
>
> Luke 11:21

The devil uses **wiles** and **devices** to cleverly and craftily capture our **will** and then our total spirit, soul, and body. He wants us to choose actions that put us onto paths, if we take them, that lead us into a preset **snare** (trap). This snare then binds us—first our spirit then our soul and finally our body. His ultimate goal is to kill us. Addictions to substances and or destructive physical and spiritual acts come to mind.

Evil spiritual beings attack each of us personally regardless of title or social status. We all must grow wise in the ways evil spiritual beings attack our spirit, soul, and body. If we are to avoid becoming controlled by evil spiritual beings intent on destroying us, we must know how they use their wiles, devices, and snares to specifically attack each of us.

Each of us must become a student of our self. Decide to study yourself and determine the truth and rightness of any action that affects you and how you respond to it. Determine whether occurrences in your life are from Jesus Christ. Then decide, with the assistance of Jesus Christ and the Holy Spirit, the right action you should take to prevent evil spirits from influencing you and cast them out when they bind us and others.

In a larger sense, I believe that efforts should be undertaken to study the histories of wars, their causes, and their prevention. World leaders, scientists, educators, religious, community leaders, and interested individuals must come together to establish peaceful ways to resolve conflicts with full recognition that what is done among mankind in the earth often has its origin in spiritual realms. We must include the existence and actions of spiritual beings in our deliberations about war and peace and seek the guidance of Jesus Christ.

More information on the history of war and mankind can be found in countless books and on the Internet. To get a sense of the enormity of warfare in the history of mankind on earth and an appreciation of the lost of lives and costs, I refer you, who have access to the Internet, to review the following source that may prove of interest:

http://en.wikipedia.org/wiki/War.

Of special note is the section under **List of Wars by Death Tolls**. An extract of information from this Web page follows. The information includes estimates of World War II casualties by country. And although these are estimates and may be open to debate, it gives you a sense of the enormous destruction and loss of lives caused by war. We must find a solution to the carnage and insane behavior we inflict upon each other—behavior that originates in demonic spiritual beings that influence us.

	Human Losses of World War II by Country					
Country	Total Population 1/1/1939	Military deaths	Civilian deaths due to war and repression.	Jewish Holocaust deaths	Total deaths	Deaths as % of 1939 Population
Albania	1,073,000	30,000		200	30,200	2.81
Australia	6,998,000	39,800	700		40,500	0.57
Austria	6,653,000		58,700	65,000	123,700	0.02
Belgium	8,387,000	12,100	49,600	24,400	86,100	1.02
Brazil	40,289,000	1,000	1,000		2,000	0.02
Bulgaria	6,458,000	22,000	3,000		25,000	0.38
Burma	16,119,000	22,000	250,000		272,000	1.69
Canada	11,267,000	45,400			45,400	0.4
China	517,568,000	3,000,000–4,000,000	7,000,000–16,000,000		10,000,000–20,000,000	1.93–3.86
Cuba	4,235,000		100		100	0
Czechoslovakia	15,300,000	25,000	43,000	277,000	345,000	2.25
Denmark	3,795,000	2,100	1,000	100	3,200	0.08
Dutch East Indies	69,435,000		3,000,000–4,000,000		3,000,000–4,000,000	4.3–5.76
Estonia	1,134,000		50,000	1,000	51,000	4.5
Ethiopia	17,700,000	5,000	95,000		100,000	0.6
Finland	3,700,000	95,000	2,000		97,000	2.62
France	41,700,000	217,600	267,000	83,000	567,600	1.35
French Indochina	24,600,000		1,000,0001,500,000		1,000,000–1,500,000	4.07–6.1
Germany	69,310,000	5,533,000	900,000–3,170,000	160,000	6,593,000–8,863,000	9.5–12.7

Country	Total Population 1/1/1939	Military deaths	Civilian deaths due to war and repression	Jewish Holocaust deaths	Total deaths	Deaths as % of 1939 Population
Greece	7,222,000	20,000–35,100	220,000–700,500	69,500	309,500–805,100	4.29–11.15
Hungary	9,129,000	300,000	80,000	200,000	580,000	6.35
Iceland	119,000		200		200	0.17
India	378,000,000	87,000	1,500,000–2,500,000		1,587,000–2,587,000	0.43–0.66
Iran	14,340,000	200			200	0
Iraq	3,698,000	500			500	0.01
Ireland	2,960,000		200		200	0
Italy	44,394,000	301,400	145,100	10,500	457,000	1.03
Japan	71,380,000	2,120,000	580,000		2,700,000	3.78
Korea	23,400,000		378,000–483,000		378,000–483,000	1.6–2.06
Latvia	1,995,000		147,000	80,000	227,000	11.38
Lithuania	2,575,000		212,000	141,000	353,000	13.71
Luxembourg	295,000		1,300	700	2,000	0.68
Malaya	4,391,000		100,000		100,000	2.28
Malta	269,000		1,500		1,500	0.56
Mexico	19,320,000		100		100	0
Mongolia	819,000	300			300	0.04
Nauru (Australia)	3,400		500		500	14.7
Netherlands	8,729,000	17,000	180,000	104,000	301,000	3.45
Newfoundland	300,000	included with the United Kingdom	100		100	0.03
New Zealand	1,629,000	11,900			11,900	0.73
Norway	2,945,000	3,000	5,800	700	9,500	0.32
Papua and New Guinea	1,292,000		15,000		15,000	1.17
Philippines	16,000,000	57,000	500,000–1,000,000		557,000–1,057,000	3.48–6.6

Country	Total Population 1/1/1939	Military deaths	Civilian deaths due to war and repression	Jewish Holocaust deaths	Total deaths	Deaths as % of 1939 Population
Poland	34,849,000	240,000	2,380,000–2,580,000	3,000,000	5,620,000–5,820,000	16.7
Portuguese Timor	500,000		40,000–70,000		40,000–70,000	8–14.00
Romania	19,934,000	300,000	64,000	469,000	833,000	4.22
Ruanda-Urundi	4,200,000		0–300,000		0–300,000	0–7.10
Singapore	728,000		50,000		50,000	6.87
South Africa	10,160,000	11,900			11,900	0.12
South Pacific Mandate	1,900,000		57,000		57,000	3
Soviet Union	168,500,000	8,800,000–10,700,000	12,254,000–14,154,000	1,000,000	23,954,000	14.21
Spain	25,637,000	4,500			4,500	0.02
Sweden	6,341,000		600		600	0.01
Switzerland	4,210,000		100		100	0
Thailand	15,023,000	5,600	2,000		7,700	0.04
United Kingdom	47,760,000	383,600	67,100		450,700	0.94
United States	131,028,000	416,800	1,700		418,500	0.32
Yugoslavia	15,400,000	446,000	514,000	67,000	1,027,000	6.67
Total	1,967,095,400	22,576,700–25,491,800	32,246,500–49,532,200	5,753,100	62,476,670–78,878,170	3.17–4.00

In May 1865, at the end of the American Civil War, the famous Union General William Tecumseh Sherman wrote in a personal letter:

> **I confess, without shame, I am sick and tired of fighting—its glory is all moonshine; even success the most brilliant is over dead and mangled bodies, with the anguish and lamentations of distant families, appealing to me for sons, husbands and fathers ... tis only those who have never heard a shot, never heard the shriek and groans of the wounded and lacerated ... that cry aloud for more blood, more vengeance, more desolation.**

General Sherman, Ulysses Grant, Abraham Lincoln, David Porter—The Peacemakers

War is insanity influenced upon mankind by demonic forces whose purpose is to destroy the divine purpose ordained by God for the destiny of the human race.

Let's end this discussion with a scripture taken from the book of Revelation in the Bible that describes war in the kingdom of heaven and the foretelling of war on earth:

> **And there was war in heaven: Michael and his angels fought against the dragon; and the dragon fought and his angels, And prevailed not; neither was their place found any more in heaven. And the great dragon was cast out, that old serpent, called the Devil, and Satan, which deceiveth the whole world: he was cast out into the earth, and his angels were cast out with him.**
>
> **And I heard a loud voice saying in heaven, Now is come salvation, and strength, and the kingdom of our God, and the power of his Christ: for the accuser of our brethren is cast down, which accused them before our God day and night. And they overcame him by the blood of the Lamb, and by the word of their testimony; and they loved not their lives unto the death.**
>
> **Therefore rejoice, *ye* heavens, and ye that dwell in them. Woe to the inhabiters of the earth and of the sea! for the devil is come down unto you, having great wrath, because he knoweth that he hath but a short time. . . . And the dragon was wroth with the woman, and went to <u>make war with the remnant of her seed</u>, which keep the commandments of God, and have the testimony of Jesus Christ.**

Rhythm and Rest

Ocean Waves

Christ Mount of Olives

Rhythm

In the first chapter of Genesis in the Bible, we observe key aspects of God's creative processes. These divine processes have a rhythm to them. They operate upon and within spiritual and physical matters in a tempo known only to God, but observable by those who have eyes to see and ears to hear.

The voice of God is the instrument by which these divine processes are started. Within His voice is the divine power and rhythmical music of creation. If you read this chapter with a sense of divine peace, you will grasp the rhythmical music of the creation. "God said" is a phrase that is repeated in a recurring rhythm that gives the impression of the distant beat of a heavenly drum sounding forth in time and space—a sound filled with awe and suspense, announcing the coming forth of something never seen or experienced before.

What proceeds from these heavenly announcements are divine processes of immense proportion upon and within spiritual and physical matters that manifest within time and space. These processes continue even today, affecting all the creation, swaying back and forth from one condition to another. We must grow our spiritual ability to see and hear these announcements.

> **And God called the light Day, and the darkness he called Night. And the evening and the morning were the first day.**
> **Genesis 1:5**

God created (called) light to contrast with darkness. The light He called day, the darkness He called night. We move back and forth between darkness and light, night and day, in our pursuit of divine peace.

Notice that the day starts with evening and ends with morning. This denotes that we begin with a mixture of darkness and light, which becomes total darkness, and arrive at the morning, which is a newness of light that increases to become total light. Likewise, we grow from a mixture of divine peace and anxiety to a condition that may appear as total despair that will become, if we are persistent, a condition of total divine peace.

In Genesis, we see how God continued these divine processes upon and within various types of spiritual and physical matters over and over again for six cyclical days, which ended with God declaring all He had made as good. And on the seventh day He rested.

In our daily life as well, we encounter all kinds of indications of these divine rhythms such as our heartbeat, our breathing, and our being awake and asleep. We see births and deaths, the aging of loved ones, the rising and setting of the sun, the seasons of the year, the ebb and flow of ocean waves—all recognize the rhythms of life.

Divine rhythms affect our external and internal worlds and our spiritual and physical beings. These rhythms are used to teach us about time and space. God's creative actions take place in spiritual and physical time and space. If we are to grow in divine peace, we each must come to realize that we operate in time and space and that everything we experience must conform to them. One important spiritual and physical quality we develop, when we grow in the knowledge of how we exist in time and space, is **patience,** or as sometimes translated **long-suffering**.

Patience is a quality inherent in divine processes. What we experience in the physical realm is first initiated in the spiritual realm; then they manifest in the physical realm. An example will help us understand this. We first think and create an idea of taking a walk. Then we act out the idea by taking the walk. So it is with divine processes: they are first created by God within Himself and then manifest in the spiritual and physical realm. We must harmonize our behavior to God's if we desire divine peace. This demands we develop patience.

God's word is true and operates in time. We first must develop the ability to see or hear God's word spiritually before we experience it working in our physical life. We must learn about the rhythms of these divine processes and harmonize our actions to them if they are to fulfill their intended purpose in our life. This requires us to relate time and patience to them. If we are impatient and take actions that are not in harmony with the announced divine processes, they will not achieve what God intends for us. The results will be a lack of divine peace in our life and deformed creations. Time and patience work together to enable us to accomplish what God intends.

God continues to work in a rhythmical and timely way on earth and in the heavens even today:

> **While the earth remaineth, seedtime and harvest, and cold and heat, and summer and winter, and day and night shall not cease.**
>
> **Genesis 8:22**

> **To every *thing there is* a season, and a time to every purpose under the heaven:**
> **A time to be born, and a time to die; a time to plant, and a time to pluck up *that which is* planted;**
> **A time to kill, and a time to heal; a time to break down, and a time to build up;**
> **A time to weep, and a time to laugh; a time to mourn, and a time to dance;**
> **A time to cast away stones, and a time to gather stones together; a time to embrace, and a time to refrain from embracing;**
> **A time to get, and a time to lose; a time to keep, and a time to cast away;**
> **A time to rend, and a time to sew; a time to keep silence, and a time to speak;**
> **A time to love, and a time to hate; a time of war, and a time of divine peace.**
> **What profit hath he that worketh in that wherein he laboureth?**
> **I have seen the travail, which God hath given to the sons of men to be exercised in it. He hath made every *thing* beautiful in his time: also he hath set the world (uncertainty of the future) in their heart, so that no man can find out the work that God maketh from the beginning to the end.**
>
> **Ecclesiastes 3:1**

There is a time for all of God's actions, and within that time, our role is to be in harmony with what God wills.

> **Peace I leave with you, my peace I give unto you: not as the world giveth, give I unto you. Let not your heart be troubled, neither let it be afraid.**
>
> **John 14:27**

This divine peace comes to us only after we follow the commandments of Jesus Christ as given to us by the Spirit of divine peace, the Holy Spirit. One key aspect of this divine peace is that there are rhythms in what Jesus Christ commands. We will experience this as we grow in our meditation exercise. We learn that inspirations from God, through Jesus Christ and the Holy Spirit, often come in waves. We will learn that we may not get the entire plan revealed unto us at once, but that we receive an initial wave of inspiration and must learn to be patient until the Holy Spirit confirms He is finished sending all the inspirations for that period or season. Then we receive more of the plan as we faithfully response to what previously had been given. And so on. It is through this process that we learn to patiently harmonize our actions in accordance with the guidance of the Holy Spirit and enter into the divine peace Jesus Christ promised.

Rest

Rest is as much a part of the activity of life as the rhythms we discussed above. But rest in the divine sense is not inactivity. Rest is an active element of patience. At times, we must patiently wait in a state of total belief that what God has set in motion will achieve its intended end. Rest, at times, is an inner restraint that we imposed upon our will in rhythm with the announced word or plan of God through Jesus Christ and the Holy Spirit.

Rest is as powerful as action. The effects of rest are necessary to permit the preceding and approaching actions to reach their intended end. This is sensed particularly in a musical score, where the entire or sections of an orchestra stops playing in the middle of a score and then begins again. (In Beethoven's Fifth Symphony, we hear an excellent example of this.)

Jesus Christ came to demonstrate God's continual desire for mankind to become divine. He has sent the Holy Spirit to help each of us achieve the purposes for which we were created. We must learn to be obedient to the guidance of the Holy Spirit if we are to understand this concept of rest. For within the guidance given to us by the Holy Spirit are moments when we must cease from our own efforts while permitting the actions put in motion by God and us as co-creators to achieve their purpose.

Rest in the Bible is used to describe the condition of faith that enables one to believe what God says and patiently waits for it to unfold. Our rest is a condition where we believe His commandment and **cease doing what we desire** but do what He has commanded us to do. In some cases, this action is to wait. In every situation, we must follow His commandment and perform any action in accordance with them. You see, to wait is as much an action as to fly or run or walk. As is described in Isaiah:

> **But they that wait upon the LORD shall renew *their* strength; they shall mount up with wings as eagles; they shall run, and not be weary; *and* they shall walk, and not faint.**
> **Isaiah 40:31**

And in Hebrew:

> **For we which have believed do enter into rest, as he said, As I have sworn in my wrath, if they shall enter into my rest: although the works were finished from the foundation of the world. For he spake in a certain place of the seventh *day* on this wise, And God did rest the seventh day from all his works. And in this *place* again, If they shall enter into my rest. Seeing therefore it remaineth that some must enter therein, and they to whom it was first preached entered not in because of unbelief: Again, he limiteth a certain day, saying in David, To day, after so long a time; as it is said, Today if ye will hear his voice, harden not your hearts. For if Jesus had given them rest, then would he not afterward have spoken of another day. There remaineth therefore a rest to the people of God.**
> **For he that is entered into his rest, he also hath ceased from his own works, as God *did* from his. Let us labour therefore to enter into that rest, lest any man fall after the same example of unbelief**
> **Hebrew 3:3–11**

There is a rest that is a quality of faith in God's word and obedience to His commandment, a rest that comes from the divine peace that guides us to think and do as God commands.

Peace and Healing

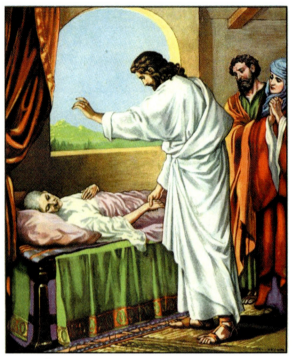
Jesus Healing

The Trinity

The Spirit of the Lord is upon me, because he hath anointed me to preach the gospel to the poor; he hath sent me to heal the brokenhearted, to preach deliverance to the captives, and recovering sight to the blind, to set at liberty them that are bruised, To preach the acceptable year of the Lord.

Luke 4:18–19

This scripture describes Jesus Christ's earthly mission. It states that the Spirit of the Lord—this word "Lord" is better translated as **God—the Spirit of God is resting on Him and gives Him knowledge, strength, and authority to do the things mentioned**:

- Preach the Gospel to the poor
- Heal the brokenhearted
- Preach deliverance to the captives
- Preach recovering of sight to the blind
- Set at liberty them that are bruised
- Preach the acceptable year of the Lord

All these actions are what Jesus Christ was sent unto earth to do. God loves the world so much that He sent His Son into the world to save those who believe in Him. These actions were the actions necessary to save those who are in the world. So Jesus Christ was empowered to do these things.

It is beyond the scope of this book to discuss them all, but I would like to spotlight the second one, "**Heal the brokenhearted**." As we have mentioned earlier, there is a correspondence of the will to the heart. When the scripture mentions a broken heart, it refers to a broken will. The will is a component of our spirit and has a connection to our physical heart. You might recall that we mentioned when discussing the will that the will is influenced by our understanding and conscience. These are all spiritual organs that have connections to our physical body and are sensed particularly in our physical heart. Our understanding is to be filled with divine truth. Our conscience is to be filled with the peace of Christ. Our will is to be filled with divine righteousness.

When these three are in harmony (that is, working in concert), our heart is whole. When they are not working in harmony, our heart becomes "broken."

When our heart is broken, it signifies that our will or spirit has become damaged and is not functioning as it should. The result is that our peace and understanding are prevented from interacting with our will as it should. This then causes our spirit, which includes all of them, to be broken. A broken spirit because of the interconnection of the spirit, soul, and body will cause damage to our soul and physical body, which will manifest as sickness and disease in them all.

Peace in our conscience affects our will, our spiritual heart, as well as our physical heart. When they are disturbed and damaged, healing is required. The remedy for healing depends on the cause. If the source or cause of the damage is physical, then the remedy should be sought in the physical realm. If the cause is spiritual, then the remedy should be sought in the spiritual realm. The great thing about the healings of Jesus Christ in this regard is He operates in both the spiritual and physical realms. His healings bring wholeness wherever it is needed.

Let's look at an example of physical healing by Jesus Christ as recorded in the scriptures:

> **And a certain woman, which had an issue of blood twelve years,**
> **And had suffered many things of many physicians, and had spent all that she had, and was nothing bettered, but rather grew worse,**
> **When she had heard of Jesus, came in the press behind, and touched his garment.**
> **For she said, If I may touch but his clothes, I shall be whole.**
> **And straightway the fountain of her blood was dried up; and she felt in *her* body that she was healed of that plague. And Jesus, immediately knowing in himself that virtue had gone out of him, turned him about in the press, and said, Who touched my clothes? And his disciples said unto him, Thou seest the multitude thronging thee, and sayest thou, Who touched me? And he looked round about to see her that had done this thing. But the woman fearing and trembling, knowing what was done in her, came and fell down before him, and told him all the truth.**
> **And he said unto her, Daughter, thy faith hath made thee whole; go in peace, and be whole of thy plague.**
>
> **Mark 5:25–34**

Notice that Jesus addresses her as **daughter** signifying His love for her and the acceptance of her as His child, though by the context of the story He has just met her. Then He informs her that her "**faith hath made thee whole**," which indicates that her efforts were vital to her healing, for it was the force of her faith that caused the healing spiritual power within Jesus to flow into her body. Then He instructed her that she must "**go in peace**"; that is, she must continue **to use** the **peace** that had just been transferred into her if she wanted to continue to be whole.

Now let's look at an example of how Jesus Christ also used His healing power to heal a man who suffered a sickness that was caused by an evil spirit:

> **And he was casting out a devil, and it was dumb. And it came to pass, when the devil was gone out, the dumb spake; and the people wondered.**
> **But some of them said, He casteth out devils through Beelzebub the chief of the devils. And others, tempting *him*, sought of him a sign from heaven.**
> **But he, knowing their thoughts, said unto them, Every kingdom divided against itself is brought to desolation; and a house *divided* against a house falleth.**
> **If Satan also be divided against himself, how shall his kingdom stand? because ye say that I cast out devils through Beelzebub. And if I by Beelzebub cast out devils, by whom do your sons cast *them* out? therefore shall they be your judges.**
> **But if I with the finger of God cast out devils, no doubt the kingdom of God is come upon you. When a strong man armed keepeth his palace, his goods are in peace:**
> **But when a stronger than he shall come upon him, and overcome him, he taketh from him all his armour wherein he trusted, and divideth his spoils.**
>
> **Luke 11:14–26**

Notice in the passage the portion that reads, "**When a strong man armed keepeth his palace, his goods are in peace**"; the use of the word "palace" signifies a wonderful building. Our being that is our spirit, soul, and body is full of wonders. The psalmist David says, **I am fearfully and wonderfully made**, and that includes all of us. But we must actively protect our spirit, soul, and body against forces that seek to do us harm.

It is possible for evil forces, who seek entrance into our being, to do so. They do this by transmitting untrue thoughts to our mind, which may cause—if we permit it—fear, uncertainty, and doubt in our mind. The result is loss confidence in our self and loss of peace and trust in Jesus Christ. As a consequence, our spiritual protection (armor) is weakened; and our spirit, soul, and body become vulnerable to devils who enter and destroy our well-being.

The good news is that we can turn to Jesus Christ for help. . He possesses the spiritual power to drive these evil spirits out of our spirit, soul, and body and restores life forces that heal us of any damage we experienced.

Jesus Christ said:

> **Peace I leave with you, my peace I give unto you: not as the world giveth, give I unto you. Let not your heart be troubled, neither let it be afraid.**
>
> **John 14:27**

Jesus Christ is always available to heal and restore us from the effects of evil forces.

The Journey Is Eternal

Our peace journey to becoming divine is intended to be eternal. It will be if you are obedient to the will of God. It will not be if you fail to follow His will. The journey is filled with wonders and challenges calling for courage and righteous sacrifices on our individual and collective parts.

Just like Jesus Christ, we are destined to leave this earth as a resurrected being, with all the attributes that will permit us to continue to worlds yet to be revealed.

We are required to recognize that we are to return to God as a completely new creation, initially under the guidance of Jesus Christ and eventually as His friend with the same power that He has. Jesus said:

> **Ye are my friends, if ye do whatsoever I command you. Henceforth I call you not servants; for the servant knoweth not what his lord doeth: but I have called you friends; for all things that I have heard of my Father I have made known unto you.**
> **Ye have not chosen me, but I have chosen you, and ordained you, that ye should go and bring forth fruit, and *that* your fruit should remain: that whatsoever ye shall ask of the Father in my name, he may give it you.**
>
> **John 15:14–16**

This also includes taking our rightful place as guardians of the earth. This role was given to mankind in the beginning of creation. Mankind still has the responsibility to care for the earth, its environment, and its inhabitants. This includes minerals, plants, animals, all races of people, water, and air. We have the responsibility while we are on earth to become a co-creator with Jesus Christ of our own divine design. In order to dwell in the new heaven and new earth that are to come, we must be filled with **Divine Peace, Divine Truth** *and* **Divine Righteousness.**

I pray you enjoy your journey. The rewards are eternal.

Stars, Lord Jesus Christ, New Earth with PEACMAKERS-Children of God

INDEX

A

Adam, 9, 14, 18, 57, 107, 123, 125, 134
angels
    categories of, 143
    definition of, 61, 143
anointing, 61

B

beliefs
    basis of, 41
    definition of, 135
    development of, 40
Bible, meditation scriptures in, 64
Book of Enoch, 144
breathing, definition of, 19

C

Carver, George Washington, 127
cause, definition of, 95
cause and effect
    divine principle of, 103
    role of, 101
Celestial Hierarchy, The (Dionysius), 143
changes, definition of, 140
charash, 88–90
Christian Meditation Outline, 70, 81
Clausewitz, Carl Von, 145
    On War, 91
conscience
    definition of, 43, 88
    occurrence of, 90
    purpose of, 115
creation, divine design and, 29–30
customs, definition of, 140

D

darkness, definition of, 33
Deming, W. Edwards, 101
devices, definition of, 146
diffusion, definition of, 20
Dionysius
    Celestial Hierarchy, The, 143
divine attributes
    definition of, 130
    kinds of, 47–48
    manifestation of, 105
divine design, creation and, 29–30
divine influence, workings of, 40
divine orders, definition of, 36–37
divine peace
    features of, 27
    form of, 31
    function of, 31
    life form of, 31
divine rhythm, definition of, 153
divine righteousness
    definition of, 133
    growth in, 133
divine truth
    definition of, 117
    measures and boundaries of, 128
    search for, 116–17
    stages of growth to, 122–26, 132i
    transmission of, 128
    understanding and, 123–24

E

ego. *See* I AM
Enoch, 144
Eve, 9, 14, 57, 107
evil spirits
    definition of, 104
    strategies and tactics of, 146–47

F

faith, definition of, 120, 125, 136

G

Garden of Eden, 9, 14, 57, 91
God
    counseling Job on understanding, 128
    creative processes of, 107, 118
    designer role of, 8–9, 11
    divine formative powers of, 32
    inflow of Word of, 90
    interventions of, 36
    as the original cause, 96
    power of spoken word of, 33
    rejection of mankind by, 10
    restoration of communication with mankind by, 11
    ultimate purpose of, 101
God, Word of, 153
Goliath, 144
good spirits, definition of, 104
grace, definition of, 111

H

hacah, 88
Harkness, Georgia, 13n
healing, peace and, 156–57
heaven
    composition in kingdom of, 97
    definition of, 34
Heaven and Its Wonders and Hell (Swedenborg), 96
Heavenly Arcana, The (Swedenborg), 93
Holy Spirit
    earnestness of, 43
    effects of, 61
    importance of, 61
    obtaining peace according to, 9
    responsibility of, 60–61
Holy Trinity, 8
human body
    definition of, 16, 62
    respiratory system of, 19, 21

human mind
   definition of, 62
   development of, 119
   as major spiritual organ, 118
   role of, 121
human soul
   definition of, 37, 62
   parts of, 38
human spirit
   definition of, 61
   existence of, 42
human thinking, meditation and, 71–72
human will, definition of, 133

I

I AM
   definition of, 62, 111–12
   effects of erroneous acts of, 133
   formation of, 133
   having potential for divine life, 105
   relationship with spirit consciousness, 121
   role of, 62, 137
intellect, definition of, 120
Ishikawa, Kaoru, 101
Ishikawa Diagram, 102i, 102

J

Jesus Christ
   as access to God, 135
   assistance in restoring mankind to God, 58
   birth of, 13
   earthly missions of, 156
   fullness of, 101
   physical healing of, 157–58
   power of, 98
   presence of spirit of, 87
   as Prince of Peace, 50, 87
   purpose of, 101
   revealing of truth by, 121
   ruling power of, 111
   on war, 92
Job, 36, 128
Juran, J. M., 101

K

Keeley, Lawrence H.
   War Before Civilization, 91
kingdoms
   definition of, 96
   types of, 96
knowledge, search for, 93

L

life force
   definition of, 23
   functions of, 26
light, definition of, 33

M

mankind
   adversaries of, 98
   becoming knowledgeable of the fruit of lives, 106
   becoming like Christ, 137
   challenge in obtaining correct understanding of, 120
   challenges of, 141
   change of nature of, 10
   cocreator role of, 50
   composition of, 45–46
   creation of, 14
   definition of, 6
   divine destiny of, 105
   ego of, 62
   five-sense knowledge of, 113
   forming divine understanding by, 120
   growing in peace, 140
   growth processes of, 108
   growth to peace of, 105
   having potential to becoming divine, 23
   increasing in spiritual knowledge, 129
   interactions of, 102
   knowledge of sin of, 55
   new birth of, 115
   peace journey of, 53
   physical body of, 108
   purpose of, 107, 109
   purpose of life of, 6
   putting on whole armor of God, 146
   reconnection with God of, 41
   responsibility of, 57
   role of, 158
   spirit of, 112
   suborgans of, 114
   thinking process of, 134
meditation
   developing ability in, 70
   exercises in, 81–83
   experiences that may occur in, 82
   God's feelings and, 75
   God's thoughts and, 74
   God's will and, 77
   human thinking and, 71–72
   human will and, 76–77
   law of love and, 76
   mankind's feelings and, 75
   peace and, 67
   peace journey and, 78–79
   place for, 82
   position in, 82
   prayer and, 65
   process of, 68–70
   purposes of, 82
   recognizing true thoughts and, 72–73
   role of, 64
   scriptures about, 64
   spiritual listening ability and, 70
   thought images and, 74
   thought voices and, 74
   time for, 82
memories, definition of, 135
Miller, M.
   Sabbath Shiurim, 51

N

nature, laws of, 36, 88
Nephilim, 144

O

On War (Clausewitz), 91

P

Paul
   on evil spiritual beings, 143
   on growth of mankind, 89
   on human body, 46
   on the threefold mature of man, 15
   on truth, 107
peace
   challenges to divine destiny of, 115
   definition of, 25, 59, 86
   features of, 27
   forms of, 28–29
   functions of, 26
   healing and, 156–57
   importance of, 147
   meditation and, 67
   New Testament use of, 90–91
   obtainment of, 6
   plowing of, 89
peace journey, intent of, 158
perception, definition of, 125
Peter, 72–73
plowing, definition of, 88
prayer
   definition of, 64
   interaction of Holy Spirit in, 65
   meditation and, 65
Psalm 23, *78*

R

reaping, principle of, 105
rest, definition of, 154–55

S

Sabbath Shiurim (Miller), 51
Sea of Galilee, 27
self-righteousness, 114, 135–37
self-truth, 113–14, 120, 122, 125, 136–37, 140–41
shalem, 86
shalom, 86
shelem, 86
Sherman, William Tecumseh, 150
sight, 17
snares, definition of, 147
sowing, principle of, 105
spiritual attributes, kinds of, 47–48
spiritual knowledge, definition of, 126
Stone, Lloyd, 13n
sunlight
   composition of, 25
   functions of, 24

Swedenborg, Emanuel
   Heaven and Its Wonders and Hell, 93, 96
   Heavenly Arcana, The, 93

T

"This Is My Song," 13

U

understanding
   definition of, 126
   divine truth and, 123–24
   functions of, 121

W

war
   accepted causes of, 143
   casualties of, 148–50, 150t
   definition of, 91, 145, 151
   principal cause of, 145
War Before Civilization (Keeley), 91
wiles, definition of, 146
will, definition of, 137
words, definition of, 17

List of Images with Captions and Credits

p. 139	Afro-American Freedom Monument / Copyright expired. Public Domain
p. 94	Ancient of Days by William Blake / Copyright expired - Public Domain
p. 52	Angels The Awakening / Copyright expired. Public Domain.
p. 52	Bible / Credit Votix as Copyright Holder. Released to Public Domain
p. 71	Bible / Credit Votix as Copyright Holder. Released to Public Domain
p. 5	Bird / Released to Public Domain
p. 63	Christ Mount of Olives / Credit Annie Cee as Copyright Holder Released to Public Domain.
p. 152	Christ Mount of Olives / Credit Annie Cee as Copyright Holder Released to Public Domain.
p. 142	Crusades / Copyright expired. Public Domain.
p. 110	DNA / Credit Thorwald as author. wikimedia project. Released to Public Domain.
p. 131	Eagle 10272011 / Copyright expired. Public Domain
p. 5	Earth / NASA / Public Domain
p. 94	Earth / Public Domain
p. 10	Expulsion of Adam and Eve / Copyright expired. Public Domain.
p. 5	Fish / public domain
p. 5	Full Moon / NASA – Public Domain
p. 94	Full Moon / NASA – Public Domain
p. 67	Gandhi meditating / Copyright expired. Public Domain.
p. 52	Gandhi Smiling / Copyright expired. Public Domain.
p. 151	General Sherman, Ulysses Grant, Abraham Lincoln, David Porter—The Peacemakers / Copyright expired. Public Domain.
p. 110	IBM Super Computer / Credit "Courtesy Argonne National Laboratory". Public Domain.
p. 52	Jesus Christ victory over the grave / Copyright expired. Public Domain
p. 156	Jesus Healing & The Trinity / Copyright expired. Public Domain.
p. 78	Lord is my Shepherd / Copyright expired. Public Domain.
p. 5	Milky Way Spiral / NASA – Public Domain
p. 94	Milky Way Spiral / NASA – Public Domain
p. 142	Nuclear Explosion / U.S. Government. Public Domain.
p. 152	Ocean Waves / Copyright by Jon Sullivan
p. 139	Peace accord End of U.S. Civil War / U.S. Government. Public Domain.
p. 49	Peace Dove / by Clippix.com. Public Domain
p. 52	Peace Dove / by Clippix.com. Public Domain
p. 60	Peace Dove / by Clippix.com. Public Domain
p. 106	Peace Dove / by Clippix.com. Public Domain
p. 131	Peace Dove / by Clippix.com. Public Domain
p. 142	Peace Dove / by Clippix.com. Public Domain
p. 85	Plowing / Copyright expired. Public Domain.
p. 52	Praying Hands / Copyright expired. Public Domain.

p. 139	*President Johnson signing Civil Rights Bill / U.S. Government. Public Domain.*
p. 142	*President Obama Peace Prize U.S. Government. Public Domain.*
p. 85	*Rainbow – double Niagara Falls / Copyright expired. Public Domain.*
p. 57	*Reflection on Lake / Credit A. Ernyes at the wikipedia project as Copyright Holder. Released to Public Domain.*
p. 4	*Sacred Heart of Jesus Christ / None - Public Domain*
p. 58	*Sacred Heart of Jesus Christ / None - Public Domain*
p. 116	*Sacred Heart of Jesus Christ/None-Public Domain*
p. 131	*Sacred Heart of Jesus Christ / None - Public Domain*
p. 85	*Snake River, Burley, Idaho / Credit Quasipalm Copyright Holder. Released to Public Domain*
p. 110	*Space Walk / NASA. Public Domain*
p. 12	*Stars & Angels with infant entering the World / U.S. Government & Copyright expired. Public Domain*
p. 159	*Stars, Lord Jesus Christ, New Earth with PEACEMAKERS – Children of God*
p. 142	*St. Michael fallen angels / Copyright expired. Public Domain.*
p. 2	*Sun / NASA – Public Domain*
p. 94	*Sun / NASA – Public Domain*
p. 139	*Susan B. Anthony / Copyright expired. Public Domain.*
p. 52	*The Quiet Hour / Copyright expired. Public Domain*
p. 142	*The Storming of Fort Wagner – U.S. Civil War / Copyright expired. Public Domain.*
p. 49	*The Trinity / Copyright expired. Public Domain.*
p. 56	*The Trinity / Copyright expired. Public Domain.*
p. 112	*The Trinity / Copyright expired. Public Domain.*
p. 94	*USA Antelope Canyon / Credit Times 3000 Copyright Holder. Released to Public Domain*
p. 142	*War in Heaven / Copyright expired. Public Domain.*
p. 52	*White Heaven Beach Water / Credit Pediant at the wikipedia project as Copyright Holder Released to Public Domain.*
p. 142	*World War II – Kamikazes Raid / U. S. Government. Public Domain.*

Copyright © 2012 by Rubin Perry. 106701-PERR
Library of Congress Control Number: 2011962745
ISBN: Softcover 978-1-4691-3736-0
Hardcover 978-1-4691-3737-7

All rights reserved. No part of this book may be reproduced or transmitted in any form or by any means, electronic or mechanical, including photocopying, recording, or by any information storage and retrieval system, without permission in writing from the copyright owner.

To order additional copies of this book, contact:
Xlibris Corporation
1-888-795-4274
www.Xlibris.com
Orders@Xlibris.com